*Women in Sub-Saharan Africa*

RESTORING WOMEN TO HISTORY
*Series Editors: Cheryl Johnson-Odim and Margaret Strobel*

*Women in Asia*
Barbara N. Ramusack and Sharon Sievers

*Women in Latin America and the Caribbean*
Marysa Navarro and Virginia Sánchez Korrol, with Kecia Ali

*Women in the Middle East and North Africa*
Guity Nashat and Judith E. Tucker

*Women in Sub-Saharan Africa*
Iris Berger and E. Frances White

# Women in Sub-Saharan Africa

## RESTORING WOMEN TO HISTORY

By Iris Berger and
E. Frances White

*Indiana
University
Press*

BLOOMINGTON AND INDIANAPOLIS

Map on p. xviii adapted from Kevin Shillington, *History of Africa*
(St. Martin's Press, 1995). Other maps from Phyllis M. Martin and Patrick
O'Meara, *Africa*, 3rd ed. (Indiana University Press, 1995).

This book is a publication of
*Indiana University Press*
601 North Morton Street
Bloomington, IN 47404-3797 USA

http://www.indiana.edu/~iupress

*Telephone orders* 800-842-6796
*Fax orders* 812-855-7931
*Orders by e-mail* iuporder@indiana.edu

Manufactured in the United States of America

**Library of Congress Cataloging-in-Publication Data**

Berger, Iris, date
Women in sub-Saharan Africa : restoring women to history / by Iris Berger and
E. Frances White
p. cm.—(Restoring women to history)
Includes index.
ISBN 0-253-33476-4 (cl : alk. paper). — ISBN 0-253-21309-6 (pa : alk. paper)
1. Women—Africa, Sub-Saharan—History. I. White, E. Frances. II. Title. III. Series.
HQ1787.B47   1999
305.4'0957—dc21                         98-53906

1  2  3  4  5   04  03  02  01  00  99

*To Allison and Anna*

IRIS BERGER

*To Adelaide Cromwell*

E. FRANCES WHITE

# CONTENTS

# SERIES EDITORS' PREFACE

This book is part of a four-volume series entitled "Restoring Women to History": *Women in Sub-Saharan Africa; Women in Asia; Women in Latin America and the Caribbean;* and *Women in the Middle East and North Africa.* The project began in 1984, bringing together scholars to synthesize historical information and interpretation on women outside of Europe and the United States of America. Earlier versions of the volumes were produced and distributed by the Organization of American Historians (OAH) as *Restoring Women to History: Teaching Packets for Integrating Women's History into Courses on Africa, Asia, Latin America, the Caribbean, and the Middle East* (1988; revised, 1990).

These volumes are intended to help teachers who wish to incorporate women into their courses, researchers who wish to identify gaps in the scholarship and/or pursue comparative analysis, and students who wish to have available a broad synthesis of historical materials on women. Although the primary audience is historians, scholars in related fields will find the materials useful as well. Each volume includes a bibliography, in which readings suitable for students are identified with an asterisk. Each volume is preceded by a broad, topical introduction written by Cheryl Johnson-Odim and Margaret Strobel that draws examples from all four volumes.

This project is the culmination of many years' work by many people. Cheryl Johnson-Odim and Margaret Strobel conceived of the original single volume, extending OAH projects published in the 1970s and 1980s on U.S. and European women's history. Joan Hoff (then Joan Hoff-Wilson, Executive Director of the Organization of American Historians), Cheryl Johnson-Odim, and Margaret Strobel wrote proposals that received funding from the National Endowment for the Humanities for a planning meeting of eight other authors, and from the Fund for the Improvement of Postsecondary Education (FIPSE) for the preparation, distribution, and dissemination of the manuscript. Under the leadership of Executive Director Arnita Jones, the OAH took on the responsibility of printing and distributing the single volume. The FIPSE grant enabled us to introduce the project through panels at conferences of the African Studies Association, the Association of Asian Studies, the Latin American Studies Association, the Middle Eastern Studies Association, and the World History Association.

Because of the strong positive response to the single volume, Joan Catapano, Senior Sponsoring Editor at Indiana University Press, encouraged the ten of us to revise and expand the material in four separate volumes. In the decade or so since the inception of this project, the historical literature on women from these regions has grown dramatically. Iris Berger and E. Frances White added important new information to their original contributions. White was assisted by Cathy Skidmore-Hess, who helped revise some of the material on West and Central Africa. Barbara Ramusack and Sharon Sievers found new material for Asia, with certain regions and periods still very unstudied. Marysa Navarro and Virginia Sánchez Korrol, with help from Kecia Ali, reworked their previous essays on Latin America and the Caribbean. Guity Nashat and Judith Tucker developed further their material on the Middle East and North Africa from the earlier volume.

This project is a blend of individual and collective work. In the 1980s, we met twice to discuss ways to divide the material into sections and to obtain consistency and comparability across the units. Each author read widely in order to prepare her section, reworking the piece substantially in response to comments from various readers and published reviews.

Scholars familiar with each region read and commented on various drafts. For this crucial assistance, we wish to thank Edward A. Alpers, Shimwaayi Muntemba, and Kathleen Sheldon for Africa; Marjorie Bingham, Emily Honig, Veena Talwar Oldenberg, Mrinalini Sinha, and Ann Waltner for Asia; Lauren (Robin) Derby, Asunción Lavrin, Susan Schroeder, and Mary Kay Vaughan for Latin America and the Caribbean; and Janet Afary, Margot Badran, Julia Clancy-Smith, Fred Donner, Nancy Gallagher, and Jo Ann Scurlock for the Middle East and North Africa. In revising the introduction, we received useful comments from Janet Afary, Antoinette Burton, Nupur Chaudhuri, Susan Geiger, and Claire Robertson. Anne Mendelson ably copyedited the OAH publication; LuAnne Holladay and Jane Lyle copyedited the Indiana University Press volumes. At various times over the years, undergraduate and graduate students and staff helped with nailing down bibliographic citations and/or preparing the manuscript. These include Mary Lynn Dietsche, Geri Franco, Jill Lessner, Lisa Oppenheim, and Marynel Ryan from the University of Illinois at Chicago, and Carole Emberton, Maryann Spiller, and Esaa Zakee from Loyola University Chicago.

This project owes much both to the Organization of American Historians and to Indiana University Press. We thank the following OAH staff members, past and present, who contributed to the project in various ways: Mary Belding, Jeanette Chafin, Ginger Foutz, Brian Fox, Kara Hamm, Joan Hoff, Arnita A. Jones, Nancy Larsen, Barbara Lewis, Michelle McNamara, and Michael Regoli. Our editor at IUP, Joan Catapano, waited months on end for the completion of our work. Without her prompting, we would probably not have taken the initiative to attempt this revision and publication of separate volumes. We appreciate her patience.

From reviews, citations, and comments at conferences, we know that scholars, teachers, and students have found our efforts valuable. That knowledge has helped sustain us in those moments when each of us, having moved on to other scholarly projects or having assumed demanding administrative positions, questioned the wisdom of having committed ourselves to revising and expanding the original materials. This kind of scholarship, what Ernest Boyer calls the "scholarship of integration," is typically not rewarded in academe as much as is traditional research, what Boyer terms the "scholarship of discovery."* For this reason we are particularly thankful to the authors for their willingness to commit their minds and energies to revising their work. Although our effort to get ten authors simultaneously to complete all four volumes sometimes made us feel like we were herding cats, we appreciate the intellectual exchange and the friendships that have developed over the years of our work together.

*Cheryl Johnson-Odim*
*Chicago, Illinois*

*Margaret Strobel*
*Chicago, Illinois*

*Ernest L. Boyer, *Scholarship Reconsidered: Priorities of the Professoriate* (Princeton, N.J.: Carnegie Foundation for the Advancement of Teaching, 1990), 16–21.

# AUTHORS' PREFACE

During the past two decades, African women's history has become a thriving field, generating numerous outstanding books and articles and raising questions that challenge other historians to revise accepted ideas about women and gender. Yet, despite the richness of this research, few scholars have attempted to synthesize its conclusions, to begin the work of constructing a narrative of African women's past. We readily acknowledge the challenges in our effort to do so, and we are grateful to reviewers of the earlier editions of this project for their suggestions.

This book and its previous versions also benefited from the ideas and criticisms of a number of colleagues. They include Edward A. Alpers, Shimwaayi Muntemba, and Kathleen Sheldon. Ron Berger's insightful and detailed editing of the section on East and southern Africa deserves credit for making the text more accessible to non-specialist readers. The time he took away from his own writing to immerse himself in another field of history is greatly appreciated. Cathy Skidmore-Hess brought important new insights to our reading of nineteenth-century West-Central African history.

As part of a collective effort to restore the voices of women in the past, in other parts of the world as well as in Africa, we also wish to recognize our co-collaborators: Marysa Navarro, Guity Nashat, Barbara Ramusack, Virginia Sánchez Korrol, Sharon Sievers, and Judith Tucker. The ideas and energy generated at our group meetings and in our joint presentations at a variety of scholarly conferences during the late 1980s helped to shape the questions we asked and our approaches to answering them.

Without the expert guidance and editorial skills of our editors, Cheryl Johnson-Odim and Margaret Strobel, this project never would have come to fruition. Only their exacting standards and their unflagging dedication made possible this pioneering effort at recovering women's history.

*Iris Berger*
*Albany, New York*

*E. Frances White*
*New York City*

# GLOSSARY

**Age grades:** Groupings of all men or women in a particular stage of life; age sets, formed at the time of adolescent initiation, had their own names and sense of corporate unity and moved together through the age grades.

**Amharic:** A Semitic language spoken widely in Ethiopia.

**Bantu:** One of Africa's major language groups, covering parts of West Africa and most of East, Central, and southern Africa.

**B.C.E.:** "Before the common era." Used in place of B.C.

**Brideservice:** Services performed by the husband for the new wife's family.

**Bridewealth, brideprice:** A gift from the husband to his new wife's family, traditionally in goods and/or services, but increasingly in money; often an exchange between the bride's father and the groom's father.

**C.E.:** "Of the common era." Used in place of A.D.

**Clitoridectomy:** An operation in which the clitoris is removed; in more extreme forms, known as infibulation, much of the tissue of the genital area is also excised. Sometimes referred to as female genital mutilation.

**Coptic Christianity:** Form of Christianity practiced in Egypt, Ethiopia, and early Nubia; believers followed the Monophysite doctrine declaring that Christ had only one nature, which was completely divine.

**Cushitic:** A group of languages centered in Ethiopia, but also found in more southern areas of East Africa; part of the Afro-Asiatic language family.

**Frelimo:** Front for the Liberation of Mozambique.

**Gandhian:** Referring to the passive resistance techniques initially advocated by Mohandas Gandhi, leader of the nationalist movement against British rule in India.

**Ge'ez:** The classical language of Ethiopia.

**Great Lakes or Lakes Region:** The area between Lake Victoria to the east and the chain of lakes on the western borders of Uganda, Rwanda, Burundi, and northwestern Tanzania.

*Jihad:* Literally, "striving." Variously used for a range of activities, from war against unbelievers to an inner striving to realize one's religious faith.

*Kgotla:* Male-associated political space in the Tswana kingdom.

*Lelemama* **associations:** Dance societies among Swahili women.

*Lobola:* Term for bridewealth in many southern African languages.

**Matrilineal societies:** Societies in which descent is traced through the mother.

**Matrilocal societies:** Societies in which a married couple lives with or near the wife's family.

**Nilotic:** A group of languages widely spoken in East Africa that forms a sub-branch of the Nilo-Saharan language family.

**Patrilineal societies:** Societies in which descent is traced through the father.

**Patrilocal societies:** Societies in which a married couple lives with or near the husband's family.

**Pentecostalism:** Designation for the practices of various fundamentalist Protestant groups, often stressing direct inspiration by the Holy Spirit.

**Polygyny:** The practice of having two or more wives at the same time.

**Proto-Bantu:** The common ancestral language of all the Bantu languages.

**Ptolemaic Egypt:** The 300-year period beginning in 332 B.C.E. when Egypt was ruled by a Greek-speaking dynasty.

**Spirit medium:** A person who communicates the messages of the spirits to others in the community.

**Structural adjustment:** A set of economic austerity measures imposed by the International Monetary Fund and the World Bank as a condition for lending money, often resulting in lower commodity prices, increased prices for imported goods, and cutbacks in expenditures for education, health, and social services.

**TANU:** Tanganyika (Tanzania) African National Union.

**ZANU:** Zimbabwe African National Union.

# MAPS

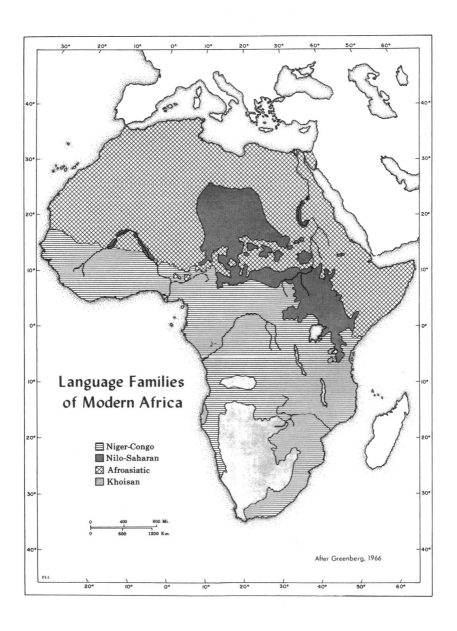

**Language Families
of Modern Africa**

- ⊟ Niger-Congo
- ▨ Nilo-Saharan
- ⊠ Afroasiatic
- ▨ Khoisan

| 0 | 400 | 800 Mi. |
| 0 | 600 | 1200 Km. |

After Greenberg, 1966

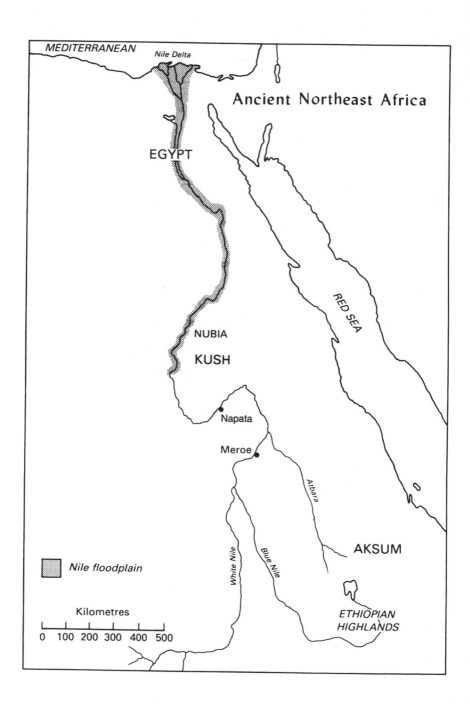

MEDITERRANEAN    Nile Delta

Ancient Northeast Africa

EGYPT

RED SEA

NUBIA

KUSH

Napata

Meroe

Atbara

White Nile

Blue Nile

AKSUM

Nile floodplain

ETHIOPIAN
HIGHLANDS

Kilometres

0   100   200   300   400   500

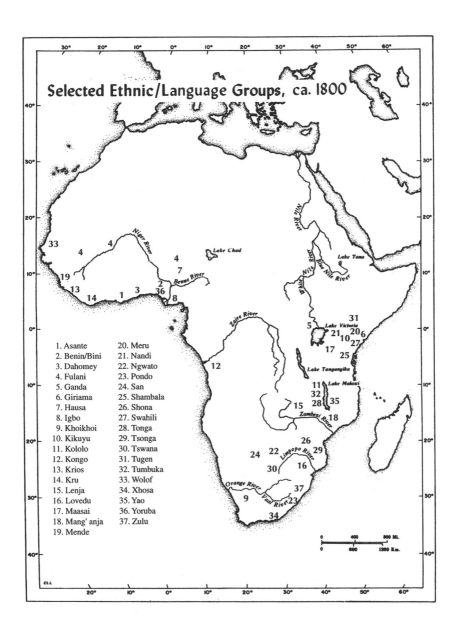

Selected Ethnic/Language Groups, ca. 1800

| | |
|---|---|
| 1. Asante | 20. Meru |
| 2. Benin/Bini | 21. Nandi |
| 3. Dahomey | 22. Ngwato |
| 4. Fulani | 23. Pondo |
| 5. Ganda | 24. San |
| 6. Giriama | 25. Shambala |
| 7. Hausa | 26. Shona |
| 8. Igbo | 27. Swahili |
| 9. Khoikhoi | 28. Tonga |
| 10. Kikuyu | 29. Tsonga |
| 11. Kololo | 30. Tswana |
| 12. Kongo | 31. Tugen |
| 13. Krios | 32. Tumbuka |
| 14. Kru | 33. Wolof |
| 15. Lenja | 34. Xhosa |
| 16. Lovedu | 35. Yao |
| 17. Maasai | 36. Yoruba |
| 18. Mang' anja | 37. Zulu |
| 19. Mende | |

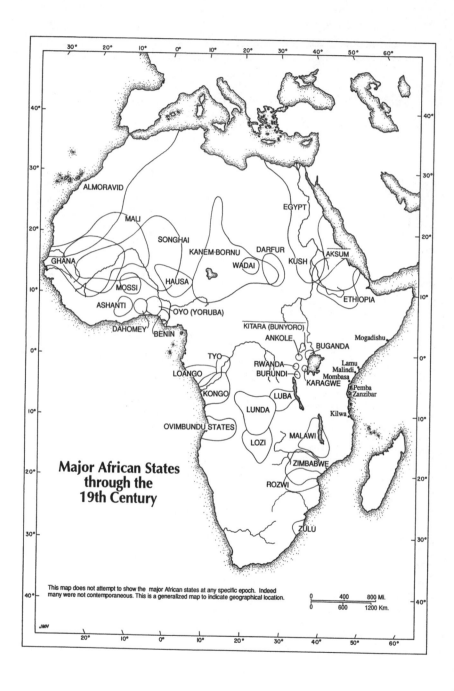

ALMORAVID

MALI

EGYPT

SONGHAI

KANEM-BORNU    DARFUR

GHANA    WADAI    KUSH    AKSUM

MOSSI    HAUSA

ASHANTI    ETHIOPIA

OYO (YORUBA)

DAHOMEY    BENIN

KITARA (BUNYORO)

ANKOLE    Mogadishu

BUGANDA

TYO    RWANDA    Lamu

LOANGO    BURUNDI    Malindi

Mombasa

KARAGWE

KONGO    Pemba

LUBA    Zanzibar

LUNDA

Kilwa

OVIMBUNDU STATES

MALAWI

LOZI

**Major African States
through the
19th Century**

ZIMBABWE

ROZWI

ZULU

This map does not attempt to show the  major African states at any specific epoch.  Indeed
many were not contemporaneous.  This is a generalized map to indicate geographical location.

| 0 | 400 | 800 Mi. |

| 0 | 600 | 1200 Km. |

JMH

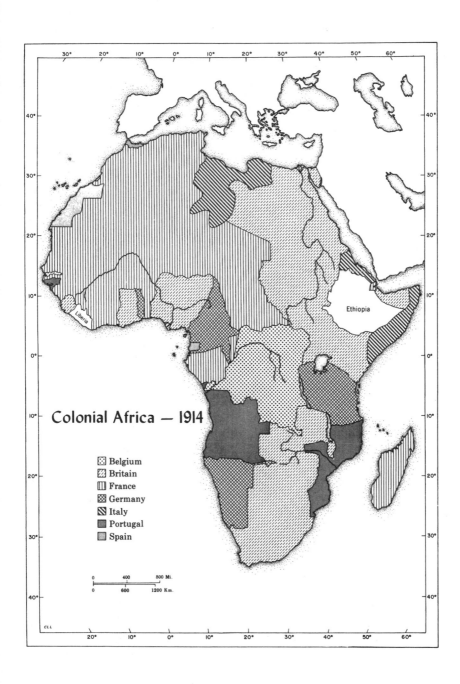

Colonial Africa — 1914

Belgium
Britain
France
Germany
Italy
Portugal
Spain

Liberia

Ethiopia

0    400    800 Mi.
0    600    1200 Km.

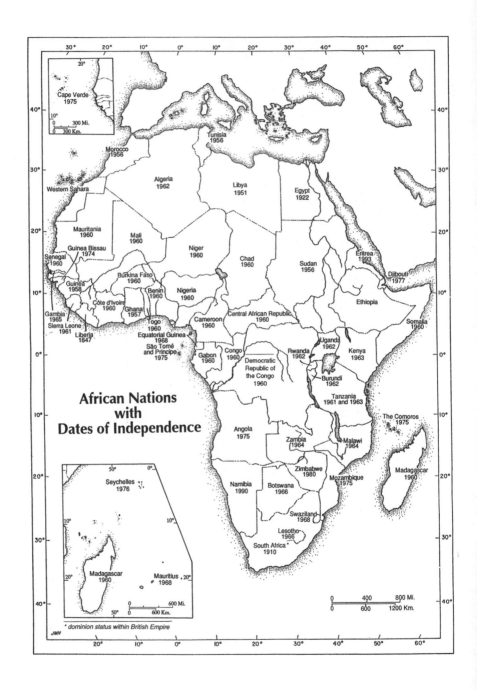

African Nations
with
Dates of Independence

# CHRONOLOGY

*Many of the dates in the early periods of this chronology are approximations.*

### B.C.E.

| | |
|---|---|
| **18,000–7,000** | Settled communities develop; wild foods harvested; hunting techniques improve |
| **7,000–5,000** | Beginning of shift from hunting and gathering to food production through agriculture and herding; indigenous domesticated plants include yams, rice, sorghum, oil palm, and millets |
| **3100** | Emergence of Nubian kingdom |
| **3100–2180** | Egyptian Old Kingdom |
| **2080–1640** | Egyptian Middle Kingdom |
| **1570–1090** | Egyptian New Kingdom |
| **800–300** | Nubian Kingdom of Kush centered at Napata |
| **500–200** | Nok culture thrives |
| **300–300 C.E.** | Kush centered at Meroe |

### C.E.

| | |
|---|---|
| **1–700** | Kingdom of Aksum develops in Ethiopia |
| **350** | Aksum adopts Christianity as official religion |
| **800–900** | Introduction of Islam to western Sudan |
| **900–1000** | Height of Ghana Empire |
| **1000–1500** | Early Great Lakes states begin to form |
| **1100s** | Decline of Ghana Empire, consolidation of early Yoruba states |
| **1200s** | Rise of Mali |
| **1200s–1400s** | Consolidation of Mali |
| **1200–1500** | Major towns built on Swahili coast |
| **1200s–1600s** | Consolidation of Hausa city-states; peak of trans-Saharan trade |

| | |
|---|---|
| **1260–1270** | Islamic conquest of Nubia |
| **1200–1400** | Great Zimbabwe constructed |
| **Late 1300s** | Oyo founded |
| **1444** | First Portuguese slave raid in Mauritania |
| **Early 1500s** | Mane invasion of Sierra Leone |
| **1505** | Portuguese establish bases on east coast |
| **1576** | Queen Aminatu of Zazzau ascends to throne |
| **Late 1500s** | Rise of Songhay; Mali begins decline |
| **1600s** | Rise of Asante state |
| **1652** | Dutch establish base at Cape of Good Hope |
| **1600s–1700s** | Oyo at height |
| **1625** | Dahomey founded |
| **1630** | Senhora Philippa controls trading center at Rufisque |
| **1655** | Nzinga of Matamba makes pact with Portuguese |
| **1700s** | Mende migration into Sierra Leone |
| **1705** | Kimpa Vita (Doña Beatrice) repopulates São Salvador |
| **1787** | Sierra Leone founded |
| **1804–1811** | Hausaland *jihad* led by Uthman dan Fodio |
| **1807** | Atlantic slave trade declared illegal by British Parliament |
| **1818–1828** | Shaka builds Zulu kingdom |
| **1834–1841** | Afrikaner Great Trek |
| **1840–1893** | Yoruba Civil Wars |
| **1856–1857** | Xhosa "cattle killing" |
| **1867** | Diamonds discovered at Kimberley in South Africa |
| **1878** | Cocoa production introduced to Gold Coast |
| **1884–1885** | Berlin Conference leads to partition of Africa |
| **1885–1905** | Madame Yoko rules as a Mende chief |
| **1886** | Gold discovered on the Witwatersrand in South Africa |
| **1898** | Revolt against British protectorate in Sierra Leone |
| **1899–1902** | South African War |
| **Early 1900s** | Abolition of slavery in various colonies |
| **1910** | Creation of Union of South Africa |
| **1913** | Women's campaign against passes (South Africa) |
| **1928–1929** | Female "circumcision" crisis (Kenya) |
| **1929** | Women's War in Nigeria |
| **1945** | Pare women's protest (Tanganyika) |
| **1949** | Nyasaland famine |
| **1952–1956** | Mau Mau Emergency in Kenya |
| **1956** | Women's anti-pass demonstration (South Africa) |
| **1957–1964** | Independence won in British West, East, and Central Africa, Francophone colonies, and Belgian colonies |
| **1958–1959** | Women rebel in Cameroon |

**1966–1968**  Southern African protectorates become independent (Lesotho, Swaziland, Botswana)

**1975**  Portuguese–ruled areas (Angola, Guinea-Bissau, and Mozambique) gain independence

**1980–1990**  Southern African countries win independence (Zimbabwe, Namibia)

**1994**  First democratic elections held in South Africa

# SERIES EDITORS' INTRODUCTION

*Conceptualizing the History of Women in Africa, Asia, Latin America
and the Caribbean, and the Middle East and North Africa*

CHERYL JOHNSON-ODIM AND MARGARET STROBEL

In this thematic overview* we hope to do, with beneficial results,
what historians are loath to do: dispense with chronology and introduce several themes common to the histories of women in the "non-
Western" world. A thematic focus will accomplish several purposes.
First, we can discuss the significance of phenomena—for example,
the existence of female networks and subcultures—so that the authors' references to such phenomena are given a broader context than
the sometimes-scant evidence allows. Second, we can introduce and
synthesize approaches and ideas found in feminist scholarship. Third,
because regions often develop distinctive sets of research questions
and ignore others, our overview may suggest new areas of exploration. Finally, we can suggest possibilities for comparative investigation.

We cannot here do justice to the specificity of the historical tradition in each region; readers may use the indexes of relevant volumes
to locate elaborations on the examples cited below. Our themes highlight the similarities in women's experience across these very diverse
regions, but the differences, not dealt with here, are equally crucial.

The intellectual justification for addressing these four regions
together rests on the assertion that most of these areas have experienced broadly comparable relationships with Western Europe and
the United States in the past five hundred years. Although these vol-

*An earlier version of this essay appeared in the *Journal of Women's History* 1, no.
1 (Spring 1989): 31–62.

umes examine the long eras in each regional area before the last five hundred years, it is because of their histories of the last five hundred years that they are broadly viewed in the United States as "Third World," or "non-Western." We understand the need to problematize viewing *most* of the world's people, in all their diversity, in such "catch-all" categories and do not mean to claim the commonality of their relationship(s) with the West as the only reason for their appearance here.

It was difficult to decide on a common terminology that allowed us to keep from constantly listing the regions under consideration. "Third World" (despite some controversy) was often appropriate as a geopolitical designation, but it left out places such as Japan that are not generally regarded as Third World due to a high degree of industrialization. "Non-Western" also seemed appropriate, except that after many centuries of contact, Latin American societies cannot legitimately be regarded as entirely non-Western. Although we prefer not to refer to people by a negative term such as "non-Western" and are aware that terms such as "Third World" are problematic, we ended up employing both terms despite sometimes imperfect usage, in addition to the cumbersome listing of all four geographic regions.

A final word about terminology: we distinguish between "sex" as a set of biological (physiological) differences and "gender" as socially constructed roles that may build upon or ignore biological sex. Hence, in place of the common term "sex roles," in this text, we will instead use "gender roles."

## THE CHALLENGE OF THIRD WORLD WOMEN'S HISTORY

It is important to avoid three common pitfalls: interpreting women as the exotic, women as victims, and women as anomalies. Stereotypes regarding the non-Western world (particularly those labeling it as "primitive," "backward," or "barbaric") are very prevalent in our society and frequently provide the only knowledge many North Americans have about other cultures. The roles, positions, and statuses of women in non-Western societies are often as central to those stereotypes today as they were when European colonizers first pointed to women's "oppression" in Africa, Asia, Latin America and the Caribbean, and the Middle East and North Africa as partial justification for their own imperialist designs. "Brideprice," women as "beasts of burden" and female genital mutilation (FGM) in Africa, *sati* and footbinding in Asia, *machismo* in Latin America, female hypersexuality in the Caribbean, and the harem and seclusion of women in the Middle East frequently represent the extent of the Western public's exposure to the lives of women in these regions. It is in fact such images of women that help fuel our pictures of these societies as exotic. Feminist historians challenge this notion of the female exotic by placing cultural practices in an appropriate sociocultural framework and by looking at a multitude of women's activities over the broad scope of their lives.

Women, just because they are women, have undeniably been disadvantaged in their access to political and economic power. Where the fact of being a woman intersected with belonging to a racial, ethnic, religious, or other minority, or with poverty or lower-class status, women could be doubly or triply disadvantaged. But women have never been a monolithic group even within the same society; class, race, and/or ethnicity could have consequences as significant for women's opportunity and status as did (does) gender. Women's history, however, is not primarily a history of disadvantage and degradation. Such a "victim analysis" fails to present a picture of the variety of women's multiple statuses and relationships (including those with other women), the dynamism and creativity of their activities, and their importance in various cultures.

Women's agency and initiative, as well as their subordination, must therefore be explored. Integrating the histories of women in Africa, Asia, Latin America and the Caribbean, and the Middle East and North Africa in part poses the same challenge as that of European and U.S. women's history: the expansion and transformation of conceptual categories that, in explaining male, rather than integrated, human experience, have treated women as anomalies. For example, political history has tended to focus on activity in the public sphere and on office holders, both of which highlight male experience. The evidence demonstrates that women also have exercised power. Historically, however, it was most often within gender-segregated settings that ordinary women were able to exercise their greatest degree of power and decision-making. And, when they acted collectively, women could exercise considerable power even within male-dominated societies. Individual women—for example, Eva Perón—were often important political actors and exerted influence, both inside and outside of formal political structures. Because women's political participation did not always appear in obvious places or ways, it has been regarded as peripheral or absent, a view that ignores the complex processes through which power is exerted in societies. An investigation of gender relationships can add a critical element of analysis to our scrutiny of history and to definitions and explanations of the operation of political power and the conceptual category of political activity.

In addition to challenging definitions of what constitutes political history, the study of women can reveal important insights into the study of an entire region. For example, if one looks at the actual impact of Confucianism on women's lives in East Asia, the system of teachings becomes a much less monolithic historical force than it has hitherto been considered.

Similarly, looking at gender clarifies our understanding of Latin American society. Scholars have long studied the development of racial division there, yet gender and class were central to that development in several ways. Sex both opened and closed racial barriers: sexual activity across racial lines was legitimized through the practice of concubinage and was sanctioned because of the unequal sex ratios among the colonizers. But concubinage, while protecting status differences between the colonizers and the colonized, also resulted in a mestizo and mulatto population whose existence undermined racial barriers. Thus the control of (female) sexuality was linked to the control of racial purity.

In the Middle East, aspects of women's position that are at the core of historical and contemporary Islamic society (e.g., seclusion and veiling) have their roots in pre-Islamic practices. Hence, Islam can be seen not only to have introduced important changes in the Middle East, but also to have built upon existing practices; the introduction of Islam does not mark as sharp a break as some scholars have claimed.

In the study of Africa, the recent emphasis on examining gender has transformed our understanding of the Atlantic slave trade, a topic of longstanding importance in African historiography. Scholars had noted that African males outnumbered females on the Middle Passage, but why this was the case received little attention. As scholars began to problematize gender roles within Africa—and noted the extraordinary role women played in agriculture—some came to view the Atlantic slave trade as being partially shaped by the desire of African slave-owning societies to accumulate female labor.

The act of including women in the histories of these regions represents a more profound challenge than the "add women and stir" approach, as it has often been identified. The mere insertion of famous women, like the insertion of only "exotic" and hurtful practices, gives a distorted and inadequate history of the bulk of women's experience in a given society.

Just as adding information about women challenges the existing histories of Africa, Asia, Latin America and the Caribbean, and the Middle East and North Africa, so too does adding information about women from these regions challenge the writing of women's history. Because the oppression of Third World women is the result of both internal sexism and externally induced dynamics (e.g., mercantile capitalism, colonialism, neo-colonialism), being citizens of the Third World is as crucial as gender. Therefore, studying women in the Third World means studying not only a less powerful category within society, but also a category within societies that have often been dominated in the international arena. Thus, some things that oppress(ed) women also oppress men (slavery, indentured labor, alienation of land from indigenous owners or conversion of land to cash crop production, export of raw natural resources and import of finished products made from those resources and even of food), though often in different ways. And many issues that are not obviously gender-related, such as lack of self-sufficiency in producing staple foods and provision of water, bear their heaviest impact on women who are disproportionately charged with providing food and water.

Finding women in the histories of the non-Western, just as in the Western, world requires persistence due to the silence or obliqueness of "traditional" historical sources such as documents written by historical actors themselves. The roles of women in agriculture, health, crafts, religion, politics, the arts, and other arenas have often been regarded as negligible, exceptional and infrequent, or irretrievable for other than the very recent period. However, far more is available than one may think; much of it lies hidden in non-obvious sources: oral testimony, mythology, life histories, genealogies, religious records, missionary and explorer accounts, archaeological excavations, language, legal codes, land tenure arrangements, oral and written literature, or cultural lore and fable. For women's histories, case studies often come after the general treatise, which frequently concentrates as much on exposing the lacunae and generating hypotheses as on synthesis. The historical literature on women in Africa, Asia, Latin America and the Caribbean, and the Middle East and North Africa has greatly increased in the years since these essays were first published, and that has led to their revision. Still, a great deal remains to be done. These general overviews are meant to acquaint scholars with the possibilities as much as to show what has been done.

## THEORIES THAT EXPLAIN THE
## SUBORDINATE STATUS OF WOMEN

Trained to look to the specifics of place and time more than to the creation of theory, historians have often left to anthropologists the task of theorizing about the origins of women's oppression or the factors that account for women's subordinate status. One basic division runs between biologically oriented and socioculturally oriented theories. The former finds significance in a relative universality of physical characteristics among humans and of a gender division of labor that assigns men to certain tasks and women to others, a division that sometimes characterizes the public sphere as a male domain and the private sphere as a female domain. This commonality is attributed to genetic or physical differences.

Environmentalists stress the equally apparent diversity of humans, physically and culturally, and claim that biology alone cannot cause this diversity. Moreover, they view "natural" features of society as fundamentally culturally and ideologically determined. Even childbirth and lactation, they argue, do not predestine women to stay at home; rather, societies can devise a division of labor that enables such women to be mobile.

Embedded in these positions are views about the appropriateness of men's and women's roles. Biologically oriented theories tend to assume that gender differences are best not tampered with. Sociocultural theories tend to see the pattern of women's subordination as subject to change; thus, the search for the causes of women's oppression becomes linked to the possibility of creating gender-equal societies. If the universality of women's subordinate status can be proved untrue, then the possibilities of creating gender-equal societies are strengthened; hence, some scholarship focuses on the search for matriarchies, or for gender-equal societies, past or present. While most scholars find evidence lacking, the discussions of matriarchy and gender-neutral societies have raised important questions about the relationship between the actual power of living women in a particular society and (a) kinship and residence patterns (e.g., matrilineality and matrilocality), (b) social structure and mode of production (e.g., patriarchy, pre-industrial), or (c) the ideological representations of women in art, ritual, or belief systems.

Another approach to the issue of the causes of women's oppression links women's power or lack of it to economic forces. Research in this area has generated questions about the link between gender inequality and levels of production or technology, class formation, women's and men's control of the products of their labor, etc. Furthermore, these theorists dispute the universality of the notions of public and private, arguing that these categories follow historically from the development of industrial(izing) societies. In the modern period discussion of women's oppression in postcolonial Third World countries must take into account the effects of colonialism and neocolonialism on the construction of gender. In several places colonialism and neocolonialism marginalized women in the economy, displaced them politically, cooperated with indigenous males to keep women socially subordinated, or increased the social subordination of women themselves.

Feminism challenges both European colonial and indigenous patriarchal ideologies regarding women. The relationship between Western and non-Western feminist thought has often, however, been adversarial. In part the tension between the two groups results from the explanation given for the oppression of women. Many non-Western women (even those who identify themselves as feminists) object to Western feminist theories that posit men as the primary source of oppression. Recently this debate has generated theories that focus on the interrelationship of multiple forms of oppression, such as race, class, imperialism, and gender.

## THE INADEQUACIES OF THE CONCEPTS
## OF TRADITIONAL AND MODERN

The concepts of "traditional" and "modern" are often both ahistorical and value-laden. It may be legitimate to talk about ways people have done/do things "traditionally" (evolving at some unspecified time in the past) or in the "modern" way (coming into use relatively recently). However, for Africa, Asia, Latin America and the Caribbean, and the Middle East and North Africa, often the term "traditional" describes everything in the long eras before European intervention, and the term "modern" describes those phenomena following European intervention. This establishes a false dichotomy, with all things indigenous being "traditional" and all things Western being "modern." This usage often implies that the traditional is static and the modern, dynamic; it fails to portray and analyze each regional history within the context of its own internal dynamics, in which encounters with the West prove to be only one element among many. Such a view also obscures the fact that most societies were not isolated and had contact with other peoples before Western contact, that they are not homogeneous, and that several traditions often co-exist (to more or less peaceful degrees) within the same society or nation-state.

Sometimes this ahistoricity results from equating "modernization" with higher levels of technology; sometimes it is cultural arrogance and implicitly defines "modern/Western" as somehow better. Since colonialist ideology in Africa, Asia, and the Middle East often used indigenous "oppression" of women as a justification for intervention in these societies, colonizers promoted the belief that the arrival of Western civilization would improve women's lives. For example, in India in the early nineteenth century, one of the central arguments British officials employed to legitimate political control based on the use of military force was that British policies would "improve" the status of Indian women. Thus the colonizers made women central to the politics of colonialism.

The study of the lives of Third World women, in fact, challenges the legitimacy of the notion of a strict dichotomy between traditional and modern. Women's lives, especially, show that traditional cultures in these regions are not static, monolithic, or more misogynist than Western culture, and that there is no automatic linear progress made in the quality of women's lives by following a Western pattern of development. Regional studies provide evidence that the "traditional" ways of doing things, especially in the political and economic arenas, were often less inimical to women's collective interests than the "modernization" that colonialism purported to export.

The concept of tradition has also sometimes been used as a rallying point in anti-colonial liberation struggles. That is, by conceptualizing their struggle against European domination in "anti-Western culture" terms, various peoples have politicized the return to tradition as a liberating strategy. Because this "return to tradition" was often formulated during eras of high colonialism, when the promotion of Western culture was inseparable from the colonial presence, women were as central to the vision of tradition that emerged as they were to justifications for colonialism. Even after the colonial presence was gone, Western culture still symbolized continuing economic dominance. Gandhi claimed that women's superior ability at self-sacrifice made them better practitioners of *satyagraha* or non-violent resistance. In response to French cultural imperialism, wearing the veil became a political act of resistance in Algeria. Similarly, veiling became identified with opposition to Western influence and to the Shah in Iran. In the 1970s, Mobutu Sese Seko of Zaire (now the Democratic Republic of the Congo) constructed his policy of *authenticité*, a major tenet of which was a return to the "traditional" value of women as mothers and housekeepers who obeyed male relatives. These are but a few examples that show women have often been on the losing end of a return to tradition—a "tradition" misused by ideologies of both colonialism and liberation. A view of culture as dynamic, as well as a better understanding of women's roles in the pre-European-contact periods, can help demythologize the concept of tradition.

## RELIGION

Religion has been a source of power for women, or a source of subordination, or both.

Religious authorities have often functioned as politically powerful figures. In Inka society, women played important roles in the religious structure, even though male priests held religious and political power. As virgins, or *aqlla*, they were dedicated as "wives of the Sun" to prepare an alcoholic beverage for religious rituals and officiate at the same. Even in less-stratified societies of a much smaller scale, indeed perhaps more often in these societies, women acted as religious/political leaders. Charwe, a medium of the spirit Nehanda, led resistance to British colonialism in late-nineteenth-century southern Rhodesia. In the eighteenth century, the legendary Nanny drew upon her mediating relationship with ancestral spirits in leading her maroon community in Jamaica. Even where they did not hold religious office, women exercised power through religion: in peasant and nomadic regions of the Middle East, women continued, into the twentieth century, to control popular religious activities and thus to exert influence through their intercession with the supernatural.

Religious beliefs may point to the equality of women as sacred beings or the importance of female life force. Female clay figurines suggest the worship of female deities in Egypt around 3000 B.C.E., but we can infer little about the lives of women in general. Full-breasted female figurines, presumed to be fertility goddesses, are associated with the Indus Valley in South Asia around 2000 B.C.E. Aztec religion embodied many goddesses associated with fertility, healing, and agriculture. The presence of such goddesses did not signal a society of gender equality but rather one of gender complementarity, as in the Inka case. One of the largest temples in Ancient Sumer, at Ur, was headed by the priestess Enheduanna, who was also a renowned poet and writer.

On the other hand, religious beliefs may both reflect and reinforce the subordination of women. Women in many religious traditions are seen as polluting, particularly because of those bodily functions surrounding menstruation or childbirth. In West Africa,

Akan fear of menstruating women limited even elite women's activities: the *asantehemaa*, the highest female office, could be held only by a post-menopausal woman from the appropriate lineage. Even though such beliefs may ultimately derive from women's power as procreators, women's status as polluting persons can restrict their activities and power. Moreover, traditions that stress the importance of male children to carry out ancestral rituals—for example, those in Confucianism—contribute to the negative valuation of female children and women. Other customs repressive and/or unhealthy to women—for example, *sati*, ritual suicide by widows—are sanctioned by religion. Finally, the traditions of Christianity, Confucianism, Hinduism, Islam, and Judaism all legitimate male authority, particularly patriarchal familial authority, over women: Christianity through biblical exhortation to wifely obedience, Confucianism in the three obediences, Hinduism in the Laws of Manu, Islam in the Qur'an's injunction regarding wifely obedience, and Judaism in the Halakhah Laws.

However much these traditions carry profound gender inequalities in theology and in office, these same traditions spawn groupings that attract women (and other lower-status people). In India, the Gupta period, in which the Laws of Manu increased restrictions on Indian women, also witnessed the rise of Saktism, a cult derived from pre-Aryan traditions that envision the divine as feminine. In this set of beliefs, the female divinity appears in three major incarnations: Devi, the Mother goddess; Durga, the unmarried and potentially dangerous woman; and Kali, the goddess of destruction. Subsequently, in the Mughal period in South Asia, women in search of help with fertility or other psychological problems flocked to devotional Hinduism, becoming followers of *bhakti* saints, and to Muslim Sufi holy men. Women in the Middle East and in Muslim parts of Africa were also attracted to these mystical Sufi orders, which stressed direct union with Allah and believed there were no differences between men and women in their ability to reach God. Among syncretic Christian offshoots in Africa, women play much more central, albeit often expressive, roles.

## SEXUALITY AND REPRODUCTION

Many theories about the origins of the oppression of women see control of female sexuality and the reproductive process (or female procreative power) as central. For this reason, it is useful to examine basic questions, if not patterns, in societies' construction of female sexuality. Just as gender is socially constructed, so too is sexuality—

that is, which sexual practices (and with whom) were considered socially acceptable and which were considered deviant are specific to time and place, and often contested. Scholarship on homosexuality, for instance, is in its infancy in many of these histories, particularly that regarding lesbianism. Some scholars, though, posit the harem or *zenana* as a site of lesbian relationships.

Throughout history, societies have generated ideological systems that link female identity to female sexuality, and female sexuality to women's role in procreation. Thus one reason for controlling women's sexuality was to control their role in procreation. Women were aware of their important role in the procreative process, and sometimes used such sexual symbolism as a power play. African women on several occasions utilized sexual symbolism to protest threats to themselves as women. For example, in the Women's War of 1929, Nigerian women challenged the offending officials to impregnate each of them, drawing upon an indigenous technique to humiliate men: they were protesting men's right to interfere in women's economic power and thus women's obligations as wives and mothers. In 1922, Kenyan women, by exposing their buttocks at a public protest of colonial officials' actions, challenged their male colleagues to behave more "like men," that is, more bravely.

Religions project varied views of female sexuality. Islam acknowledges women's sexual pleasure, as it does men's, while advocating that it be channeled into marriage. In contrast, the Mahayana Buddhist views female sexuality as a threat to culture. In this religious group, women have been associated with bondage, suffering, and desire; female sexuality, then, is to be controlled by transcendence (or by motherhood).

Often the control of female sexuality and reproduction is linked to concerns about purity. The Aryan notion of purity was reflected throughout Hindu ritual and beliefs, but in particular it provided the impetus for early marriage and for *sati*. Colonial constraints upon Spanish women's behavior in the New World derived from the elite's desire to maintain "blood purity."

Expressed through virginity and chastity, in several cultural traditions a woman's purity had implications for her family. A Muslim woman's behavior affected her family's honor, for example, resulting in the ultimate penalty of death for adultery. Infibulation (briefly, the sewing together of the labia and one form of female genital surgery), found in both Muslim and non-Muslim areas, is commonly associated with virginity and the control of female sexuality. Although virginity was of little consequence in Inka society, adultery on the part of noblewomen was punishable by death. In seventeenth-century China, chastity was raised to a symbolic level not found in Japan or Korea. The 1646 Manchu rape law required women to resist rape to the point of death or serious injury; otherwise, they were considered to have participated in illicit intercourse.

The point here is not to list the multitude of ways in which women have been unfairly treated, but to understand the cultural construction of female sexuality. These examples, all drawn from religious traditions or the ideological systems of states, highlight the control of female sexuality. But the earlier African examples remind us that sexuality and sexual symbolism, like all cultural phenomena, are a terrain of struggle, to be manipulated by women as well as used against them. In their critique of Japanese society, the Bluestockings, a group of literary feminists in early twentieth-century Japan, saw sexual freedom as an integral aspect of women's rights.

Societies have sought to control men's sexual access to females through a combination of beliefs, laws, customs, and coercion. At times men enforced these sexual rules; at other times women policed themselves as individuals or curtailed the activities of other women— peers, younger women, daughters-in-law. Male control of sexual access to females has sometimes been a violent assault upon women, such as in enforced prostitution or rapes associated with wars. During the conquest of the Americas, for instance, Amerindian women were raped, branded, and viewed in general as the spoils of war. Also, enslaved women were often the sexual prey of their male owners, valued as both productive and reproductive laborers. Sexual tourism in the twentieth century, particularly in Asian and Pacific regions, exploits young girls primarily for the benefit of expatriate "tourists."

Concubinage, another institutionalized method of controlling female sexuality, existed in all the regions covered in this survey. Concubinage legitimated a man's sexual access to more than one woman outside of marriage. Although it clearly represented a double standard, concubinage as an institution offered certain protections or benefits to women. In the New World some Amerindian women gained substantial wealth and status as concubines; in addition, slave concubines might be manumitted at their owner's death and their children legitimized. Similarly, Islamic slave owners manumitted some concubines, encouraged by the belief that such action was rewarded by God. The protections offered by the institution of concubinage, albeit within a grossly unequal relationship, were lost with its abolition, and compensating institutions did not always replace concubinage. Hence, abolition in parts of Africa left poorer women, former concubines, without the legal rights of wives or concubines but still dependent financially. In contemporary Africa, women who in the past might have become concubines because of their economic or social vulnerability might today have children outside of formal marriage without the previous assurance that their children will be supported financially by the fathers.

Historically, prostitution has occurred under a variety of conditions that reflect different degrees of control of female sexuality. Prostitution may be seen as a strategy for a family's survival: impoverished Chinese families in the nineteenth century sold their daughters as prostitutes in the cities to earn money. Elsewhere in Asia, prostitutes functioned as part of larger institutions, or even imperial expansion. Hindu *devadasi,* or temple dancers, served as prostitutes tied to temples. In the nineteenth century the British, in an attempt to limit military expenditures, provided prostitutes rather than wives for non-commissioned British troops in India. During the period of imperial expansion in the 1930s, Japanese prostitutes were sent to service brothels in outposts of the empire, a process described in the film *Sandakan No. 8* (Brothel Number 9). Under these circumstances, prostitution did not mean increased autonomy for women, whether or not it provided subsistence.

In some places and times, however, prostitution has offered an alternative of increased autonomy. New colonial towns in Africa created spaces for women to escape from abusive or unwanted marriages. There, operating as entrepreneurs rather than under the supervision of pimps or other authorities, they supported themselves and their children by selling sexual and other domestic services to men, who frequently were migrant laborers. In addition, prostitutes were able to keep their children, an option that was not available to women in patrilineal marriages, where offspring belonged to the husband's patrilineage and were lost to a woman who divorced or absconded. Even under circumstances in which prostitutes had more control over their sexuality and their lives, it is important not to romanticize prostitution. It has been, and remains, an option for some women within a context of gender and class oppression.

The production of offspring (especially male offspring in strongly patrilineal societies) is often a measure of a woman's value. In some African societies, this value is represented by bridewealth, the gifts that a groom must give to the bride's family in order to obtain rights to the offspring in a patrilineal society. The production of male off-spring is essential for some religious rituals, for example, in Confucianism.

We have little historical information about control of reproduction. But even prior to the recent rise of reproductive technology, women found ways to limit birth. For example, in Congo in the late nineteenth century, slave women limited the number of children they had. In the complex conditions created by the internal African slave trade, slave women saw few advantages to producing children who belonged to their owners and who could not be expected to care for their mothers in old age. Advances in reproductive technology such as amniocentesis, which project the sex of an embryo or fetus, have sometimes been used to select male children and abort female children.

Recently, with the advent of population control programs adopted by nation-states and promoted by international agencies, control of reproduction has shifted away from individually initiated actions to highly bureaucratized operations. In that shift, the balance has slipped from birth control, which empowers women by giving them options, to population control, which regulates female reproduction in the interests of a nation-state or a donor country. Women may be encouraged or coerced to have babies for the nation, or the revolution, or conversely they may be manipulated or coerced into limiting childbirth. Stringent population policies were introduced in India, prompting protests by women's groups, and in China, where urban couples recently have been allowed to have only one child. In Puerto Rico one-third of the women of childbearing age were sterilized by the 1960s in one of the early attempts at widespread population control following policies initiated by the U.S. government. The white regime in South Africa promoted "birth control" among blacks as part of the larger plan of apartheid. In none of these population policies does birth control unambiguously empower women, since the elements of choice and safety have been compromised.

## HOUSEHOLD RELATIONS

Household relationships are at the heart of most societies, since families act as the primary culture-bearing unit. In pre-industrial societies the family is also an important economic unit. Indeed, the way that families are organized is linked as much to the relations of production as to culture. Among other factors, a sedentary, nomadic, or hunting-and-gathering lifestyle, sex ratios, or the availability of land can affect family organization—and all of these factors also help determine the relations of production and culture. With few exceptions (Japan, for instance), the areas under discussion are still in the process of industrializing. Even while allowing for different levels of industrialization and cultural specificity, we can make some general observations.

In the Third World, historically and presently, domestic relationships have involved far more people than a nuclear family. The family most often functionally (not just emotionally) encompassed a wide range of relatives, including grandparents, parents, children, brothers and sisters, cousins, aunts and uncles, etc. Even when these people do not all inhabit the same household or compound, the sense of communal responsibility, obligation, and authority is wide-ranging and strongly felt and encouraged. The importance of the individual, as a general value, has been subordinated to that of the collective. Thus, domestic relationships and decision-making even between a husband and wife and their own children are often influenced by a wide variety of individuals and situations. Issues of polygyny, birth control, sexual conduct, education, allocation of economic resources, and so on are often group decisions, with elders frequently carrying more weight than younger members. The authority of a wide group of people who know about and sanction or approve behavior is accepted. Increasingly, however, factors such as class, personal mobility, and the proliferation of ideas about greater individual freedom are beginning to disrupt this pattern.

Historically, marriage was an important alliance that could not be viewed as a relationship between individuals, but between two kin groups, because the family was a primary unit for economic production and the concentration of wealth, for the allocation and legitimation of political power, and for conflict resolution. Consequently, marriages were often arranged for both women and men by other family members or by marriage brokers. Among the Aztecs, for instance, marriages were arranged by a go-between known as a *cihuatlanque*. Among the Spanish and Portuguese in Latin America, however (until 1776 when the Crown enacted new laws requiring parental consent for marriage), so long as a girl was twelve and a boy fourteen they could marry without such consent. Still, marriage was generally seen as an alliance between families by both the Spanish and the Portuguese, especially by those of the upper classes, where property was at stake and marriage between relatives was common. In the nineteenth-century Middle East, families exercised close control over marriage arrangements, and first-cousin marriage was commonly used as a method for ensuring political alliances and centralizing wealth. Arranged marriages seem to have held less importance for the poor, however, reflecting less wealth to protect and perhaps even the need to decrease the number of dependent kin. In Africa, also, arranged marriages were a prevalent means of ensuring the continuity of the transfer of resources. As men undertook wage labor their ability to pay their own bridewealth and hence arrange their own marriages increased, but rarely would this have been done over family objections to choice of a mate.

Gifts passed between families (and still do in many places) and between the bride and groom at the time of marriage. Dowry was brought by a bride to her marital home, and other transfers, such as bridewealth or brideservice, went from the groom (or his family) to the bride's family. The degree of access to and control over these gifts exercised by a bride varied greatly among the societies discussed here.

The institution of dowry served an important economic as well as social function. The dowry (or *dote*) was not a requirement for marriage among the Spanish and Portuguese in Latin America, but it served as a way of both compensating a husband for assuming the economic burden of a wife as well as providing a woman with some economic independence. Though it was administered by a husband, it remained the property of the wife and could not be alienated without her consent. If the husband mismanaged the dowry, a woman could petition in court to control it herself, and in the case of divorce, the dowry had to be repaid. In the case of the wife's death, however, the dowry was either divided among the children or returned to the wife's parents. In India, dowry encompassed both *stridhan*, which was usually jewelry and clothing belonging to the bride alone, and a broad array of household goods and other valuables that were gifts to the couple and to the groom's family, with whom they lived.

In various societies, wealth moved in the reverse direction, from the groom and his kin to the bride and hers. The system of bridewealth found in Africa was generally a gift from a man to the parents of his bride and signified their compensation for the loss of their daughter as well as his rights to the children of the marriage and, to varying extents, her labor. Among matrilineal peoples in Central Africa, a groom had to perform brideservice, (that is, labor in the bride's family's fields). Forms of bridewealth varied (including cloth, beads, cattle, and, after the introduction of wage labor during the colonial period, cash), and, in the case of divorce, it frequently had to be returned. In some places in Africa, women assumed control over a portion of their bridewealth. Some East Asian and Middle Eastern societies had both dowry and bridewealth. Under Islamic law, women retained rights to the personal ownership of their bridal gift, or *mahr*.

Polygyny, or the taking of more than one wife, was commonly practiced in a number of places. Sometimes, as noted above, it had an important political function in cementing alliances. In Islamic societies in the Middle East, Asia, and Africa, men could legally wed up to four wives. In non-Islamic areas of Africa and among some early Amerindian societies, such as the Inka in Latin America, polygyny also existed, but the number of wives was not limited. Judaism allowed polygyny by c.e. 70 in the Middle East. The economic obligations entailed by taking more than one wife could operate to curtail the degree to which polygyny was actually practiced; however, since women also produced wealth through trade, agricultural activities, and production of crafts, as well as by the exchange of bridewealth, it was often true that polygyny could be economically advantageous to men. Polygyny could sometimes be economically advantageous to women by allowing them to share household duties and obligations and by affording them more freedom to engage in trade and craft production.

Concubinage or the forging of sexual (and sometimes emotional) extramarital alliances was common in all four regions. Though concubines, as discussed above, were generally in a very vulnerable position, sometimes there were indigenous laws governing their treatment, and because these women often came from poor families, concubinage could represent a way of improving their economic position and even status. For example, Khaizuran, concubine of Caliph al-Mahdi during the Abbasid period in Iraq, saw two of her sons succeed their father as caliph, and she herself intervened in state affairs.

Since one of women's primary responsibilities was considered the production of heirs and the next generation, infertility could be a devastating circumstance and was the subject of many religious practices aimed at prevention or cure. Infertility was most often blamed on women until fairly recently. In Sumeria (3000–2000 b.c.e.) men could take another wife if their first did not bear children, historically a fairly common practice worldwide. Among the Aztecs a sterile woman could be rejected and divorced.

Some form of divorce or marital separation has existed for women nearly everywhere. (Among Zoroastrians, only men could divorce.) Although in general divorce was easier for men than women, there were exceptions to this rule. Extreme physical cruelty and neglect of economic duty were fairly common grounds by which women could petition for divorce. Adultery and a wife's inability to produce children, among a much wider range of other less consequential reasons, were common grounds on which men exercised their right to divorce women. In the early Spanish societies of Latin America, marriages could be annulled due to failure to produce children. Legal separation, known as *separación de cuerpos* (or separation of bodies) was also available on grounds of extreme physical cruelty, adultery, prostitution, or paganism, but such a separation forbade remarriage. From the sixteenth century onward, women were often the initiators of divorce in Spanish Latin America. In Southeast Asia women easily exercised their right to divorce, a situation some historians speculate was due to their economic autonomy. Prior to the twentieth century, however, divorce initiated by women was much harder in other parts of Asia, such as China and Japan. The ease with which divorce could be obtained was sometimes related to class. For instance, the divorce rate among the urban poor in nineteenth-century Egypt was higher than among the upper classes, for whom the economic components of marriage were more complicated. In Africa, because divorce often involved the return of bridewealth, women were sometimes discouraged from divorcing their husbands.

The treatment and rights of widows varied widely. During the Mauryan era in India (322–183 B.C.E.), widows could remarry, although they lost their rights to any property inherited from their deceased husbands. During the Gupta era (320–540), however, the Laws of Manu severely limited women's rights in marriage, including the banning of widow remarriage. Though its origins are unknown, the ritual suicide of widows among the Hindu known as *sati* is one of the most controversial treatments of widowhood. A complex practice, it appears to have economic as well as socioreligious foundations. Among the Aztecs widows not only retained the right to remarry but were encouraged to do so, especially if they were of childbearing age. In the colonial period in Spanish America, widows had the rights of single women who, after a certain age, were considered to have attained a legal majority. They could acquire control over their children or remarry. In parts of Africa, Asia, and the Middle East, widows were sometimes "inherited" by male kin of their deceased husbands. This practice, known as the levirate, could entail conjugal rights, but could also mean only the assumption of economic responsibility for a widow and her children. Women sometimes retained the right to refuse such a marriage. Among the Kikuyu of East Africa, for instance, women could opt instead to take a lover.

In many places women's activity in reform and nationalist movements, especially in the twentieth century, has been characterized by their struggle to liberalize laws governing marriage and family relationships. The Egyptian Feminist Union, led by Huda Sha'rawi, agitated for reform of laws governing divorce and polygyny in the 1920s and 1930s. Women (and men) of the May Fourth generation struggled in early twentieth-century China to make the reform of marriage and family law and practice central to their revolutionary effort. Even after the success of the Cuban revolution and the passage of a family code that explicitly gives women the same rights as men in economic and political arenas as well as in the family, women's organizations, with state support, continue to work to implement equality. In Africa women and men activists in liberation movements, such as the PAIGC in Guinea-Bissau in the 1960s and 1970s, clearly articulated the need to transform domestic relations as an important tenet of revolutionary ideology.

Women's roles, statuses, and power within the family have varied both through time within the same society and from one place to another. As reflections of material culture, they tell us more about societies than about women's place in them. For the regional areas under discussion, we can see the common threads, but we can also distinguish the wide variation.

## WOMEN'S ECONOMIC ACTIVITY

In virtually all societies, the gender division of labor associates women with family maintenance. Overwhelmingly, gender segregation and domestic subsistence production have characterized the lives of women in the economic sphere, although before industrialization there was little distinction between the private and public economic spheres as most production took place in the family and in and around the home. In Nubian civilization in ancient Africa, for example, there is evidence that women were involved in the production of pottery for household use, while men specialized in producing wheel-turned pottery for trade. At times there were disincentives for women to be economic actors. In medieval Islamic society, elite urban men were cautioned not to marry women who engaged in economic activities in the public arena. But such observations should not be construed as an indication of lack of importance and variety in women's roles in agriculture, craft and textile production, the tending of livestock, trade, and other areas. In fact, many women engaged in economic activity that not only supplied subsistence but generated wealth, especially in agricultural and trade sectors of the economy.

In nearly all of sub-Saharan Africa, women historically played and continue to play important roles in agricultural production. In one of the few areas of sub-Saharan Africa where private property in land pre-dated European arrival, among the Amhara of Northeast Africa (present-day Ethiopia), women could control the entire agricultural production process. They owned, plowed, planted, and harvested their own fields. Amerindian women were important in agricultural production in Latin America before the arrival of the Spanish and Portuguese, who then sought to enlist men as agricultural laborers in cash crops. Although for the early centuries of the Atlantic slave trade the sex ratio was heavily imbalanced toward males, African women performed important agricultural labor, which was essential to the economies of colonial Latin America, the Caribbean, and what would become the United States. Women were cultivators in much of Asia, usually in family-centered production units. Even where women did not cultivate, they often performed other roles associated with agricultural production. For instance, in nineteenth-century Egypt, women did not plow land, but they worked at harvesting and in pest control activities.

Women undertook various kinds of manufacturing activities. In the Chewa-Malawi area of nineteenth-century East Africa, women were involved in producing salt and in other manufacture. In the eleventh-century Pagan Empire in Southeast Asia, women were important in the spinning of yarn and weaving of cloth. In eighteenth- and nineteenth-century Egypt, women were important in the textile crafts, though they were squeezed out by industrialization. In the nineteenth century, partially due to demand created by a European market, women became important to the growth of the silk industry in Lebanon and the carpet industry in Iran. Women were important weavers among the Inka, where they also worked in the mines. In the sixteenth and seventeenth centuries, women among the Shona of southern Africa worked in the gold mines.

Perhaps the most ubiquitous economic activity undertaken by women was that of trading. In Africa, Asia, Latin America and the Caribbean, and the Middle East and North Africa, women traded a number of items, including agricultural products, cooked food, cloth, beads, and handicrafts. Although women's trading activities were sometimes on a small scale, often referred to as "petty trading," that was not always the case. In Southeast Asia, women in twelfth- and thirteenth-century Burma were engaged in trade that included the large-scale buying and selling of rice and other commodities. They were also identified with the production and trade of a particular foodstuff, betel leaf, for which they made elaborate jewelled containers. Sometimes women engaged in long-distance trade that required their absence from home for extended periods of time. Among the nineteenth-century Kikuyu of East Africa, women engaged in long-distance trade and retained control over some of the wealth they accumulated. Even where women engaged in local, small-scale trade, they could be very important to the growth and development of long-distance trade and of port towns and urban centers. Such was the case with women traders along the west coast of Africa in the eighteenth and nineteenth centuries.

Residence in a harem and the practice of seclusion placed restraints on women's ability to engage directly in public-arena economic activity, thus forcing them to use intermediaries to conduct their business operations. This use of intermediaries, and the higher economic status that seclusion usually implied, meant women sometimes held considerable wealth and became significant economic actors. In the nineteenth century in parts of the Middle East (notably Cairo, Istanbul, Aleppo, and Nablus), upper-class women employed agents to conduct their business transactions in the public arena. They also invested capital as "silent partners" in other ventures and loaned money to men. Among the Hausa of northern Nigeria, Islamic women who were secluded used prepubescent girls to trade for them in public.

In some places, however, the strict gender segregation of Islamic societies in fact expanded women's economic alternatives, since only women could perform certain services for other women. In nineteenth-century Egypt women of lower economic status served as entertainers, cosmologists, and midwives to women of higher economic status who were in seclusion. Strict gender segregation opened up the professions (medicine, education, etc.) to women in the late twentieth century, especially in countries where economic resources are plentiful, such as Saudi Arabia.

The absence of male heirs, or the fact of widowhood, could also create economic opportunity for women. Under such circumstances women ran businesses and were important in trades. In sixteenth-century Mexico, Mencia Perez, a *mestiza*, married a rich merchant. When he died, she took over the business and became one of the wealthiest merchants in the province. In Syria, the *gedik*, a license that allowed one to practice a trade, was normally inherited by sons from their fathers. In the absence of a male heir, women could inherit the *gedik*, and although prevented from practicing the trade, they could sell, rent, or bequeath the license. In coastal West Africa creole women traders descended from African mothers and European fathers served as cultural intermediaries and often became very successful and wealthy businesswomen.

Yet women's tremendously varied and important roles in economic activity did not translate into economic, legal, or political equality with men. The more economic autonomy women had, however, the greater their freedoms. Whatever the origins of women's inequality, the complex processes through which it has been perpetuated will not fall in the face of economic parity alone.

## POLITICAL POWER

In general histories of the Third World, political access is not normally discussed with gender as a factor of analysis, although frequently class, race, ethnicity, and other factors are considered. And being of a particular class, race, or ethnicity could influence women's power and status as much as gender. Still, the type and degree of women's political participation both as individuals and as a group have been underreported, and the present has frequently been mistaken for the past.

One of the most obvious ways women exercised direct power was by ruling. In the ancient African kingdom of Kush, women assumed power in their own right as well as sometimes co-ruling with their sons. There were women who ruled in early Austronesian societies from Polynesia to Madagascar, including the Philippines and Indonesia. In tenth-century Abyssinia in Northeast Africa, Gudit was a powerful queen of the Agao. Two African queens ruled in the sixteenth century, Queen Aminatu or Amina of Zaria and Queen Njinga of Matamba. The Mende of West Africa also had a tradition of women chiefs. Mwana Mwema and Fatuma ruled in Zanzibar in the late seventeenth and early eighteenth centuries, and Mwana Khadija ruled in Pate on the East African coast in the mid-eighteenth century. In India, several Hindu and Muslim women ruled small kingdoms during the late eighteenth century. In fifteenth- and sixteenth-century Burma and the Malay peninsula women also ruled.

What the existence of women rulers has to say about women's power qua women is a complex question. Most women who ruled were elite by birth, but then so were ruling men. However, Queen Njinga certainly achieved rather than inherited her power, moving from the position of palace slave to that of a reigning monarch. Although the existence of women rulers indicates that women were not universally absent from the highest seats of power, having a woman ruler did not necessarily reflect the status of other women or empower them, any more than it does today.

Women also exercised direct power within arenas viewed as the female province; these varied based upon material culture. In Africa female networks seem to have arisen from the gender division of labor, and over many centuries women exercised considerable power and autonomy within society as a whole through all-female organizations. Women leaders of women such as the *iyalode* among the Yoruba and the *omu* among the Igbo are examples of such power. The *coya*, known as the "queen of women" among the Inka, is another example; she even had the power to rule in the absence of the male ruler. Women exercised considerable power within the royal harem in both Turkey and Iran.

Women exercised power as members of collectives of their own sex organized for particular purposes. Practices similar to the Nigerian institution of "sitting on a man" are found in various African societies. This phrase describes organized political activities of women who gathered as a group to protest policies or protect another woman by confronting a man and ridiculing him or making demands, sometimes even destroying his property as a punishment for some act against a woman or women as a whole. Women directed this practice against recalcitrant husbands and colonial officials alike. There is also evidence of the existence of this kind of activity in early twentieth-century China, where women forced husbands who had maltreated their wives to march through town wearing dunce caps.

Perhaps the most ubiquitous example of women's indirect and influential power is the existence of the queen mother, normally the progenitor of a male ruler although sometimes a woman appointed as his "mother." These women had power over women and men. Their power resulted not only from their access to the ruler, serving as his "ear," so to speak, but also because they often commanded formidable financial and personnel resources and/or had specific responsibilities over the governed. Queen mothers existed in ancient Kush, India, the Ottoman Empire, and West, East, and Northeast Africa, to name a few places. Some queen mothers, such as Shah Turkan of thirteenth-century Delhi, could be very instrumental in installing their sons on the throne, and consequently exercised considerable state power. Others, like Mihrisah, mother of the Ottoman ruler Selim II, who ruled in the early nineteenth century, exercised considerable power through largesse; she built a mosque and a medical school. Yaa Kyaa, mother of the West African Asante ruler Osei Yaw, also exercised considerable state power, even signing a peace treaty between the Asante and the British in the 1830s, and Yaa Asantewa led a large revolt against British rule. The *magajiya*, the title given to the queen

mother in several of the Hausa states of the western Sudan in West
Africa, even had the power to depose the ruler, or *sarki*. The queen
mother, however, usually owed her power to her relationship to a
male ruler and not to her relationship to other women. Even though
she might be regarded as "queen of the women," she did not necessarily represent women's interests as a whole. Still, these women were
often at the center of power, and many displayed formidable political
acumen.

We also cannot discount the power and influence of women who
were the wives, sisters, daughters, and consorts of powerful men.
Precisely because of the intimate context in which such situations
occurred, they are admittedly hard to document, but evidence exists.
Women such as Inés Suárez, who accompanied Captain Pedro de
Valdivia as his lover in his campaign to conquer Chile, played an important role as a spy and confidante and eventually took part in the
conquest. Wives of emperors in the Byzantine empire wielded considerable political influence. Nineteenth-century Confucian reform-
ers in China were influenced by increased contact with literate women
at court and in elite families. The nineteenth-century Islamic reform
movement led by Uthman dan Fodio in West Africa was certainly
influenced in its ideas on greater education for women by the women
in Fodio's own family, which produced five generations of women
intellectuals who left bodies of written work in Fula, Arabic, and Hausa.
In the West African kingdom of Dahomey, by the eighteenth century
at least, no man could become king without the support of the powerful palace women. Royal women in nineteenth-century Iran also
exercised considerable power and independence, even from inside
the harem. There are many other examples which suggest to us that
women's influential roles in politics were consequential.

Women's military participation as individuals and as organized
corps of women fighters was also widespread. In many places women
accompanied male troops, such as in Aksum and early Ethiopian kingdoms, in early Arabia, in Latin America, and elsewhere. But women
were also actual combatants. The African Queen Amina of Zaria led
troops into battle, as did the renowned Nguni warrior Nyamazana, of
early nineteenth-century southern Africa, and Indian women in Delhi
and Bhopal in the second half of the eighteenth century. In c.e. 40
two Trung sisters in Southeast Asia (in present-day Vietnam) led an
army, including female officers. In eighteenth-century Jamaica, slave
women played important roles as combatants in maroon societies
composed of runaway slaves. One woman, Nanny, is still revered as a
fighter and ruler of one of the most famous maroon communities,

Nanny Town. Actual corps of trained women soldiers also existed, such as those in Java and in the West African kingdom of Dahomey, where they formed the king's bodyguard and were an elite unit of "shock troops." In eighteenth-century Egypt, women went into battle against Mamluks and the French. In the nineteenth century women fought in Japan, in the T'ai p'ing Rebellion in China, and in the Mexican Revolution. In early twentieth-century China, corps of women fought as the "Women's Suicide Brigade" and the "Women's National Army." Twentieth-century anti-colonial and liberation struggles are replete with examples of women as combatants, for example, in the 1950s "Mau Mau" rebellion in Kenya, the Frelimo liberation army in Mozambique, and the Cuban and Nicaraguan revolutions.

In addition to serving in military roles, women organized in other capacities with men and in women's groups against colonial policies that they viewed as inimical to their interests. In India at the turn of the twentieth century, women were active in the *swadeshi* movement, which sought to encourage the use of indigenously made products as opposed to European imports. In the 1930s Indian women participated in anti-colonial protest marches in Bombay and elsewhere. In 1929 the "Women's War" of the Igbo and Ibibio of eastern Nigeria was a massive uprising of women against the threat of female taxation by the colonial state. In 1945 the market women in Lagos, Nigeria were very instrumental in a general strike against economic and political policies of the British. Women in Egypt, Iran, and the Ottoman Empire worked with men in organizations promoting independence from European imperialism by participating in street demonstrations, public speaking, and writing. In the Algerian War of Independence against the French (1954–62), women were couriers of weapons, money, and messages, as well as actual combatants.

Women's participation in general strikes, major protest marches, economic boycotts, and armed rebellion was prevalent everywhere there was an anti-colonial struggle. As with any major societal upheaval resulting in challenges to existing authority, colonialism both created opportunities for and oppressed women. In the final analysis, however, the vast majority of women have opted to work for the independence of their societies and to pursue the issue of gender equality in the context of an independent and autonomous state.

Despite all of this, and despite the fact that improving women's status has often been a central point of anti-colonial ideology, women have usually not become the political and economic equals of men in newly evolving independent societies. In fact, the development of nationalist movements, at least in the nineteenth and twentieth centuries, has often operated to subordinate women. In nineteenth-century Japan the growth of nationalism and patriotism tended to subjugate women, requiring that they be good wives and mothers as their first "patriotic" duty. Although initially instituting reforms that served to empower women, within a few years the Kuomintang nationalist movement in early twentieth-century China began to repress a developing feminist movement that had supported its rise to power. The 1922 Egyptian constitution denied women the right to vote and barred them from the opening of Parliament, despite the active role they had played in the nationalist movement. After the success of the Algerian Revolution, women's roles in the war were viewed as validation of their "traditional" roles of wife and mother. After gaining independence, the Indonesian nationalist movement encouraged women to go back into the home to provide "social stability." In Nigeria, although the nationalist movements of the mid-twentieth century had courted women and counted them as strong supporters in the independence struggle, women remained generally excluded from political power after independence and especially under military rule. In many disparate places and cultures, nationalism left women unrewarded after independence was achieved.

There are exceptions, as some national liberation movements have challenged sexist ideologies regarding women. Frelimo in Mozambique criticized both the traditional initiation rites that included notions of female subordination as well as the colonial exploitation of women's labor. This kind of struggle was termed "fighting two colonialisms" by the PAIGC, a comparable liberation movement in Guinea-Bissau. In Cuba the government also sought to address the issue of women's equality in the post-independence period in a written family code that explicitly delineates women's equal status compared to that of men. The revolutionary Nicaraguan government of the 1980s also attempted to officially stipulate women as the equals of men. The positive difference in these countries, however, seems as related to women's continued organization as women (such as the Organization of Mozambican Women and the Cuban Federation of Women) as to state-supported revolutionary ideology.

## CENTRALIZATION, BUREAUCRATIZATION, AND STATE FORMATION

Women's role in centralization, bureaucratization, and state formation poses some challenging questions. In the processes of state formation and centralization, women often have tremendous importance and potential for autonomy and power as marriage partners who centralize wealth, cement alliances, merge cultures, and produce heirs. In the Middle East the practice of first-cousin marriage helped establish the family as a base of centralized wealth and political solidarity. In the pre-colonial West African kingdom of Dahomey, the king took wives from wealthy and powerful families to cement political alliances. Among both the Hindus and the Muslims in India, marriages reinforced political bonds with the nobility and among rival states. In Latin America the Spanish sought unions with elite Amerindian women to legitimize and consolidate their control over indigenous societies. However, it appears that when the state begins to bureaucratize, making these relationships less important to state organization, women lose much of their potential for being central to state power. In the Middle East the growth of the state meant that the great family houses that had served as centers of societal organization and power lost much of that role. Similarly, in the West African kingdom of Dahomey, kinship ties became much less important in power relations as the state solidified and shifted to a merit system based more on service to the king than lineage connections.

Nationalist struggles in the nineteenth and twentieth centuries mobilized women nearly everywhere in the Third World. But once the state was established (or gained its independence from external conquerors), women often seemed to lose in the process. Particular and comparative research with gender as a central analytical factor can test this hypothesis and may open new windows on studies of state formation and the development of nationalism.

## WOMEN'S CULTURE, NETWORKS, AND AUTONOMOUS SPACE

In male-dominant societies, women's activities, values, and interactions often form a "muted" subculture: their worldview is non-dominant and does not generally claim to represent that of the entire society of men and women. This subculture is reinforced by a strong gender division of labor that results in women and men spending most of their time in same-sex groupings and, occasionally, is augmented by ideological formulations or social rules (e.g., notions of pollution, or purdah).

At times, women demanded the separate space or took advantage of it as a refuge from oppressive features of their society. For example, the sisterhoods of silk workers in southern China, who pledged to resist marriage, provided an alternative to the patriarchal family. Bud dhism allowed women to pursue the monastic life, albeit as less than equals to male monks. Still, Indian Buddhist nuns taught religion to other women and composed religious poetry. (Jainism accepted nuns as the equals of monks.) Women who joined Buddhist nunneries in China were criticized for ignoring female responsibilities of motherhood, although these nunneries, we might suspect, provided a space less controlled by male authority than the rest of Chinese society. Convents in colonial Latin America housed single women with various motives: some sought to escape marriage, others searched for religious fulfillment, and a few sought access to education. And not all who resided in a convent lived by vows of poverty and chastity.

Whatever its source or structural manifestation, this social space and the resulting female-controlled institutions offered women rich opportunities. Among the most important of these opportunities was the potential for female solidarity. Various African societies institutionalized female solidarity through activities such as "sitting on a man" (a Nigerian practice noted earlier). In Mende society in West Africa, the women's secret society known as Bundu (parallel to a men's secret society) provided a political base for female chiefs (it also perpetuated, as a central initiation ritual, the practice of clitoridectomy).

In addition to encouraging female solidarity, the separation of women and men had economic consequences at times. Islamic seclusion provided the impetus for the development of occupations serving the women of the harem or *zenana*, such as midwives, educators, entertainers, musicians, or cosmologists; for reasons of honor and modesty, these occupations were filled by women. The same rationale prompted the expansion of professions open to women: medicine, nursing, and teaching.

The physical separation of women contributed to a flowering of artistic, oral, and written culture from the female subculture. The world's first novel, *The Tale of Genji*, is only one example of the fine literary work of Japanese women writers in the eleventh century. Unlike men, who were restricted by gender norms to writing rather arid, but higher-status, poetry in Chinese characters, these women composed prose in *kana*, the language of indigenous expression of sentiment. Even where excluded from education and certain cultural outlets, women's networks produced a fine and rich tradition of oral expression, as in Bedouin communities in North Africa.

Women's networks and women's subculture, because they often derive from the marginalization of women from the centers of power, have been controversial in the scholarship. Even in extreme forms (perhaps more so there), the separating of women can provide a source of psychological support and connectedness and protection. In assessing the actions of women among themselves, the important issues of victimization and agency are played out and we must ask certain questions: On whose initiative are the women grouped? How do women respond to this grouping? How does the clustering of women, apart from men, empower and/or limit women? Is this a condition that encourages women's oppression of other women (since there are now distinctions of power drawn between women) as much as it encourages female solidarity?

## WOMEN IN CROSS-CULTURAL CONTACT

Women are important intermediaries for cultural exchange. For several reasons, they are likely to end up marrying outside their community of birth. First, patrilineal societies outnumber matrilineal societies, and in patrilineal societies a woman marries into her husband's patrilineage and generally resides with her husband's kin (patrilocality).

Second, women have often been exchanged, as wives and as concubines, to cement alliances. In eighteenth-century Dahomey in West Africa, lineages were required to send their daughters to the king. During the same period in Java, the male ruler gave various women from his court to noblemen as wives. In sixteenth-century Japan, warrior families cemented alliances by the exchange of wives.

Third, in cases of European expansion into the Third World, the gender division of labor in Europe resulted in most explorers being male, which in turn created particular conditions for indigenous women to link with these men as sexual partners. Perhaps the best-known individual woman in this category was the slave Malinche (or Malintzin), who became the first Mexican mistress of Cortés. She served as translator in Maya, Nahuatl, and Spanish and apprised Cortés of the inland empire of Moctezuma. In the seventeenth century, the *signares* along the West African coast became wealthy traders and intermediaries through their relations with European men. Their mulatto children, familiar with two worlds, served as power brokers. Similarly, initially in the seventeenth century, the Dutch administration encouraged the marriage of its junior officers to Indonesian women to provide a form of social order through mestizo culture on the frontiers of Dutch colonization. By the nineteenth century, the status of these mixed-race individuals had declined. The same gender division of labor, in which men were the agents of expansion, is also characteristic of societies outside of Europe. Most conquerors were male—for example, in the nineteenth-century Zulu expansion through southern and East-Central Africa, and among the Muslims who infiltrated Nubia from the sixteenth century on.

Women were thus well placed—as socializers of children, farmers, or traders—to transmit new ideas about social practices or mores, technology or techniques, religion, kinship, and so on to their new community. Female African slaves, valued for their horticultural labor and transported far from their natal villages, brought with them ways of planting or cultivating, thus encouraging agricultural innovation. Women, for the same reasons, were well placed to resist the cultural aspects of imperialism by perpetuating indigenous culture and customs. Amerindian women in Latin America, for example, continued indigenous religious practices in the face of Catholic proselytizing, as did African female slaves.

Women may become empowered by their intermediary position: it may give them pivotal control of information or material resources. On the other hand, as intermediaries they are sometimes marginal within their society of origin. They may lose the protections from their natal group accorded by custom without gaining those granted to indigenous women. As in-marrying strangers, they may suffer isolation. It is important to note, too, that the individuals and cultures resulting from these cross-racial liaisons were not valued everywhere: Anglo-Indians were shunned by both the English and the Indian communities during the Raj. The female intermediary risked being polluted by contact with outsiders and subsequently cast out or made a scapegoat when illness or other negative circumstances plagued a community. And some women who served as intermediaries—for example, Malintzin, or Eva in seventeenth-century southern Africa—have been labeled historically as traitors because they were seen as helping to facilitate conquest of their people by outsiders.

## GENDER PLUS CONQUEST:
## COLONIALISM AND IMPERIALISM

Contact resulting from conquest held vast implications for women as a group. Customs were transferred from one society to another. New practices that restricted women's physical mobility might be forced upon the indigenous groups or adopted by them in emulation. For example, although the *jihad* of Uthman dan Fodio improved conditions for Hausa women in numerous ways, such as providing greater access to Qur'anic education, it also led to the increased seclusion of elite women and a loss of their religious and political power.

Recent scholarship on women in European-dominated colonial societies presents evidence that there was no one colonial experience for all women, even within the same national boundaries. However, the position of most women declined under the aegis of colonialism both because of its sexist bias and because women were members of politically dominated and economically exploited territories. In general, women were dislocated economically and politically within a weakened indigenous order, and in those spheres at least, women were rarely compensated in the new order. Nevertheless, though women were often the victims of colonialism, they also took initiative both in resisting policies they viewed as harmful to them and in using new situations to their advantage. And sometimes the social fluidity created by the colonial experience allowed for the creation of alternative roles for women. As one scholar suggests, however, studies of gender need to be located as much in the changing relationships of production as in the political and social policies engendered by colonialism. Another scholar underscores this point in emphasizing that it was the integration of the Middle East into a global economic system which is the real canvas on which we must paint an analysis of women's changing economic roles.

Women were members of colonizing as well as colonized societies, and members of the former group eventually accompanied colonizers to conquered territories. For most of the regions under consideration here, these women were a small minority in colonial territories. In the initial phase of conquest, they were nearly absent; then a trickle came to join husbands; then more came, depending on the degree of expatriate settlement that the colonizers encouraged and the needs and size of the colonial bureaucracy.

In Latin America (and South Africa), however, the era of European conquest was marked by the rise of commercial capitalism rather than the industrial capitalism that would fuel the colonialist thrust of the nineteenth century, and it also pre-dated (by several hundred years) the colonization of other regions. After the initial phase of conquest, during which few women from the Iberian peninsula were in residence in Latin America, much larger numbers began to migrate there. The Amerindian population of Latin America was decimated due to European diseases and attempts at their enslavement (the Khoi Khoi of South Africa suffered a similar fate). Though the population of African slaves grew considerably from the sixteenth to the nineteenth centuries in Latin America, European immigration outstripped it. The region was effectively colonized centuries before widespread colonial penetration into other areas. Thus, by the nineteenth century, Latin American nations were gaining their independence, and the descendants of Europeans in Latin America were the predominant people in the population of the continent. In many regions Latin American culture became an amalgam of African, Amerindian, and European cultures, shaped on the anvil of a centuries-old slave mode of production and forced Amerindian labor. Therefore, the following discussion of women under European colonialism does not apply to Latin America after the early decades of the conquest.

Imperial and colonial expansion had economic, social, and cultural consequences for women. The greater development (or in some places the introduction) of wage labor that accompanied colonialism predominantly involved men, whom it drew away from work on the land, increasing women's subsistence agricultural labor. Among the Tonga of Zambia the absence of male laborers had a particularly deleterious effect on the agricultural labor of older women, who were no longer able to depend upon help from sons and sons-in-law. This situation was also common in West and West-Central Africa. Sometimes, however, women left alone on the land exercised greater power in the economic decision-making process. An example is late-nineteenth- and early twentieth-century western Kenya, where Luo women were able to experiment with new crops and agricultural techniques that improved their economic position.

In some places the existence of widespread wage labor among men eroded the importance of the family economy and women's role in it. In forcing male migration to wage labor in mining and other work among the Aztecs, Inkas, Mayas, and Arawaks, the Spanish eroded the significant role women performed in the pre-Columbian family economy. In Morocco during the French colonial era, women were only seasonal wage laborers but were still dislocated in the family economy.

The development of the cash-crop system created greater interest in establishing private property in areas where it had not previously existed. This change to private property often distorted land tenure arrangements and usufruct (usage) rights and seems to have operated overall against women's interests. In Morocco the French, pursuing a policy of consolidating landholdings, helped destroy a family-based economy in which women played an important agricultural role. The Swynnerton Plan, begun by the British in 1954 in Kenya, was a policy of consolidating and privatizing landholdings that severely disadvantaged women and set the stage for their loss of rights to land after independence. In West and West-Central Africa women also lost out in the privatization of land occasioned by the growth of wage labor and cash crops. In a few instances women were able to resist erosion in their economic viability; from the 1920s through the 1940s, women in the cotton-producing areas of Nyasaland (now Malawi) were able to utilize cash cropping to their advantage. There, remaining collectively organized, women delayed the privatization of land, participated in cotton production, and maintained their pre-colonial agricultural autonomy.

Competition from European imports often displaced women occupationally and pushed them to the margins of areas in the economy where they were formerly quite important. For instance, in the Middle East and North Africa, European cloth imports in the nineteenth century devastated local textile production in which women had been heavily involved. Among the Baule of the Ivory Coast, French monopolization of local cloth production, and its alienation to factories, displaced women's former predominance in producing cloth and related items, such as thread. Sometimes the colonial economy created jobs for women, and though they were often overworked and underpaid, this independent income still provided women with some autonomy. Often it was the situations fostered by the colonial economy, especially in the urban areas, that created room for women to establish their own occupations. These urban areas often had large populations of single adult men (or men separated from their families) and entrepreneurial women engaged in occupations that provided them with services normally provided by the family. Although sometimes these occupations were marginal (such as beer-brewing, selling cooked food, and doing laundry) or even dangerous and possibly degrading (such as prostitution) women seized whatever opportunity was available to stabilize themselves, and often their children, economically and to gain independence from men and other adult family members.

The colonial need to control the economy also marginalized women who had often exercised control over the production, pricing, and distribution of agricultural, textile, and household goods. In southwestern Nigeria, for instance, the British were constantly in disputes with Yoruba market women over the location of markets, their internal control, and the setting of prices for staple commodities—all areas women had formerly controlled and which the colonial state sought to regulate.

A small number of women in some places were able to benefit economically from an increase in market scale that accompanied European contact and colonial rule, such as Omu Okwei of Nigeria. This benefit came to few individuals and often at the expense of other women, since women's economic power had historically emanated from their operation in collectives.

Political independence in many countries did not eliminate economic dependence on former colonial powers and was often followed in the post–World War II period by the arrival of multinational corporations. Since colonialism situated women overall as an easily exploitable class of labor, this situation has had profound economic implications for women. On the one hand, a number of multinational industries, especially electronics and textiles, have shown a marked preference for female labor. This has meant women have been drawn into the formal wage-labor force and therefore have had independent income. On the other hand, it has also meant the severe exploitation of their labor at depressed wages in unskilled and low-skilled jobs with little stability or possibility of promotion, and under unhealthy conditions.

Yet colonialism was not merely an economic and political relationship; it was a social relationship as well. By the eighteenth and nineteenth centuries, European colonizers hailed from societies that had rejected prominent and public political roles for women and that empowered men to represent women's interests. Alternative colonialist definitions of femaleness reflected a European gender division of labor and sexist bias. Women's education was viewed as a vehicle for making them better wives and mothers, since women's role was to be domestic and dependent. The schools of colonial Latin America shared with those of colonial Africa, the Middle East, and India an emphasis on education for domestic roles. The provision of suitable wives for the male Christian elite and the importance of mothers as socializers of their children dominated the colonial agenda, as articulated by both the colonizers and the indigenous male elite. Colonialism sought to impose not only political dominance and economic control, but also Western culture.

Seeking to legitimate their presence, and based upon European views of women in society and their own notions of the value of human life, some colonizers and missionaries criticized polygyny and such indigenous women-oriented practices as clitoridectomy, *sati*, foot-binding, and seclusion. In the area of family law, especially relating to marriage and inheritance, Europeans did sometimes seek to provide women with increased individual rights. Among the indigenous Christianized elite in Nigeria, for instance, Christian marriage was initially popular with women for these very reasons; but because it also promoted women's economic dependence and reinforced a pre-existing sexual double standard without the historical protections provided by the extended family, women soon began to chafe under its restrictions. The arbitrariness with which European family law was often administered and its confinement primarily to urban centers combined with other factors to leave a number of states with more than one legal code—European, customary, Islamic, and so on—a situation still in the process of being reconciled in many places.

Gender—the roles, perceptions, ideologies, and rituals associated with sex—is constructed by society. All societies have broad experiences in common (everywhere people construct shelter, trade, procure food, resolve conflict, etc.), but they approach these tasks in vastly different ways. Similarly, with women, writ large, there is much that is the same in the construction of gender; writ small, there is much that is different.

Even accounting for the cultural and historical context, the commonalities in the construction of gender point to women as generally less privileged human beings than men. Women's sexuality has usually been more regulated than that of men. Women have been far more associated with household labor than are men. Women have been less likely to rise to the highest positions of political and/or religious power. Women as a group have exercised less control over wealth than men as a group. Even within the same space and time, gender has been constructed differently for certain women depending on class, race, ethnicity, religion, and other elements. Thus we must view constructions of gender related not only to sex, but to a number of other factors—mode of production, culture, religion, to name a few—that can sometimes operate to bond women and at other times operate to separate them. The fundamental construction of gender everywhere, however, has been to separate women from men—in role, status, privilege, access, and other ways.

# INTRODUCTION

## Iris Berger and E. Frances White

Over the past twenty-five years, scholarly interest in the history of African women has increased dramatically. We have learned a great deal since the 1970s, when Denise Paulme published her important collection *Women of Tropical Africa* (1971) and Nancy Hafkin and Edna Bay released their influential work *Women in Africa* (1976). And we have sharpened our theoretical analysis since Ester Boserup's path-breaking book *Woman's Role in Economic Development* (1970) set the stage for a more sophisticated understanding of African women. Early studies in women's history explored a range of topics, from queen mothers and dance societies to slaves and prostitutes. The impact of capitalism and migrant labor on economic systems and family life provided the context for much of this work. Still within this framework, scholarship expanded in the 1980s to include domesticity, mar-

riage, sexuality, motherhood, and the legal dimension of family relationships. More recently, many historians have turned from women
to gender, seeking to understand how ideas of "female" and "male"
shape all areas of society. This work has provoked substantial theoretical debate, particularly concerning the relative impact of internal
and external forces on women's lives and the balance between economic and cultural interpretations of social change.

Major gaps in our knowledge remain, however. Most sources were
produced by men, who seldom recorded women's activities. They are
also the product of European observers, whose strong Western biases
about appropriate gender roles often distorted their understanding of
African women. Since African women left few records of their activities, it is often difficult to discover how they viewed their own lives
and the historical circumstances of their times. Although we have
information about queen mothers from many parts of the continent,
we know little about how other women viewed their power. Documentary sources are particularly sparse for the precolonial period.
Through creative use of oral tradition, archaeology, linguistics, and
other non-conventional sources and methodologies, historians of Africa have sought to make up for scant written documentation. But
however pioneering this work has been in certain respects, its primary focus on political history has meant an absence of interest in
gender relations or women's experience, apart from that of politically
powerful leaders. In the scholarly division of labor that emerged in
African studies, it was usually anthropologists rather than historians
who explored economic and social questions that inevitably concerned
women. Yet the "ethnographic present" in which most early anthropologists wrote makes their work problematic for historians seeking
to reconstruct the precolonial past. Deciding how to use this work in
a historically sensitive manner is among the most demanding meth-
odological tasks of African social historians, since recent research documents substantial change during the nineteenth and early twentieth
centuries in bridewealth, marriage patterns, the division of labor, and
other areas central to women's history.

Periodization is another problem. Like other areas of social history, women's history often challenges standard divisions of historical time and space, calling into question the politically oriented
framework that has provided historians with an accepted chronological canon. In an effort to shift our historical vision, Marcia Wright
has creatively used changes in bridewealth to delineate periods of
social history for one area of Zambia (Wright 1983). Here, however,

we have attempted to follow widely accepted chronological and regional divisions to facilitate the inclusion of this material in existing courses. Doing so is difficult because of the special problems of evidence and because of the concern of women's history with non-traditional topics: kinship and marriage systems, household relations, sexuality, and the construction of gender identity, both individually and collectively.

Women's history challenges us to find ways of exploring the unspoken and private realms of past experience and to relate these aspects of society to changes in political and economic power and relationships. Although we have tried to accomplish the difficult task of reconstructing African women's history within an accepted framework, we hope that both our presentation and the questions we raise will point the way to a new and more challenging synthesis.

# Part I

## WOMEN IN EAST AND SOUTHERN AFRICA

### Iris Berger

### EAST AND SOUTHERN AFRICA TO 1880

*African Society and Culture: Unity and Diversity*

Early African societies and cultures were remarkably diverse, but they also shared common features that differentiate the continent from many other regions of the world. Most fundamentally, although private property in land emerged early in human history, profoundly shaping class and gender relationships, kin-based communal groups and/or political authorities maintained control over land in most of sub-Saharan Africa. These land tenure patterns contributed to relatively low levels of economic division on the basis of property rights. Yet gender divisions were substantial. Although most farmers were women, senior men controlled access to land and labor and were the exclusive owners of cattle, another source of wealth and power. By

exchanging cows for wives through bridewealth, men rich in livestock could acquire the labor to cultivate larger areas of land.

Although land was communally controlled, women gained the
right to farm only indirectly, through men. In patrilineal kinship systems, where sons inherited from their fathers, women cultivated land
belonging to their husbands' families; in matrilineal systems, by contrast, where family ties were established between a mother's brother
and her children, women possessed greater rights in their communities of birth. In both cases, however, marriage granted men access to
women's labor and reproductive capacities. Since more children added
to the strength and prestige of the lineage, polygyny was common.
Bridewealth, a gift to the woman's family from the family of her prospective husband, strengthened the bond between the two groups,
while also stabilizing the marriage and compensating for the loss of a
group member.

Because the idea of fertility lay at the heart of communal and
even national well-being, marriage, religious ceremonies, and other
rites of passage often expressed symbolic and ceremonial concern with
regulating women's conduct. Yet age was as important as gender in
African societies. The idea that older members of the group (women
and men) should command respect from the young permeated all
social relationships: between rulers and family heads, patrons and
clients, and husbands and wives. But such principles also influenced
relationships among women. Thus mothers-in-law held authority over
wives, as did older over younger co-wives. Indeed, women's acces-
sion to positions of greater power in the family as they aged makes it
hazardous to generalize about their status in society.

Although fathers and husbands exercised varying degrees of "patriarchal" power, such patterns derived from local norms and beliefs,
except in areas of orthodox Islam or Christianity, rather than from a
single dominant religious system. Furthermore, the great variation in
gender relationships over time and space in African Muslim societies
suggests the prominent place of local economic, political, and cultural norms in determining the full impact of Islam for women. Islamic law guaranteed women basic rights in marriage, divorce, and
property, but the degree to which Muslim women were separated
from men, veiled, and kept from public places was not uniform (Strobel 1995).

While political institutions in the region varied, women often had
substantial access to public power and authority, through both
single-sex associations and specialized political and religious offices:
as queen mothers, royal wives, priestesses, healers, and spirit medi-

ums, and as the members of older women's age grades. In some areas, women who attained wealth and power became "husbands" to other women, for whom they paid bridewealth. The ability to acquire followers in this way has led scholars to portray precolonial African conceptions of gender as highly situational, subject to change during an individual's life cycle, and generally more flexible and less tied to biology than in modern Western societies (Amadiume 1987; Berger 1994a).

### Early Foraging Communities: An Egalitarian Past

During the long history of foraging societies, communities developed that were considerably more egalitarian than in subsequent stages of human existence. People dependent on gathering and hunting (including fishing where possible) are universally recognized as the earliest inhabitants of the African continent. They lived in small, fluid bands, establishing patterns of women's political, social, and economic equality that remain today in isolated pockets among the forest-dwelling Mbuti of eastern Congo and the !Kung on the desert fringes of Botswana, Angola, and Namibia. Ancestors of the latter peoples, known collectively as the San, once covered the savannahs and light woodlands of most of Africa south and east of the forest belt. Evidence of past geographical distribution of the Mbuti outside their present location is scant. Among both groups, technology was relatively simple, and access to land was collective and non-exclusive. Although there may be hazards in suggesting the continuity of social institutions and relationships over such a lengthy period, most anthropologists and historians until recently assumed that because of narrow environmental constraints, many aspects of these cultures, including gender relations, had undergone remarkably little change. By contrast, Ed Wilmsen's work has challenged accepted views, attributing the culture of southern African foraging communities to systematic dispossession and underdevelopment (Wilmsen 1989).

From contemporary examples, anthropologists have developed models of foraging communities that depend jointly on the economic contributions of women and men, who make decisions collectively and take an equal part in ceremonial life. Although some sexual differentiation exists among the !Kung and the Mbuti, it does not lead automatically to gender inequality. !Kung women contribute 60 to 80 percent of the food supply by gathering a great variety of wild plants. Women alone control all aspects of gathering and distribution, requiring neither the assistance nor the permission of men. Like hunting, gathering is a collective activity that takes small groups of women away from the village for several days a week, while other adults assume responsibility for childcare in their absence. Women and men each have distinct domestic tasks, the former maintaining subsistence tools, doing housework, fetching water, collecting firewood, making dwellings, and preparing and serving food. Though fathers take part in childcare and are intimately involved with their children, they spend less time at it than women. Whatever the differences in customary responsibilities, however, fluid conceptions of gender roles make many tasks interchangeable. Under these conditions, women have high status in the community, take a major part in family and band decisions, and share in the ownership of waterholes and foraging areas. Despite this practical equality, the culture defines them as less powerful than men, perhaps because of the high value placed on the meat provided by male hunters (Draper 1975; Lee 1979; Shostak 1983).

Mbuti society places greater emphasis on age than on sex, although gender is central to the division of labor. But cooperation and mutual assistance dominate all group activities. With separate responsibilities, both women and men gather and hunt, and females and males of each age group participate collectively in decision-making. Only the reproductive events of adulthood produce any real opposition between the sexes, which is reflected in ritualized conflict over male sexual behavior during the breastfeeding period, when intercourse is forbidden. The interdependence of the sexes is ceremonially expressed in the month-long *molimo* ceremony held at the death of an important person (female or male). Although male elders appear to regulate the ritual, by interrupting near the end of this highly charged occasion, women are able to assert their control (Turnbull 1962, 1981).

Research on another foraging society, the Hadza of Tanzania, also illuminates relationships among women across generations. Concerned initially with explaining the evolutionary advantages of menopause, anthropologists working in this area began to document precisely the activities of postmenopausal women. Doing so led them to formulate the "grandmother hypothesis," which centers on the critical role of grandmothers in increasing their daughters' reproductive success. By helping to provide food for small children who have been weaned when their mother is nursing another infant, these older women play a critical role in ensuring the children's welfare and survival (Hawkes et al. 1997).

These examples of highly egalitarian societies not only provide important insights into the African past but also challenge any notion that childbearing automatically relegates women to an inferior position in society. Clearly, it is the material and social conditions under which birth and mothering occur that determine their significance. A group of !Kung who have recently adopted a more settled existence, living by agriculture, animal husbandry, and intermittent gathering, provide an apt illustration. Their new way of life has undermined the egalitarianism of the past: sex roles are defined more rigidly, women and girls have become increasingly home-bound with the demands of time-consuming food preparation and a richer material life to maintain, and men are often absent from the village. Through their travels, men acquire an aura of authority and sophistication that sets them apart from women and children (Draper 1975).*

*Women in Antiquity: Northeast Africa to c.e. 600*

African women's history at present is similar to the structure of oral traditions, with substantial information on the early period, a growing wealth of material on the late nineteenth and twentieth centuries, and significant gaps in the middle. Yet, as with precolonial history prior to the 1960s, the problem is not simply a lack of data, but an absence of serious concern with gender as an issue for research. For the early civilizations of northeast Africa (Egypt,** Kush in the Nile Valley, and Aksum and its predecessors in the Ethiopian highlands), inscriptions on stelae (upright stone monuments) and tombs, plentiful archaeological remains, and documentary descriptions—both in local languages (as yet incompletely understood) and by outsiders—offer the possibility of new historical insights on the status of women.

The Nile Valley was linked culturally to the "Green" Sahara, providing fertile fields for its people as desiccation occurred. Along with the Ethiopian plateau, the Sahara was probably a center in which the earliest indigenous crops were domesticated. They included finger millet, sorghum, and the specifically Ethiopian contributions: *teff* (a tiny grain), *ensete* (a banana-like staple), and the oil plant *noog*. Because women were central to African agricultural production, they probably played a major role both in the lengthy process of innovation and experimentation that preceded agriculture and in the later diffusion of plants and technical knowledge. As settled farming systems emerged, they created the potential for surplus production and greater class division. Ironically, then, women's creativity contributed

---

*In addition to the works cited within this section, see Leacock 1981; Sacks 1982; Slocum 1975.

**Ancient Egypt is covered in this volume; the remainder of Egyptian history is discussed in the volume on the Middle East.

to economic changes that expanded domestic labor, thereby laying the foundation for new forms of inequality that increased women's subordination.

The relationship between gender and class in the early years of human civilization has generated intense debate among feminists. Some (Leacock 1981) have followed Engels's contention that class distinctions led to women's subordination; others (Lerner 1986) have argued that gender differences provided the earliest model of social inequality. Although we do know that existing African foraging societies combine a clear division of labor between women and men with only minimal inequality, this is not conclusive proof that all such societies on the continent followed these models. Sacks's carefully executed comparative anthropological study of Africa (1982), however, does suggest that increasing class division intensified women's subordination. This model needs to be tested more fully in the historical transformation of individual societies.

While current knowledge does not permit a resolution of the debate on the origins of women's inequality in Africa, the history of ancient Egypt and of the Nubian kingdom of Kush suggests that increasing gender differentiation accompanied the development of class-divided, urbanized trading societies and centralized political systems. Yet in Egypt, the best-known of these civilizations, women held positions of relative equality; and in all these states, as in later societies elsewhere on the continent, royal women had substantial political influence. Suggesting another similarity with later African cultures, some texts indicate that a prospective husband was required to make a gift to the woman's father.

Elite women's power is well documented in Egypt, the earliest center of urban civilization in Africa. At least five pharaohs were women, and evidence from royal cemeteries, inscriptions, and rituals suggests that queens, representing the female principle of the universe, wielded considerable authority. In the Old Kingdom (ca. 3100–2180 B.C.E.), many upper-class women were priestesses of Hathor, the goddess of fertility, sexuality, and childbirth. Like their counterparts in neighboring Nubia, later princesses and queens held the ritual office of "divine wife" of the god Amun-Re, acquiring greater independence and power over time. By the first millennium B.C.E., princesses sent south to rule his temple at Karnak were virtual monarchs, acting as priestesses and controlling large administrative staffs and vast estates. This position was initiated during the New Kingdom (1570–1090 B.C.E.), when the power of queens reached its height. Possessing their own palaces and administrations, they could collect taxes and dispose of their own resources. A pharaoh who wished to see his wife had to travel to her palace.

Although women occasionally assumed the culture's premier office, with its aura of divinity, posterity treated two of the female pharaohs as usurpers. The reign of the most powerful of them, Hatshepsut, illustrates the contradictory aspects of their position. Judged strong-willed and capable, she strengthened the country's defenses, led armies into Nubia, sent her fleets south into the land of Punt (present-day Eritrea), and initiated spectacular construction projects. Her temple at Deir el-Bahri remains the greatest surviving monument to a woman in antiquity. Yet in order to legitimize her position, Hatshepsut also took male titles, dressed as a man, and proclaimed herself "king." Thus, rather than undermining the principle of male domination of political life, the position of these few women pharaohs reinforced existing norms.

In most respects, however, women experienced a high degree of equality. They possessed full legal rights and the right to own and administer property and to initiate divorce. Underlining this ethos of gender equity, both nobles and their wives during the Middle Kingdom were accorded the pharaonic privilege of becoming gods after death. As elsewhere in Africa, high infant and child mortality enhanced the prestige of motherhood for all women. Indeed, Isis, the ideal wife and mother, was the kingdom's most popular goddess. But motherhood did not restrict women to the home. Unlike women in many ancient societies, Egyptian women enjoyed substantial freedom of movement in public places. Like male citizens, they were compelled to work in factories or on construction sites as part of the taxation system. Paintings depicted women working alongside men in the fields and buying and selling in the marketplace. As the primary spinners and weavers of cloth, they produced a valued export and a primary commodity of exchange. When government expanded outside the royal family during the Middle Kingdom, women also assumed varied professional positions as scribes, reciters of stories and myths, and supervisors of estates. In the role of diviner, village women helped solve community disputes and heal the sick.

Yet this equality was not absolute. Just as female pharaohs occupied an anomalous position, women were denied formal positions in the state's bureaucracy, and literary sources portrayed them in only two stereotypical roles: as honorable wives and mothers or as dishonorable violators of social norms (El-Nadoury 1981; Lesko 1998; Robins 1993; Watterson 1991; E. Wells 1969; J. Wilson 1951; Yoyotte 1981).

The population of Nubia included early sedentary peoples, who probably engaged in farming and herding, and later pastoralist migrants. Recent archaeological discoveries suggest that kingship emerged in the area at about the same time as in Egypt (c. 3100 B.C.E.), or even a few centuries earlier, possibly influencing the development of royal institutions and symbols to the north. From the third millennium before our era, when Egypt established its preeminence in the ancient world, until the fifth century B.C.E., Nubia was closely linked to Egypt through intensive trade and conquest. Although at times this contact prompted intensified urbanization and class formation in the south and the Egyptianization of some aspects of courtly culture, Nubian cultural patterns retained their hold. The Nubian kingdom of Kush, for example, dating to the first millennium B.C.E., had a distinctively African culture. References to women are scant for this period. While the presence of female clay figurines in graves of 3100 B.C.E. to 2780 B.C.E. suggests that female deities were venerated, women and children suffered disproportionately from the large-scale human sacrifice indicated in graves of the second millennium (1730 B.C.E. to 1580 B.C.E.). They constituted a majority of the two hundred to three hundred persons buried alive with the owner of a grave.

From the ninth century B.C.E. an independent royal line emerged at Napata, moving southward to Meroe four centuries later. These cities became the center of a wealthy Nubian civilization known as the Kingdom of Kush. Kushitic prosperity was based jointly on cultivation along the river banks and animal husbandry, although for much of its history pastoral pursuits were more important than agriculture, and kings, aristocrats, and temple priests measured their wealth in cattle. The connection of cattle with predominantly male forms of authority suggests the early evolution of a tradition different from that in the Middle East, where women regularly cared for livestock. Other important economic activities included fruit cultivation, cotton growing, the spinning and weaving of cloth, gold production, and, at Meroe, iron smelting. The gender division of labor in these pursuits and among the large class of crafts workers is largely unknown. In pottery-making, however, women produced hand-made wares in their households, while men dominated the specialized and lucrative production of wheel-turned pots for trade. The prevalence of women among slaves probably indicates the importance of their domestic activities, although a definitive conclusion would require more information on women's agricultural work. The geographer Strabo observed that women as well as men were armed, using bows as weapons. Probably spreading from Ptolemaic Egypt, worship of the Egyptian Mother Goddess, Isis, became extremely popular in Meroe.

Substantially more is known about the royal women of Kush, who possessed considerable authority, both religious and secular, and were able to augment their power skillfully over the course of time. The entourage of high-status men included their mothers, wives, sisters, and female cousins, and succession occasionally passed to the son of one of the queen's sisters. These features are sometimes interpreted as reflecting a tradition of matrilineal succession during the peak of Kushite civilization at Napata and Meroe. At the major religious sanctuaries, princesses were consecrated as the musicians of Amun, the great god of the dynasty. Although these priestesses claimed quasi-royal privileges, forming a kind of parallel dynasty with succession from aunt to niece, they had less authority than the king.

As in many later African kingdoms, the queen mother was a significant political figure. She played an important part in the choice and coronation of the next ruler; and through a complicated system whereby she adopted the wife of her son, her daughter-in-law also became a part of the royal family. In later periods these women began to assume power in their own right, sometimes as co-rulers with their sons, becoming known in the Greco-Roman world as "Candace" (from the Meroitic title *k(t)dke,* meaning "queen mother"). This power notwithstanding, it is notable that the tombs of queens, while of the same general style as those of kings, were considerably smaller and less elaborately embellished. Thus, by the time neighboring Aksum conquered Kush in the early fourth century c.e., a complex heritage of both female power and female subordination had been established.

Like Kush, Aksum developed a highly cosmopolitan civilization, in close contact with the Middle East and the Mediterranean. Inhabited in prehistoric times by pastoral peoples who possessed large herds of humpless long-horned cattle, the Ethiopian plateau became an early center of African agricultural development in the third or fourth millennium b.c.e. By the fourth and fifth centuries b.c.e., a complex urban commercial society had emerged, displaying particularly close contacts with the southern Arabian peninsula. During the second and third centuries c.e., Aksum also became a political center, its prosperity based not only on trade and crafts, but on terraced and irrigated agriculture with ox-drawn plows and iron tools. As in Kush, large herds of cattle were a significant form of wealth.

For ordinary women, this increased social complexity probably produced forms of inequality similar to that in Kush. But a full understanding of this process would require closer knowledge of gender relations in the pastoral societies predating the development of agriculture. The plow-based farming system in Aksum also might yield new insights on the division of labor in areas of plow agriculture, which Boserup (1970) assumes to be universally associated with men.

Considerably less is known about women in Aksum than in Kush, although they figure prominently in the kingdom's origin myth, the *Kebra Nagast,* which identifies Makeda, the earliest Ethiopian queen, with the biblical Queen of Sheba. According to legend, she transformed the custom that only a young girl could reign, decreeing when she transmitted the throne to her son that from then on only men would rule. Kobishchanov (1979) suggests that the tradition probably reflects an early pattern whereby queens were co-rulers of the state along with their sons and brothers, their title "queen of queens" (*negeshta nagashtat*) symbolizing their sovereignty over all the women in the kingdom. But the relationship between an apparent shift in succession patterns and the position of female rulers remains unclear.

Little else is known about women during this period, apart from an inscription that speaks of women accompanying troops on military campaigns, a custom also found in later Ethiopian kingdoms. The Christian term for God indicates that religion probably centered on female agricultural cults. Although now translated as "Lord" of the Earth, the original root of the term is feminine.*

### Communities of the Interior to 1500

Representing the region's main language families, the varied populations that displaced and assimilated foraging societies in East and southern Africa (Bantu-speaking farmers, Cushitic herders and cultivators, and Nilotic pastoralists in the Rift Valley grasslands and the Great Lakes region) carried their own traditions of gender relationships. High levels of continuing change within these societies as a result of internal development, trade, intermarriage, and other forms of contact with each other and with outsiders make it hazardous to reconstruct the position of women based on later descriptions. I have therefore refrained from projecting non-historical accounts back into the past, making the pre-nineteenth-century material necessarily fragmentary. Nonetheless, the kind of linguistic analysis hitherto applied to questions such as the diffusion of cattle-keeping also might illuminate aspects of society involving women (age grades, initiation ceremonies, religious ceremonies, and women's authority structures, for example).

*In addition to the works cited within this section, see Adams 1977; Hakem 1981; Leclant 1981; Sherif 1981.

The spread of Bantu-speaking farmers over much of the continent was central to the history of all of East and southern Africa and is credited with innovations in agriculture, ironworking, and pottery styles. Whereas historians and archaeologists once dated this population movement to the early years of the first millennium C.E., evidence now suggests that proto-Bantu speakers arrived in the western Great Lakes region early in the last millennium B.C.E., and that the height of the early Iron Age synthesis of the agricultural expertise of Bantu-, Sudanic-, and Cushitic-speaking peoples dates to between 500 B.C.E. and 500 C.E. By around the second century C.E., Bantu speakers had spread rapidly throughout much of the central and southern regions of the continent, reaching as far south as Natal in present-day South Africa (Schoenbrun 1993).

The significance of these demographic, agricultural, and technological developments for women and gender relations remains speculative. Given women's centrality to cultivation throughout the region, the emergence of complex farming systems based on iron technology must have rested in part on their skills. In this new agrarian environment, population levels probably increased, contributing to a more settled life and larger social units, although a high level of differentiation within the same language families and varied pottery traditions suggest that settlement density remained low. While women probably continued to exercise control over the food they produced, the case (noted earlier) of the !Kung who became farmers suggests possible negative repercussions as well. If the demands of agrarian life meant greater time spent in food preparation, women may have become more tied to household responsibilities than men and less able to benefit from new resources when long-distance trade developed. On the other hand, the low level of class division in early Iron Age societies may have produced relatively high levels of gender equality.

Oral traditions, linguistic analysis, and other historical material suggest that shifts in kinship systems occurred during this period. Linguistic evidence implies that the earliest Bantu speakers followed bilateral forms of descent, recognizing maternal and paternal kin; matrilineal and patrilineal forms followed more recently. In the Great Lakes area, patrilineality developed in response to environmental conditions that drove people to seek greater control over such resources as cattle and land. In other regions, early Iron Age societies were more likely to be matrilineal and matrilocal. A Kikuyu myth, for example, which speaks of men plotting to impregnate all the women at once in order to seize power from them, may symbolically document a shift from matrilineal to patrilineal kinship patterns. Thus, a primary source of cultural and technological interaction among peoples of different language communities came from women incorporating men of other groups through marriage or maintaining strong ties to their natal homesteads when they became wives in patrilineal communities (Ahmed 1991; Kenyatta 1979; Schoenbrun 1993, 1997).

Mixed farming and herding communities also developed new religious syntheses centered on creative deities believed to control natural forces associated with agrarian productivity (Posnansky 1981). Women's connection to agricultural and individual fertility was at the center of these cosmological systems in early Iron Age societies. Religious ceremonies rested on a symbolic fusion of male and female power expressed within a context of male-controlled social and symbolic structures. Thus rulers, responsible for fertility in the widest sense, were dependent on actual and symbolic female regenerative power for their success. Similarly, fundamental transformative activities such as ironworking and royal investiture invoked both male and female strengths. This dual ritual emphasis reflected the development of social systems in which the need to control reproduction in order to maximize fertility led older men to regulate the lives of women and younger men. Only as women's fertility waned with age did rigid gender boundaries dissolve (Herbert 1993).

In two regions of East and southern Africa, the northern area from the coast through the Lake Region and present-day South Africa, the complex interaction and acculturation between different groups of peoples continued to form the dominant theme of history between 1000 and 1500. In the Lake Region and in the south-central area, the emergence of class inequalities and centralized states also became important factors in shaping local societies. The implications of these developments for women's history remain uncertain, however.

In the northern interior, the interaction among people linguistically identified as Bantu, Cushitic, and Nilotic and earlier foraging populations continued as a dominant historical theme, as the ancestors of many present populations began to settle in their contemporary areas. As a result of this interaction, a number of Bantu-speaking peoples adopted clitoridectomy, in some cases apparently from Cushitic speakers and separately from formal groupings based on age. In other areas, the practice came from Nilotic neighbors and was adopted as an integral part of age-set structures (J. Murray 1974).

The agricultural adaptiveness of this period undoubtedly involved women as farmers and may have encouraged shifts in the division of labor and the structure of kinship, a hypothesis supported by Luise

White's correlation of particular groups of crops with distinct forms of kinship organization (1984). These changes in production included the shift from root crops to millet and sorghum in central and western Tanzania, which allowed the eventual absorption of the area's Cushitic and Nilotic populations, and the development of intensive highland agriculture with bananas as the staple crop in the mountain regions of Kilimanjaro and Kenya. The coexistence of different economic pursuits in these highland agricultural economies produced the area's only formal markets. As among the Kikuyu of central Kenya in the nineteenth century, many of those who exchanged food for livestock probably were women (Ehret 1984).

In the Great Lakes region and in Zimbabwe, as the sparsely populated, relatively unstratified societies of the early Iron Age gave way to more complex and differentiated social forms, relationships between women and men probably changed accordingly. The degree and nature of these changes for women is critical to our understanding of whether increasing political and economic differentiation led to a deterioration in women's position in African societies, as Karen Sacks has argued (1982).

The societies and economies of the Great Lakes rested on the relationships that developed between the predominant agricultural communities and small numbers of pastoral people who possessed immense herds of long-horned cattle. As access to cattle became a primary source of political and economic authority, new ruling classes emerged. The dramatic transformations of the early second millennium c.e. are recorded in the Bacwezi legends, which use intermarriage as a principal metaphor for dynastic change and show female ceremonial figures as a vehicle for transmitting tradition from one group to another. It is likely that many of the new dynasties dating to this period looked to priestesses and to the women's religious ceremony of *kubandwa* as sources of legitimacy. This religious tradition was linked to ancient practices of dedicating young girls as spirit wives. Queen mothers also were significant in the region from an early period (Berger 1981, 1994b).

Emergent centralized states in the Zambezi and Limpopo basins were based on both internal change and external influence, in this case long-distance gold exports to the east coast. The resulting concentration of power and wealth, centering most dramatically on the massive stone monument at the Great Zimbabwe, but also on smaller political centers, led to new political and economic inequalities. Although little is known of the implications for women, Sacks's model can serve as a useful guide to future research. As part of an argument that Zimbabwe declined in part because regional resources were insufficient to support the expanding central area, Beach (1980) suggests that women became reluctant to walk the increasingly long distances necessary to tend the fields and cut firewood.

Farther south, the dominant regional force was the emergence of a group of foragers turned pastoralists who became known as the Khoikhoi. They kept cattle and fat-tailed sheep and used oxen to pack their belongings. Linguistic evidence suggests that as they expanded rapidly from present-day Botswana to the Cape, and then outward again to the east and the west, their pastoralism left a great impact on the Bantu-speaking peoples of the eastern Cape and Natal. The results of this expansion for gender relationships are not entirely clear, however (Ngocongco with Vansina 1984).

## Transitions to Islam

In northeastern Africa and along the east coast, the spread of Islam transformed the lives of Christian Nubians and Bantu-speaking coastal peoples alike. In both areas, as in parts of the interior, cultural change rested in part on the ability of matrilineal kinship systems to absorb male outsiders into new communities.

Information on Nubian women during the Christian period, which began in the sixth century, is scant. The power of queen mothers probably was affected as the monarchy began to follow a pattern of strict succession from father to son. After the eleventh century, however, kings reverted to an older system whereby a sister's son succeeded his uncle instead of the king's own son. This shift suggested that matrilineality had not entirely disappeared. Although most land remained in small family holdings, women's part in cultivation is unclear. They did, however, produce handmade baskets, mats, and pottery at home. Since many European Christian attitudes toward women were based on writings of the Church Fathers that came after the elaboration of Coptic Christianity in Egypt, the gender roles that became embedded in the Nubian and Ethiopian churches probably developed locally. In neither case, for example, do discussions of monasticism refer to female members of these orders, which became such important centers of women's power in early medieval Europe.

Two key aspects of women's history emerge in Nubia from the late twelfth to the early fifteenth centuries. As the Christian kingdoms of Makurra and 'Alwa came gradually under northern domination, women were intimately involved in the ensuing processes of

Arabization and Islamization. (Early in the history of Islam, Egypt was drawn into the cultural, and often the political, orbit of succeeding Middle Eastern dynasties.) Encouraged by a matrilineal descent system, intermarriage between Arab men and Nubian women became an important vehicle of culture change, for the offspring of such unions were able to gain access to property and leadership positions. Over time, however, another shift with implications for women occurred: a change to patrilineal kinship organization. Thus, women must have been significant in both transmitting and resisting new forms of culture. The implementation of Muslim law came only from the early sixteenth century onward. Little information on Abyssinian women is available during this period, apart from references at the end of the tenth century to a powerful queen of the Agao named Gudit (Yodit) who rebelled against the Aksumite state and rejected Christianity (Kropacek 1984).

On the east coast, where a process of ethnic and religious transformation similar to that in Nubia was occurring (resulting in the emergence of a specifically Swahili cultural tradition), women again became agents of change based on intermarriage with Muslim men. In the first millennium of our era, the east coast was settled by Bantu-speaking peoples who lived in small villages, fishing, farming, keeping some livestock, and trading among themselves. From about 1000 onward, trade increased, and from the twelfth century towns began to grow, gradually becoming centers for the transmission of Islam. The traditions of most of these towns were similar, although only those of Mombasa identified the first ruler, Mwana Mkisi, as a woman. All centered on the process by which traders identified as "Shirazi" (to highlight their claimed Persian ancestry) married local women, taking advantage of matrilineal links to obtain rights to settle and access to land. This pattern remained typical of coastal Swahili traders, who continued to take local Bantu-speaking wives as a means to establish economic and political connections. In a somewhat different way than in Nubia, intermarriage became a route to political power, based on pre-Islamic patterns of closed aristocratic clans whose women could transmit the royal title through marriage. This practice was apparently at the root of a tradition in Pate, Kilwa, and other coastal towns whereby men acquired power by marrying the ruler's daughter. Eventually, however, royalty and prestigious families (*waungwana*) adopted a system of patrilineal kinship, which enabled them to restrict more closely the status of their descendants. No longer could the children of outsiders inherit their mothers' social standing.

Since Muslim law was adopted only gradually, first among the trading community, it is difficult to know how women's position was affected. The emergence of a new cultural tradition that centered on rich merchants and the old coastal aristocracy probably intensified class divisions among women; but their place in this mercantile trading culture remains to be investigated. It may be significant, however, that Arab and Portuguese sources describe coastal women as finely dressed in silk and gold garments, laden with jewels, earrings, necklaces, bangles, and bracelets. Seclusion was never mentioned (Matveiev 1984; Nurse and Spear 1985).*

*Opportunities and Constraints, 1500–1800*

As yet, few historically based studies of women in this period exist; but the effort to explore oral sources and to correlate this information with both contemporary written accounts and anthropological information should be a high priority. The few efforts to do so verify the need for great caution in simply projecting anthropological data backwards to reconstruct a so-called "traditional" past. Although many historians have explored this era through oral tradition, the resulting descriptions of population movements and the rise and fall of political systems rarely speak of women or of gender. In Muslim areas women became more secluded, while in centralized kingdoms increasing differences emerged among women of different ranks. External commercial and political influences also began to shape new patterns of opportunity and constraint.

In the Funj kingdoms of Nubia, the gradual implementation of *shariʿah* (Muslim law) beginning in the early sixteenth century contributed to changes in the position of women. They began to withdraw from public life but remained involved in family-oriented ceremonies such as weddings. Yet the low level of popular adherence to Muslim orthodoxy makes it uncertain how widespread these changes were. A remarkable account in 1813 by the explorer J. L. Burckhardt (discussed in Adams 1977) portrays women as worn down by continual labor in the household, including the crafting of mats and pottery by hand, while men exclusively worked in the fields. Women controlled a portion of their bridewealth, which must have given them a certain level of economic independence. But it was not uncommon for women suspected of adultery to be put to death, which suggests a high level of patriarchal control over their sexual and reproductive behavior. Prostitution was tolerated only at Derr, a bus-

*In addition to the works cited within this section, see Fagan 1984; Phillipson 1974; Sutton 1981.

tling commercial center; those involved were not local women but destitute emancipated slaves, an illustration of the social and economic vulnerability of women who lacked family protection.

A similar pattern emerged on the east coast, where Muslim beliefs about women began to provide a conceptual justification for ousting most women from public life. By the seventeenth and eighteenth centuries, women were secluded and required male mediators in their dealings outside the household. Absent from nearly all positions of political authority, they were also forbidden to hold such religious offices as judge or leader of prayer in the mosque. Occasionally, however, royal birth might lead to unaccustomed privilege, as in the case of Mwana Mwema and Fatuma, both queens of Zanzibar in the seventeenth and early eighteenth centuries, or Mwana Khadija, the ruler of Pate from 1764 to 1773. Women rulers also were recorded in Pemba and Tumbatu. Religious strictures against women were confined to orthodox Islam, however, for women participated in folk versions of ceremonies and in pre-Muslim communal celebrations, while older women continued to wield authority in family matters (Caplan 1982; Gray 1962).

In several interior regions of East Africa, differences were developing among women of different ranks. Ethiopian queen mothers exercised considerable power, and women at court were visible in ways that European observers found curious. Army camps were not occupied by soldiers alone, but by the queen, all the ladies at court, and the wives of important men. Other women ground meal and transported honey wine and large earthenware jars of honey. Occasionally, women also fought. During wars against the Oromo (Galla) in the late seventeenth century, the Ethiopian king was alarmed to discover women dressed as men taking part in campaigns. Repeating the Nubian pattern of male agricultural labor, most peasant women remained at home, grinding corn and grain and cooking and spinning, while men worked in the fields, wove cloth, and washed heavy clothing in the river. One traveler's tantalizing reference to a "sizeable village" populated almost entirely by market women suggests that further investigation of female traders may reveal novel forms of collective organization (Pankhurst 1961).

In the politically centralized kingdoms of the Lakes Region, wealth in livestock was creating an aristocratic cattle-owning class. The women among them were relatively idle, apart from creating finely woven basketry. High-ranking women included queen mothers, the wives of prominent men, and female ritual specialists. During this period, new groups of rulers gradually took over some of the myths and symbols of popular, predominantly female religions known as *kubandwa*, while in some areas household and lineage heads came to use the authority of these fertility religions to enhance their own power (Berger 1981). In Buganda, with an economy more dependent on land than on cattle, polygyny intensified among members of the political elite in conjunction with growing state power. As control of labor and land came under the joint sway of the royal family and bureaucratic chiefs, women's position was redefined. They lost their place in political leadership as the husbands or guardians through whom they obtained land became the patrons of other men, placing peasant women at the bottom of a new hierarchy. Perhaps most important, as wives became important symbols of prestige, women became a commodity for wealthy men to accumulate. At the same time, however, royal princesses grew freer and more powerful in their own domains. Though granted great sexual freedom, they were not allowed to marry or to bear children (Musisi 1991).

In other parts of East and southern Africa, intensified foreign commercial and political penetration, which often created increased economic competition among different African peoples, began to influence women's lives both directly and indirectly. In the Shambala kingdom of Tanzania in the seventeenth and eighteenth centuries, for example, where the entry of immigrant groups intensified the struggle for resources and eventually created a new centralized state, the accumulation of women and children was one of the aims of plunder and conquest. As the level of trade increased, men became more involved in the production of exchange goods, leading women to intensify their labor in growing food for subsistence (Mbilinyi 1982). Similarly portentous for women was the increase in raiding, warfare, and the general level of violence over the whole of southern Africa beginning in the late eighteenth century.

To the south, intensive coastal trade and the presence of Europeans left some contemporary documentation on women. Among the Shona in present-day Zimbabwe during the sixteenth and seventeenth centuries, the division of labor was distinct, but not rigid. Although women worked in the fields and fetched water and firewood, and men worked in other branches of production, later sources refer to hunting as a joint activity. Under a system of polygynous, patrilocal marriage, most men, in fact, could afford only one wife, since bridewealth payments were high. Though divorce was common, it was limited by the need to return bridewealth, usually paid in cloth, beads, hoes, and cattle (Schmidt 1988).

Along the southern coast, new commercial influences affected women more directly. Near Sofala, women grew rice, selling the surplus to the port population, and worked in the gold mines. (In areas controlled by *prazeros,* landowners of Portuguese origin, squads of female slaves mined gold, and to a lesser extent iron and copper.) Once again, the wives of male rulers, one of whom was the king's full sister, were extremely powerful in their own right. In southern Mozambique, where commercial influences intruded early, women's economic position began to erode in the seventeenth century. As ivory and horns came to be valued in international trade, men's hunting activities yielded new prestige goods and larger herds of cattle, which they could invest in additional wives. Women's activities were not unchanging, however; they used their agricultural skills to adopt new crops such as maize, cassava, and groundnuts (Beach 1980; Isaacman 1972; Young 1977).

In the Khoikhoi or Khoena communities that covered large areas of South Africa when the Dutch arrived in 1642, the extent of women's political power is unclear; but through ridicule they were able to exercise some control over the actions of those in authority. The wives of important people, however, were vulnerable to abduction, apparently for reasons of political prestige. Their recapture was a frequent cause of warfare. Although herding was the paramount economic activity (supplemented by gathering), women were not as disadvantaged as in many African pastoral societies. Milk, a more important food source than meat, was supplied by women. They did most of the milking and apparently had some control over the cattle given for them as bridewealth. But daughters inherited large numbers of livestock only if there were no living sons (Elphick 1985).

Contrasting patterns emerged in the few areas of southern Africa that experienced direct European settlement. The Africanization of the Portuguese *prazeros,* resting on intermarriage with local women, probably involved little cultural change for the women concerned. For Khoikhoi women in South Africa, the situation was rather different. Taken into Dutch homes from the earliest period of settlement at the Cape, they were trained as domestic servants. Most were probably very young, however, and returned to their own communities when they married. As the Dutch began to employ more highly skilled household slaves from the East Indies, the Khoikhoi were gradually displaced, reappearing in large numbers as domestic workers in frontier areas during the eighteenth century. Many fewer Khoikhoi women were Christianized, and to some degree Europeanized, during the early years of Dutch rule. For Eva, the best-known of these women, the results were tragic. She became a servant of Jan van Riebeeck, the first commander at the Cape. Having learned Dutch and Portuguese, she acted as a mediator between the colonists and her own Khoikhoi group and eventually married a Danish surgeon. When he was killed within four years of their marriage, she began drinking heavily, turned to prostitution, and ended her life in banishment on Robben Island (Elphick 1985).*

*Nineteenth-Century Transformations*

During the nineteenth century, women in most societies remained central to production, trade, and other economic pursuits and had considerable autonomy in controlling the products of their labor. In centralized kingdoms, queen mothers and members of royal families wielded significant power and authority. As healers, priestesses, and spirit mediums, other women addressed individual and communal afflictions, while older women directed life-cycle rituals for girls that helped to create cohesion in values and institutions. Substantial variation remained, however, in the levels of women's political and legal authority and in the degree of submissiveness and deference demanded of them. Furthermore, where the influence of European missionaries, settlers, and traders was increasing, the ensuing changes in economic, political, and religious life were disrupting established relationships in profound, sometimes disturbing ways.

In the kingdoms of northeast Africa and on the East African coast, women's position was highly influenced by class relationships: in Ethiopia, between the nobility and the peasantry; in the Sudanese state of Dar Fur, between royal women, nobles, commoners, and slaves. Among the Amhara of Ethiopia, where private property in land formed the basis of society, class distinctions and gender both governed access to land. In contrast to most areas of plow agriculture worldwide, women owned, plowed, planted, and harvested their own fields. Despite formal equality in controlling property, however, a male-dominated legal system left them in a disadvantaged position in the late eighteenth and early nineteenth centuries. A similar balance of formal legal rights and social and political disadvantage prevailed in Dar Fur, Muslim-dominated from the last half of the seventeenth century. Here a small number of royal women held substantial political power, while other women's social and sexual autonomy was increasingly restricted as they rose on the social scale. Despite a higher de-

*In addition to the works cited within this section, see J. Wells 1998.

gree of freedom than was customary in Muslim societies elsewhere, women were expected to display an extreme degree of deference and subservience in public encounters with men.

Poverty and detachment from kin were particularly detrimental to women. Throughout the Sudan, the incidence of slave raids and slavery rose dramatically. Mainly women, these slaves became concubines and agricultural and domestic laborers in Muslim areas of the north. In response to the dislocations of the slave trade, some African women moved to urban areas and took up new occupations. Many of the Somali women who moved to the Arabian port of Aden lived by casual labor and prostitution, activities that became common in African cities during the twentieth century (Alpers 1986; Crummey 1982; Kapteijns 1985; Sikainga 1995; Spaulding 1982).

The island of Zanzibar was similar to Dar Fur as a Muslim society in which women were allowed a certain degree of religious, economic, and political participation. During the course of the century, however, lower-class women began to perceive seclusion as a sign of respectability. Evolving ideological norms of women's domestic subordination and subservience found expression in Swahili literature, particularly in Mwana Kupona's depiction of the duties and behavior of the model wife, which she composed for her daughter around 1860 (Strobel 1979). The lengthy poem concludes:

> Read, you who are sprouts of wheat    obey your menfolk    so that you
>     may not be touched by the sorrows    of the after-life and of this.
> She who obeys her husband    hers are honour and charm wherever
>     she shall go    her fame is published abroad. (Harries 1962, p. 85)

Only in the nineteenth century do we begin to have historically grounded information on gender relations for a wide variety of societies in East and East-Central Africa. The most detailed historical description of women during this period comes from Shona communities in Zimbabwe. Although Shona women exercised considerable influence in their households and lineages, only a few women, through their religious or political positions, occupied a status equivalent to that of men; and women of the lowest socio-economic ranks might be pawned to pay debts during times of famine and hardship. Women's status increased over the course of their life cycles, however, first as they married and bore children, and later as they exercised authority over co-wives and daughters-in-law. Yet as outsiders in their husbands' families, women were vulnerable to accusations of witchcraft. Only as postmenopausal elders, close to the ancestors and considered more like men than women, might they attain respect and power.

Basic to these life-cycle changes was an ambivalent attitude toward fertility and sexuality as fundamental to survival, yet dangerous and in need of patriarchal control. Despite their subordinate position, women could confront their superiors both publicly and privately through gossip, child-naming practices, and critical songs that compared marriage to slavery or condemned the laziness of a daughter-in-law (Schmidt 1992).

Elsewhere in the region, historians and anthropologists generally depict women with a high level of economic and ritual authority, though under conditions that were shifting rapidly. Among the relatively egalitarian Kikuyu, organized politically and socially into age sets, male elders exercised authority over the entire community, while women's authority extended only to other women. Yet as cultivators, traders, prophets, and diviners, women had considerable economic independence, and a widow could circumvent the practice of remarrying her husband's brother by taking a lover or by paying bridewealth for another woman. Sometimes called "woman-to-woman marriage," this practice, found in many African societies, allowed one woman to benefit from the labor services of another (C. Clark 1980). Mang'anja women in the Lower Tchiri Valley (now in Malawi) had a similar degree of economic power and autonomy in a system based on matrilineal village communities in which married couples lived with the woman's family. Men and women were equally important to agriculture and local trade, although they divided non-agricultural production on the basis of gender. In religion, women assumed greater prominence than men in both household and community rituals and in the veneration of the region's guardian spirit, Mbona, who protected the land from natural disasters (Mandala 1984, 1990). In Yao society in Mozambique, also founded on matrilineal villages, motherhood was at the core of women's position. Though entrusted with important ritual roles, women were considered helpless and dependent on men in conducting daily affairs (Alpers 1984b). Among the Nandi of Kenya, a clear historical progression occurred during the nineteenth century: as small decentralized communities rapidly accumulated livestock and became more centralized, men attained greater control over women's productive and reproductive capacities by elaborating a new ideology of women's inferiority (Gold 1981; Oboler 1985). A similar ideological devaluation of women prevailed in Kikuyu society. Origin myths, folk tales, and proverbs, though difficult to pinpoint to a specific era, document a value system that associated men with civilization, skill, wealth, and important pursuits, while representing women as wild, cruel, and irrational—at best unfaithful servers, and at worst ugly and inconsequential (Ciancanelli 1980; C. Clark 1980; Robertson 1997b).

Many societies to the south combined cattle-keeping, state systems, and greater domination of women, a relationship that calls for additional historical exploration. Though Tswana women produced and controlled their own crops, their exclusion from all public and legal matters and the demand for strict obedience to husbands and elders may have been connected with the society's great vulnerability to drought and economic scarcity (Kinsman 1983). Zulu women experienced similar forms of subordination, intensified by the development of a highly militaristic state in the early nineteenth century. Through their poetry, however, they retained the ability to comment shrewdly and uncompromisingly on the world around them. And among the many Zulu commanders who led attacks far to the north in the 1820s and 1830s was a woman named Nyamazana, described as a remarkable warrior (Gunner 1979; Guy 1980; J. Wright 1981). Xhosa women also controlled the crops they produced, but they could not own cattle, and they remained legal minors subject to male control throughout their lives. In the frontier wars with white settlers, which lasted from 1779 until the mid-nineteenth century, Xhosa women provided food and ammunition, carried messages, and suffered along with their children from the hunger and exposure that were among the unintended results of combat (Peires 1989). Only in the northern Transvaal, the realm of the famous Lovedu "rain queens," did a relatively flexible political and social system empower women more generally as district heads, owners of livestock, and healers (Krige and Krige 1948).

As merchant capitalism spread, and new areas of Africa were rapidly integrated into a European-controlled worldwide economic and political system, the relative position of women and men began to shift in complex ways. In some societies, the impact of Christian missionaries on gender relations dates to this period. Among the Tshidi, a Tswana sub-group in South Africa, for example, women were among the marginal groups to convert first to the new religion (Comaroff 1985). Indeed, if most scholars agree that women's overall position has declined during the twentieth century, recent studies suggest that in many areas this decline began during or prior to the nineteenth century. This insight suggests the need to locate studies of gender as much in changing relationships of production as in the political and social policies of colonial rule. For much of the century, however, some regions remained relatively isolated from external forces.

Where commercial capitalism penetrated into new areas of the interior, striking changes occurred in women's lives. While historians have only begun to explore the gender-related effects of such changes, some excellent case studies agree that the erosion of women's position dates to this period. In the context of emergent commercial values and institutions from the mid-eighteenth century onward, women in the Nile Valley kingdom of Sinnar found it increasingly difficult to retain their rights to land ownership; their social vulnerability in the new urban, commercial society often forced them to sell their land. In Dar Fur, the increasing, though still only partial, seclusion of noblewomen was becoming a joint sign of wealth and of Muslim orthodoxy. Claims to religious adherence also influenced the growing fashion of clitoridectomy, although Islam did not require the practice (Kapteijns 1985; Spaulding 1982). Separate case studies from the Lake Nyasa–Lake Tanganyika corridor and from present-day northern Sudan, Kenya, Zanzibar, and Mozambique all argue that the new commercial order privileged men, leaving women increasingly disadvantaged by comparison. Only in Sinnar and on the Swahili coast were efforts made to prevent free women from farming. As part of this trend, more restrictive clothing came into fashion, and new beliefs emerged that disparaged women's capabilities.

Throughout many parts of East Africa, the new economic forms intruded through the trade in slaves, which drastically increased women's vulnerability, as the personal histories collected by Alpers (1997) and M. Wright (1993) movingly illustrate. Slavery and the slave trade, by distorting and commodifying the value of women's productive and reproductive labor, created conditions that, while dangerous and insecure for everyone, left women with many fewer options than men and often forced them to seek new forms of male protection. Among the Yao, these developments exacerbated earlier ideas of women's helplessness and dependency. Zanzibari women, responding also to rising pressure for Islamic orthodoxy, initiated a new spirit-possession cult in which these constraints on women were ritually enacted (Alpers 1984a).

Because women were so central to agricultural production, new technology and increasing commoditization changed their position in many areas. In present-day Malawi, although Kololo conquerors in the 1860s assumed control of the female sphere of salt trading, they preserved women's agricultural autonomy, which allowed them to retain economic authority vis-à-vis their husbands. But introduction of the plow in nineteenth-century South Africa, as part of the trend toward commercialized agriculture and the growth of a prosperous peasantry, affected women adversely. Both in the ethnically diverse northeastern Cape and among the Tswana, the plow increased men's work in food production, granting them rights to the crops they grew, and sometimes expanding their control over women's labor. Among the Pondo, the use of ox-drawn carts for transport had similar effects (Beinart 1980; Bundy 1980; Kinsman 1983; Mandala 1984, 1990).

One way in which capitalist relationships began to pervade the most intimate aspects of personal life was through changes in bridewealth. In some areas these customary gifts were converted into cash; elsewhere they were changed first into other commodities with a higher value in international trade, and only later into cash. The resulting inflation could have far-reaching implications. Among the Tsonga of southern Mozambique, the substitution of hoes (received from the Portuguese in exchange for ivory) for cattle greatly inflated *lobola* (bridewealth) payments. The rising value of bridewealth intensified distinctions between the rich and the poor and further confined women to reproductive labor as men became more tied to providing luxury items for trade. Payments shifted to cash later in the century as increasing numbers of young men began to work as migrants in the sugar fields of Natal and the gold mines of the Transvaal. The Pondo, responding to the economic aftermath of Zulu incursions rather than to international forces, began to substitute grain for cattle in bridewealth payments, thereby contributing to men's greater involvement in agricultural production (Alpers 1984b; Harries 1994; Young 1977).

Increasingly sophisticated analysis of nineteenth-century material also provides new insight into the ecological dimension of African historical change, revealing the relationship between women's history, health, and demography. The population expansion in Kikuyuland, leading to the occupation of newly cleared forest regions, rested partly on complex connections among land-clearing, women's processing and distribution of food, and the authority of male elders (C. Clark 1980). In the Natal region of South Africa, a scarcity of resources probably contributed to the rise of the tightly organized, militaristic Zulu state, which rested partially on manipulating the social conditions of women's fertility. In Tswana society, the ever-present threat of drought helped to shape local forms of male domination and female submissiveness.

Among the Xhosa of the eastern Cape, an epidemic of cattle lung sickness created the conditions that gave rise to a devastatingly influential woman prophet, Nongqawuse, whom local women supported overwhelmingly. A vision she had in 1856, which inspired her to instruct people to kill all their cattle, to destroy their grain, and to refrain from cultivation, led to massive starvation and depopulation, finally breaking Xhosa resistance to the colonial Cape government (Peires 1989). This upheaval, also closely connected with missionary influence and British colonial control, led to profound social and moral disruption in the Xhosa area of South Africa. A close examination of the status and language of the prophet Nongqawuse suggests that as the shortage of cattle through lung sickness made marriage more difficult, sexual transgressions (including incest and adultery) increased, thereby symbolically contaminating men and defiling the cattle that were linked through bridewealth to female reproduction (Bradford 1996).

Thus, as the formal period of European colonial rule dawned in the 1880s, East and southern African women were by no means in a pristine and unchanging "traditional" state. The preceding two millennia had produced continual shifts in institutions affecting women and gender relations, and individual women had played an important part in influencing historical developments. In foraging communities, relatively egalitarian gender relationships were maintained over a long period of time. The urbanized commercial centers of northeast Africa and the Swahili coast, by contrast, produced intensified class divisions with significant effects for women: the adoption of patrilineal inheritance patterns, efforts to confine more prosperous women to the household (justified on religious grounds), and attempts to restrict women's right to own land. Barred from mixed-sex ceremonies and from religious office, Muslim women in these areas developed their own, exclusively female observances.

In the farming and herding communities of most of East and Central Africa, where patterns of historical change remain more elusive, production, politics, and trade stand out as the major factors influencing gender relationships and women's place in society. Most fundamental, perhaps, were economic shifts, all of which had broader social consequences: in staple crops (root crops, grains, bananas), in the division of labor in non-farming activities (fishing, gathering, salt and iron production), and in the place of cattle in particular economic and social systems. Where farming predominated, local cosmologies linked women's fertility with that of the land, thereby legitimizing male control of women's reproductive powers in the name of communal well-being. The ecological pressures felt throughout southern

Africa from the late eighteenth century also influenced women directly and indirectly. These material factors undoubtedly contributed to shaping important features of social organization, such as the apparent switch from matrilineal to patrilineal inheritance patterns in some areas and the strong control over women in a number of southern cultures.

Political concentration and long-distance trade built on the economic base of community life, often profoundly altering established relationships. In centralized states in which men, and a few women, acquired substantial authority and access to resources, control over large numbers of women and their labor became one of the requisites and signs of power. Perhaps more critical were long-distance trade and the advent of commercial capitalism, which, in the two centuries preceding direct colonial rule, offered some men new, highly lucrative opportunities and led in selected areas to bridewealth inflation and to a devaluation of women's activities. In these regions of East-Central Africa and in directly colonized parts of the south, where men became plow-using peasant farmers, the events of the eighteenth and nineteenth centuries had effects on women that foreshadowed the transformations of the twentieth century.*

## EAST AND SOUTHERN AFRICA, 1880 TO THE PRESENT

### A Time of Transition, 1880–1920

Relatively fluid social, economic, and political relationships characterized the early decades of colonial rule. As Marcia Wright has observed (1993), it was a period in which the centralizing authority of the state was relatively weak and not yet routinized, but the ethnic and lineage communities disrupted by merchant capital during the nineteenth century had not yet assumed their colonial form. Though the international economy in the nineteenth century had unsettled women's lives far more in some areas than in others, the notion of transition is crucial to understanding this period.

Closely connected with economic and political transformations during the early decades of colonial rule were equally critical changes in the conceptualization of marriage and sexuality. Central to these shifts was the possibility for all people, but particularly for women, to begin to think of sexuality as an individual matter outside the context of lineage authority. While lineage relationships in the past had closely defined the networks for channeling sexual desire, during the

*In addition to the works cited within this section, see Hanretta 1998.

colonial period the combination of government legislation, wage labor, the commercialization of bridewealth, and the emergence of new urban communities transformed the context for sexual relationships. As individual rights came to have legal and social standing, the authority of male elders over women and younger men was undermined (Jeater 1993).

## RURAL COMMUNITIES

The degree of rural change varied enormously, depending on whether white farmers laid claim to local land, on how missionaries involved themselves in particular communities, and on how local colonial officials pressed their claims to labor and taxes. But certainly the most powerful cause of rural dislocation came from the disproportionate reliance on men to work on European-owned farms and plantations, to build roads and railways, and, most significant of all, to mine the gold, diamonds, and copper that became the economic backbone of southern Africa. Women's continuing presence in the rural areas was necessary to subsidize the low wages of African men, to reproduce a new generation of laborers, and to provide the care to ill and aged workers that capital and parsimonious colonial states were equally unwilling to fund.

Although male labor migration left its mark virtually everywhere in southern and East Africa, its effects were far from uniform. In parts of East Africa, for example, some rural women found the onset of colonial rule economically advantageous. During the late nineteenth and early twentieth centuries, Luo women in western Kenya experimented creatively with new crops and agricultural techniques and expanded seasonal local trade; the most successful female innovators, often Christians, were able to convert their agricultural surplus into large herds of livestock. Although missionary emphasis on hard work and agricultural training led some male converts to do a greater share of agricultural work, thus easing women's burden, labor migration attracted mainly young, unmarried men, whose absence did not appreciably change the division of labor in farming (Hay 1976).

In other areas, however, changes were less beneficial for rural women. Among the matrilineal Tonga of Northern Rhodesia (later Zambia), where the position of women depended on their ability to command the labor and allegiance of sons and sons-in-law, missionary and settler competition for male labor threatened older women in particular. Furthermore, as herds recovered from the rinderpest epidemic of the 1890s, bridewealth became more important than brideservice, and the balance between female-controlled resources (male labor) and male resources (cattle) tilted in favor of the latter. Yet, in strictly economic terms, women did not yet fare badly. In both the Tonga and the Lenja regions, the distribution of plows was too limited to have a significant influence on the division of labor, and women continued as active producers, gaining added independence by beginning to trade agricultural products (Muntemba 1982; M. Wright 1983). In the northern Sudan, however, the importance of enslaved women as field laborers increased under colonial rule as enslaved men successfully deserted their owners or gained manumission (Sikainga 1995).

A complex relationship between labor demands and marriage patterns also affected women in the Delagoa Bay hinterland of Mozambique. As male migration to the mines of South Africa combined with infecundity from the rapid spread of venereal disease to cause a fall in the birth rate and a decline in agricultural production, chiefs responded by dramatically lowering the marriage age to the period of early puberty. Women, now mothers at a much earlier age, became solely responsible for household production and maintenance (P. Harries 1994).

Urban Communities

If many case studies portray rural women as victims of structural changes over which they had little control, women in cities and small towns were better able to take advantage of vaguely enforced colonial policies and fluid social relationships to create economic opportunities for themselves. Often relying partly on the conceptual and social framework of Christianity or Islam, they tried to forge new norms and new communities to handle the problems their environment presented.

Again, patterns differed according to the size and function of towns, the political economy of the colonial territory, and the consequent division of labor by race and gender. Abercorn in Northern Rhodesia (later Zambia), a polyethnic, commercial community, attracted rural women who sought social refuge from male domination. Their marriage choices in particular reflected both the possibility of mobility and an opportunistic attitude. As early as 1903, however, colonial authorities began to support local men in regaining control over women by close regulation of the rules governing bridewealth and marriage (M. Wright 1993).

Studies of other urban areas document above all the restricted and exploitative economic opportunities for women in the formal wage economy, which undoubtedly influenced their preference for jobs in which they maintained independence, flexibility, and, under certain circumstances, the ability to support themselves extremely well. Most notable in this regard were the Nairobi women who took advantage of a skewed demographic situation to garner considerable savings through prostitution and brewing. Working independently, they invested their earnings in houses and came to form a significant percentage of African householders in the city by the 1920s (Bujra 1975).

Economic options for black South African women were extremely limited. In Johannesburg, where the sale of sexual services was heavily controlled, proletarianized women of European origin, both local and foreign, dominated prostitution in the early years of the twentieth century. Black women were drawn in only when severe rural crises forced them into town in exceptionally large numbers. There was some demand for their services in domestic work, and in both urban and rural areas of the eastern Cape and the Orange Free State, large numbers of African women entered these jobs. But in the Transvaal and Natal, neither women nor their relatively protective families favored this choice. Thus, most African women ended up brewing beer to support themselves and to supplement their household incomes. Even where the demand for black female domestic workers was substantial, many women preferred to do laundry on an informal basis. In Cape Town, as clothing production increased during World War I, young coloured (mixed-race) women were drawn into this nascent industry. Wages and working conditions were abysmal; but many preferred factory labor to cooking and cleaning in affluent households (Berger 1992; Gaitskell et al. 1983; van Onselen 1982).

Although economic choices for women in colonial urban centers were relatively narrow, they found myriad ways to re-create their cultural, social, and religious environment, drawing jointly on new and old norms, institutions, and ideologies. In some cases, Islam, associated with trade and urban life, provided the basis for this cultural redefinition; in others, Christianity did so. Earlier religious traditions also influenced these responses. Prostitutes in Nairobi, often estranged from their rural kin, became Muslims in large numbers in the quest for a new source of community; but they also drew on ethnically based notions of blood "brotherhood" and woman-to-woman marriage to create fictive kinship ties (Bujra 1975). Less deliberately, perhaps, slave women in Mombasa, because they were intimately involved in the extended households of their owners, tended to become assimilated to the dominant Muslim culture (Strobel 1997).

Just as Islam provided Nairobi prostitutes with alternative social relationships, Christianity offered many women a new source of community and new cultural norms. This support was vital to the emerging black petty bourgeoisie of South African towns, since missionaries, critical of polygyny and of older ritual systems, forced converts to separate themselves from their non-Christian kin and neighbors. Yet conversion also provoked conflict. In the absence of older controls over their daughters' sexuality, South African women were unable to live up to the domestic norms so critical to the mission churches. Prayer associations, formed first in Natal in 1912 in response to this crisis, gave women a supportive setting in which to lament their failings and their difficulties. For many Central African women in marginal positions, such as slaves and widows, Christianity expanded individual options by providing a refuge from slavery and an alternative conceptual and authority system. This open environment did not last long, however, for colonial authorities quickly responded to the abolition of slavery by promoting marriage and male dominance as a means of social control (Gaitskell 1982; M. Wright 1993).

## LEADERSHIP AND RESISTANCE

As in revolutionary periods, when strong female leadership often emerges in otherwise patriarchal settings, the early colonial era created the social space for a number of women to attain prominence at the head of resistance movements. Muhumusa in northern Rwanda (struggling jointly against foreign oppression and the central Rwandan state); Charwe, a medium of the spirit Nehanda in Rhodesia (Zimbabwe); and the Empress T'aitu Bitoul in Ethiopia all combined "traditional" claims to spiritual or political authority with unique personal strengths. The Empress, unusually well-educated in Ge'ez and Amharic for a woman, took to the battlefield against Italian troops (Rosenfeld 1986), while Muhumusa's invented connection with Rwandan royalty and her marginal position as a kinless individual in a lineage-based society augmented her position (Berger 1976; des Forges 1986; Freedman 1984). Mekatilili, a leader of the Giriama uprising in eastern Kenya, had no prior claim to authority. She combined personal charisma with an ability to articulate deeply felt fears and grievances against the colonial administration. Women, fearful of losing land, and their sons were among her strongest followers (Brantley 1986). Charwe was unusual to begin with as a female medium. After she was hanged, her spirit Nehanda attained continued fame as a primary symbol of anticolonial defiance (Lan 1985).

In South Africa, a longer history of imperial rule, Western education, and Christianity contributed to the emergence of new sources of authority and new types of reformist protest. Prominent among these middle-class leaders was Charlotte Maxeke, a teacher in the eastern Cape, who was the first black female university graduate in the country. An executive committee member of the South African Natives National Congress (later the African National Congress), she was a prominent leader of the successful women's campaign against passes in 1913. The movement drew its strength from women's fears of being forced into domestic labor, its tactics from the Gandhian model of passive resistance, and its model of female action from the British suffrage movement (J. Wells 1986). Discontent was also apparent among young black proletarianized women in Johannesburg. Those who took part in male-led Amalaita gangs that robbed homes in wealthy white suburbs were rejecting their oppression in a manner more threatening, though ultimately less effective (van Onselen 1982).

*State, Capital, and the Reconstruction of "Tradition," 1920–1945*

The close of World War I ushered in an era of fully developed colonial rule in East, Central, and southern Africa. As capitalism, Christianity, and imperialism made deeper inroads into African life, colonial states began to formulate new ways of controlling those outside the boundaries of recognized "traditional" authorities. Thus, this period combined continued erosion of preestablished economic and political relationships and institutions with efforts to reconstruct the social controls inherent in those relationships. In the process, both colonial administrators and local rural authorities began to conceptualize women as inherently immoral and in need of regulation.

URBAN COMMUNITIES

Though the larger colonial cities remained areas of gender imbalance, increasing numbers of women were migrating to urban centers such as Nairobi and Johannesburg and to the towns of the Northern Rhodesian (Zambian) copperbelt. The formal jobs open to women remained extremely limited, but they retained their hold in petty trade, marketing produce and prepared food, brewing beer, and selling various combinations of domestic and sexual services. Where the size of white settler populations created a greater demand for domestic labor than black men could fill, women worked as *ayahs* (children's nurses) in Kenya and Mozambique and as household workers in parts of South Africa. (In Johannesburg, however, most married women preferred to do laundry at home or to do housework on a daily basis rather than to commit themselves to full-time domestic labor.) The few female industrial openings, confined to South Africa, went to poor young Afrikaner women or, at the Cape, to those defined as coloured. Only small numbers of women had managed to attend school long enough to qualify for entry on their own into the petty bourgeoisie as teachers or nurses, although Nairobi prostitutes were able to do so economically by purchasing property (Berger 1992; Gaitskell 1979b; Gaitskell et al. 1983; Stichter 1975–76).

As the female population in towns began to increase, so did the concerns of both colonial officials and African male authorities, albeit sometimes for different reasons. Since many of the women who migrated to cities were deliberately escaping the control of husbands, elders, or fathers, they sought urban relationships that left them some degree of flexibility, thus involving themselves as often in short-term informal "marriages" (in Northern Rhodesia earning themselves the label of "piecework" women) as in long-term relationships (Ault 1983; Chauncey 1981; Parpart 1986). These unions were often little different from the *malaya* prostitution common in interwar Nairobi, in which the women involved provided their partners with a wide range of domestic services (Luise White 1990a).

In a period in which colonial authorities in many areas were making new and concerted efforts to curb unrestrained urban development for reasons of health, crime, and social control, a specific focus on women was not unexpected. While Nairobi officials, in the name of health, drove African prostitutes from the streets, South African legislators passed regulations in 1930 and 1937 that began the process of controlling women's movement to the cities. They still were not required to carry the passes mandated for men, however. It was here and in Northern and Southern Rhodesia where the joint interest of colonial officials and "traditional" authorities in legally controlling women has been most closely documented (Kimble and Unterhalter 1982; Simons 1968; J. Wells 1982). In South Africa, the strongly patriarchal Natal Code, which established women as legal minors, was extended to all black women in 1927. In the Rhodesias (later Zambia and Zimbabwe), by a more gradual process of codifying "customary" law, male chiefs and headmen helped to reshape "custom" in an effort to reclaim their authority over women and younger men. The problem was particularly acute in colonial Zambia, because mine owners were finding it necessary to allow workers to live with their families in order to attract sufficient male labor. By encouraging female movement to urban centers, this decision put mining interests at odds with colonial officials and male elders, who sought to keep women in rural areas (Chanock 1982, 1985; Chauncey 1981; Schmidt 1992).

In such older cities as Mombasa, women's dance societies reflected and expressed the changes of the period. Newly popular *lelemama* associations took on names such as Kenya Colony and Land Rover as their leaders assumed European titles. As elite Muslim women loosened the restrictions of seclusion, thereby lessening the social distance between themselves and lower-class women, many elements of slave life became increasingly integrated into Swahili culture (Strobel 1979).

## RURAL COMMUNITIES

The position of women in rural areas continued to vary, depending on a number of factors: the effects of cash crops, technology, and changing patterns of land tenure; the demands of white settlers; and women's previous economic position. This diversity suggests that the widely assumed correlation between cash cropping and a decline in women's status was neither universal nor uniform, and that women at times struggled successfully against changes detrimental to them. Overall, however, most studies verify that the rural shifts during this period were disadvantageous to women.

In the Tonga area of Northern Rhodesia, where maize-growing became widespread after World War I, many men began to use a cheap light plow in the late 1920s. By 1945, the resulting changes had led to a decline in married women's rights to land, and to a decrease in their autonomy as producers and marketers. This negative impact came both from the new technology and from efforts to address the problems of overstocking and soil erosion that ignored the separation between women's and men's fields (M. Wright 1983).

In southern Nyasaland (later Malawi), contradictory shifts occurred in the relationships between women and men. Africans living on the privately owned Bruce Estates had a matrilineal tradition in which women were the main food producers and guardians of fertility. But practices on the estates gradually eroded women's autonomy by making most women dependent on their husbands for access to land, and by allowing men to pass on their land through the male line. With the demise of matrilineal inheritance, female elders lost their political influence, and after 1925, when women were forbidden to marry men who lived off the estate, the resulting rivalry for husbands eroded earlier patterns of female solidarity (Vaughan 1985; Landeg White 1987).

Neighboring Mang'anja women, by contrast, succeeded in retaining and even improving on their precapitalist autonomy. In a period of intense cotton cultivation that lasted up to the 1940s, although the power of female headpersons and elders eroded, women remained strong enough collectively to hold back the tendency toward the privatization of land (through religious powers associated with fertility) and to resist the separation of male and female farming labor. Cotton production gave women an economic base, allowing autonomy to female household heads and new opportunities for petty commodity production. The popularity of *mabzyoka*, a female-led spirit-possession movement, symbolized women's efforts to maintain their visibility. By requiring husbands to contribute funds to the expensive ceremonies, women struggled to prevent wealthy men from becoming economically independent of their wives (Mandala 1984, 1990; Vaughan 1985).

In Kenya, varying regional economies influenced women's options in different ways. Luo women in the western province continued to experiment with new crops and tools. In the prosperous years before the Depression, some women were sufficiently successful to pay bridewealth for "wives" to help them to cultivate more intensively. But the conditions under which women worked were increasingly unfavorable to them. In the larger official trading centers that replaced local markets in the 1920s, Indians owned the permanent shops, while local men supplanted women in open-air selling. When local markets were reestablished in the 1940s, Luo men bought the shops as investments, and women assumed men's places in outdoor commerce. Although trade and marketing had become a regular part of women's daily lives, the difficulties of the late 1920s and early 1930s (when depression and locusts led to drought and famine) firmly established the belief that economic security lay not in farming, but in formal education and long-term wage employment outside the home. Both options were less available to women than to men. Thus, although women were able to maintain their position in agriculture and trade, these were no longer the most lucrative or viable sectors of economic activity (Hay 1976). For rural Kikuyu women in central Kenya, where foreign settlers had appropriated vast areas of land, wage labor was available picking coffee on European farms. Women on these estates held the most menial, lowest-paying positions and, particularly in the 1920s, suffered from a high level of sexual harassment (Presley 1986).

## IDEOLOGY, RELIGION, AND SOCIAL CONTROL

Colonial ideologies of social control, generally expressed through mission-sponsored education, aimed to cast African women in the mold of late-Victorian wives and mothers. Elite girls' boarding schools, aspiring to shape a generation of married, Christian African mothers, assumed strong control over their pupils' puberty and marriage in an obsessive effort to keep their charges from the shame of premarital pregnancy. Trained for domesticity, they were to become wives to the new African bourgeoisie of teachers, ministers, and evangelists. For urban missionaries in South Africa—where Christianity was, in Gaitskell's words, as much about new family forms as about faith in Christ—shielding girls from premarital sex and pregnancy was a similarly intense preoccupation. Yet here the missionaries displayed some ambivalence about whether young women were being trained for lives of domesticity in their own homes or in those of white employers. This contradiction notwithstanding, the colonial-sponsored cult of domesticity resonated also with African women, gaining them prestige and respect at a time when their families faced the threat of disintegration from both internal and external pressures. Whether in the form of boarding schools, urban-based hostels, youth organizations, or adult education classes, mission-sponsored organizations aimed to fill the educational gap left by the demise of ethnically based circumcision and initiation schools (Gaitskell 1979a, 1982, 1983; Hansen 1992; Morrow 1986).

Where such ceremonies remained, as in the Kikuyu area of central Kenya, missionaries condemned clitoridectomy and related rites of passage. In attacking rituals that were fundamental to Kikuyu identity, they incited conflict both with individuals who believed in these practices and with early nationalist organizations. Presley (1992) argues that most women at the time identified with the nationalist position and acted by leaving mission churches and supporting the establishment of alternative primary schools for the children (Davison 1996; Murray 1976).

The colonial imprint on domestic life also included a profound reshaping of sexuality and fertility control. As the standing of rural authorities diminished, women refused to undergo virginity examinations and insisted on choosing their own lovers, while young couples rejected the non-penetrational sexual practices that had governed courtship behavior in many societies. At the same time that prolonged breastfeeding and sexual abstinence for one to two years after childbirth were becoming less common, especially in the cities, women's knowledge of and access to earlier methods of abortion diminished (Bradford 1991).

In answer to such challenges, less orthodox forms of Christianity often were more appealing than the mission churches. In the Kigezi district of southwestern Uganda, the highly successful *balokole* revival movement responded to women's tensions over issues of family life and sexuality, and to individual difficulties at meeting the rigid standards of official mission churches. Through new "families" created among communities of converts, women also sought refuge from the pressures of more "traditional" non-Christian relatives (Robbins 1979).

The appeal of independent churches to women should not obscure the profound importance of mission Christianity in some regions, however. For Ngwato women in colonial Botswana, the Christian ideology of *thuto*, "teachings," offered a means of access to the public political space of the *kgotla*, formerly the exclusive domain of men. By sharing with the BaNgwato kings a commitment to the "realm of the word," women played a major part in constructing a new national identity based on Christianity and literacy. Though they remained unable to take part in daily political and legal activities, on Sundays they preached in the *kgotla* to men and women alike (Landau 1995).

Despite the official hegemony that Christianity was acquiring in many areas, earlier religious traditions also continued to respond to women's needs and interests: a new spirit cult in Nyasaland led by female doctors helped women to maintain visibility in their communities (Mandala 1990); *chisungu* initiation ceremonies in East-Central Africa remained central to religious life (Richards 1956); and the powers of the Lovedu rain queen continued as a form of religious expression and ecological control in South Africa (Krige and Krige 1943). Among Tumbuka women in Malawi and Zambia, spirit-possession ceremonies became almost exclusively female, providing a therapeutic outlet for family tensions resulting from migrant labor and a relatively recent transition to patrilineal descent. In the following song, empowered by possession, a woman fearlessly condemns her father-in-law.

> My father-in-law slanders me.
> I shall do the same!
> He is a mad fool!
> My father-in-law insults me.
> I shall insult him also! (Vail and White 1991, p. 254)

## POLITICS AND RESISTANCE

In an era of wide-ranging popular protest, women played a fuller part in local resistance movements than in early nationalist organizations. Nonetheless, women were not absent from political action, particularly in Kenya and South Africa, where their campaigns have been documented more fully than elsewhere. Furthermore, many individuals who migrated to cities to escape the power of elders and husbands took part in personal contests for control that are not usually deemed "political." In matrilineal societies, the limited powers remaining to female authority figures virtually disappeared during this period.

Women in colonial Malawi suffered in particular from the decline of women's position in matrilineal systems. Among the Mang'anja, female elders continued to lose authority as political leaders beyond the village community. This loss corresponded with the decline of female non-agricultural activities (cloth-making, iron and salt manufacturing) and the rise of household-based cotton production. Perpetuating the anti-woman bias of earlier Kololo conquerors, the British replaced the few remaining female headpersons with male appointees. Yet women elders retained sufficient influence to hold back the detrimental effects of commercialized farming for women. On the nearby Bruce Estates, closely controlled by private owners, elder women lost to colonial authorities their former right to ratify the choice of village head (Mandala 1984, 1990; Vaughan 1985; Landeg White 1987).

In South Africa and Kenya, historians have traced women's involvement in various forms of collective protest. In the Herschel District of the Cape in the early and mid-1920s, rural Christian women organized and sustained boycotts of local shops and schools. These attacks on the state and local capital reflected new pressures on women from high rates of male migration and limited polygyny, and their opposition to taxation and land registration. Women based their strength on rural female networks, including *manyano* (prayer groups), and later on the Africanist, anti-white spirit fostered by the African Methodist Episcopal Church (AME). Other communal protests of the 1920s, such as campaigns against lodgers' permits in urban townships, attracted considerable female support (Beinart and Bundy 1987; J. Wells 1993). Protests also were common in Kenya, where female coffee pickers organized labor stoppages to press for higher wages and an end to physical and sexual abuse. They relied not only on their new work-based networks, but on traditional sexually based means of humiliation: turning their backs to an opponent and lifting their skirts. During World War II, prostitutes in Nairobi took temporary collective action to control their working lives under the new conditions of wartime (Presley 1986; Luise White 1990a).

In more formal nationalist and labor movements, women's place was more ambiguous. Barred from joining the African National Congress (ANC) of South Africa until 1943, women in the auxiliary organization, the Bantu Women's League, mainly catered food and organized entertainment. The National Council of African Women, which superseded the Women's League in 1935, was more concerned with welfare than with politics, although anti-pass leader Charlotte Maxeke was among its founders. In times of crisis, however (as in the period immediately following colonial conquest), women's subordinate position could shift. Prior to a six-month strike in East London in 1930, the militant Industrial and Commercial Workers' Union (ICU) had perceived women mainly as tea makers, social organizers, and workers' wives. By the second week of the stoppage, led by the Independent ICU, their position had changed. Women became fully involved as workers, and the organization began to voice their wage demands as domestic laborers and washerwomen (Beinart and Bundy 1987; Bradford 1987; Kimble and Unterhalter 1982; Walker 1992).

Occasionally, early nationalist organizations took up issues of concern to women, as when the Kenya-based East African Association (EAA) made the beating and sexual harassment of women on coffee estates one of its concerns in the early 1920s. In 1922, when the same organization gathered to protest the arrest of its leader, Harry Thuku, the women in the crowd reviled the men for being too hesitant. After turning to traditional forms of sexual display to express their scorn and irritation, they led the assembled crowd to the police station. When European settlers drinking on the verandah of the nearby Norfolk Hotel joined police in firing on the crowd, the women's leader, Mary Muthoni Nyanjiru, was the first to die. Women's courage won them no immediate place in political affairs, however. Excluded from meetings of the successor group to the EAA, the Kikuyu Central Association, women in 1930 formed the Mumbi Central Association; the organization dissolved three years later, when women gained the right to take part in the KCA (Presley 1992; Robertson 1997b).

*Economic Restructuring and the Push for Independence, 1945–1965*

The period following World War II brought more intensive and deliberate colonial intervention in local economies, often in the form of programs to "modernize" agriculture. These efforts invariably operated to the detriment of women. Although during this period colonial states assumed greater responsibility for welfare and educational programs once primarily the work of missionaries, they brought to their efforts domestic ideologies of womanhood not dissimilar to those of religious groups. Indeed, these assumptions were probably reinforced by the new domesticity prevailing in postwar Europe. As changing conditions throughout the world created a continent-wide drive for independence, women, although often overlooked in standard historical accounts, took an active part in the effort to end colonial rule.

## RURAL COMMUNITIES

During the 1950s, women's authority and their economic position continued to erode. A decisive turn to male domination in the family and economy was particularly marked in formerly matrilineal regions. In the lower Tchiri Valley of Nyasaland (Malawi), the failure of the peasant cotton economy, in which women and men had shared equally, left women limited to precarious subsistence production, while men became increasingly involved in the cash economy, including migrant labor. As wage labor allowed boys to escape brideservice, marriage (increasingly patrilineal) came to involve a cash exchange. Once men's economic and political equals, by the 1960s women occupied a weak and marginal economic position and found divorce increasingly impossible because of the difficulty of repaying bridewealth money. As another sign of their newly emerged patriarchal power, men also took over the grassroots spirit-possession cults, once the province of female leadership, while women turned to pentecostalism to express their concerns. Similarly, in the Tonga area of Northern Rhodesia (later Zambia), a shift to bridewealth as a lump-sum payment was increasingly interpreted as entitling a husband to overriding rights in his wife and children; by the mid-1950s, this conception of paternal power meant that any property accumulated in the marriage went exclusively to him. In 1949, when severe famine struck Nyasaland, women without access to male-generated cash incomes were extremely vulnerable, particularly when the administrators who distributed food assumed that they were entitled to male support (Mandala 1984, 1990; Vaughan 1987; M. Wright 1983).

Women also suffered a decisive setback in areas making the strongest effort to "modernize" agriculture in response to such problems as soil erosion, overstocking, and presumed agricultural inefficiency. As colonial states increased their assistance to local male farmers, men's control over new technology and their easier access to government finances and markets made many rural women more economically dependent on their husbands. The trend has continued under independent governments. An integral aspect of development plans, best documented for Kenya, has been the policy of registering and consolidating land and granting titles to individuals, almost always men.

Begun in 1954 as the Swynnerton Plan, the policy continued unchanged through independence, substantially weakening rural women's autonomy in the economy and in the family. At first, however, the implications of the plan provoked severe opposition in the Luo area from male elders; engaged at the time in codifying "customary" law in response to female demands for greater freedom in matters of marriage and sexuality, they were anxious about losing control over young women (Okeyo 1980).

While such changes in policy and family structure partially account for the increased number of women leaving rural areas in the postwar period, particularly in South Africa and other areas of European settlement, women also were responding to intensified rural poverty. With young men increasingly absent, infant mortality high, and the productivity of land declining, many African reserves no longer provided women, children, and the elderly with a viable subsistence base. Although in a number of countries local officials made efforts to curb women's movement, only South Africa adopted a coherent national policy backed by sufficient force to have more than a limited effect.

## URBAN COMMUNITIES

As larger numbers of women moved to cities during the postwar period, the urban demographic imbalance began to shift to more equal proportions of women and men. In most cities, some new female jobs in the wage economy began to open up; but the vast majority of women continued to work casually and independently as petty traders, beer brewers, and prostitutes, despite the risks involved in many countries for brewers in particular. In South Africa they faced continual harassment and jail sentences, in Mozambique up to a year of forced labor (*chibalo*). In some cities, such as Dar es Salaam, however, informal labor provided women with sufficient resources to invest in urban housing, as Nairobi prostitutes had done earlier in the century (Berger 1992; Geiger 1987; Penvenne 1983).

Domestic service, the only formal female occupation in some areas, was the lowest paid, most exploited of all urban jobs, often requiring a live-in commitment that was difficult to combine with caring for one's own family. Nonetheless, where rural social relationships were most severely disrupted as a result of labor migration, land alienation, and resulting land shortage, increasing numbers of African women became household workers. Where local industries existed, as in South Africa, Kenya, and Mozambique, some women also began to work at processing food and tobacco and at manufacturing clothing, all extensions of female domestic skills. Following a typical wartime model, the Kenyan women employed in industrial jobs during the Emergency of 1952–56 ceased to interest employers when men again became available (Berger 1992; Penvenne 1983; Sheldon 1996; Stichter 1975–76; Stichter and Parpart 1988).

As an African middle class developed in numbers and self-consciousness during the years leading to independence, very small numbers of Western-educated women began to work in the acceptably female professions of teaching, nursing, and social welfare. In Muslim communities such as Mombasa, the sex segregation prescribed by Islam, while limiting women's mobility, also required female professionals in these roles. Thus some Swahili women were encouraged to pursue education and employment (Strobel 1979). Although most urban women continued their involvement in income-producing labor of some kind, throughout East and southern Africa a culture of domestic dependency was growing among a small Christian elite.

To colonial authorities, the increased pace of female movement to towns was not a neutral process. Rather, they associated urban women with prostitution, venereal disease, adultery, alcoholism, divorce, and high illegitimacy rates. Many officials included greater female independence and the growing number of women-headed families on their list of moral and social ills. In response, governments turned both to legal restrictions and to educational efforts to alter the moral and social climate of women's lives through education. The government of Northern Rhodesia, for example, tried to ensure that occupants of African housing had legally registered marriages, while South Africa in the 1950s took the first steps toward extending the pass laws to women, initiating the most stringent controls on their movement anywhere on the continent (Parpart 1986; Walker 1992; J. Wells 1983).

As part of the effort to promote the "advancement" of African women and to supply a growing male elite with suitably trained wives, colonial states began to take a more active role in promoting girls' education. Although the number of girls attending school increased rapidly in some areas, boys continued to outnumber them by a substantial margin. These formal efforts at female education combined academic subjects with a heavy emphasis on domestic science. They were matched by a vast network of official and voluntary programs designed to promote women's "domestication" on a European model (Hansen 1992). In both urban and rural areas, instructors in these projects taught basic literacy and math, cooking, sewing, health, hygiene, and childcare. Whether initiated and promoted by women's clubs in Tanganyika, the Maendeleo ya Wanawake (Women's Progress) movement in Kenya, "improvement associations" in Mombasa, *foyers sociaux* (housekeeping schools) in Usumbura (Burundi), or mining companies in Northern Rhodesia, all conveyed a morally laden message emphasizing women's primary place in the home and family. The message was by no means unwelcome, however. Some groups, even while European-run, created positions for African women, and others, such as Maendeleo ya Wanawake in Kenya, were rapidly taken over by African women (Geiger 1987; Hunt 1990; Parpart 1986; Strobel 1979; Wipper 1975, 1975/76).

## WOMEN'S ORGANIZATIONS AND NATIONALIST POLITICS

Although most African women in the 1940s and 1950s continued to express their economic concerns through informal organizations such as rotating credit associations, some members of the tiny group of women wage laborers were beginning to join emerging trade unions: *ayahs* (children's nurses) in Mombasa and Nairobi, teachers and nurses in the Sudan, and food and clothing workers in South Africa. These trade union women in South Africa formed a high proportion of the original organizers of the Federation of South African Women, the group that led the protests against passes for women in the second half of the 1950s (Berger 1992; Fluehr-Lobban 1977; Stichter 1975–76).

Recent research documents the fact that as nationalist movements swept the continent in the late 1940s and 1950s, women were as prominent as they had been in earlier forms of anticolonial protest. They expressed their political sentiments both through major political parties and through local resistance movements, both rural and urban. The strength of such popular, often spontaneous protest provides an important reminder of the grassroots ferment that underpinned the nationalist movements, even while Western-educated elite men emerged as their official voices.

Local women's protests often focused on colonial efforts to rationalize and "modernize" administration and agriculture. Thus in 1945, Pare women in northern Tanzania marched to the district headquarters to voice their opposition to new taxes seen as disruptive to family and agricultural life. They attacked the local chief and issued the symbolic demand that the British district officer impregnate them all, since his policies undermined the position of their husbands. Significantly, although these protests contributed to the enactment of local government reforms, no women were included in the decision-making process (O'Barr 1975/76). Similarly, in Usumbura, Burundi, in the late 1950s, Muslim women organized an effective revolt against a special tax on single women. Protestors, who refused to pay this exaction for several years, were incensed at the implication that all widowed, divorced, and polygynous women were *malaya* (prostitutes) (Hunt 1990).

In the Meru area of Kenya, located on the northeastern slopes of Mt. Kenya, thousands of young girls defied both African male authorities and colonial officials in a highly provocative fashion. After a locally enforced ban on clitoridectomy was passed in 1956, adolescent girls sought to initiate their own transformation into womanhood by attempting to excise each other. Using razor blades in place of special-purpose knives, and abandoning the public celebrations normally associated with the occasion, these girls exerted peer pressure throughout the district to encourage others to join them, sometimes with the collusion of their mothers and grandmothers. Occurring at the time of the "Mau Mau" insurgency against the British colonial government, the excision controversy became a test of this age group's collective strength and determination at a time when many people were being tortured in prison or killed in the forest (Thomas 1996).

Significantly more volatile, if no more dramatic, were the spontaneous uprisings of South African women in Natal in the late 1950s. Rural women, enraged at forced removals, stock control, and a new system of land allocation under which women no longer were guaranteed their own fields, smashed dipping trucks, burned fields, and attacked available symbols of the state. Women in Durban, responding to restrictions on domestic beer brewing and to government support for municipal beer halls, were equally vehement: they invaded and burned beer halls, clashed with police, picketed, and engaged in ribald gestures. Though different in certain respects, all of these actions were intense, spontaneous, and relatively short-lived, the responses of peasant or poor urban women to perceived threats to their livelihood or to a disruption of customary relationships with local authorities (Lodge 1983).

Alongside these localized responses, women's active and hitherto neglected part in nationalist movements should make names such as Bibi Titi Mohammed, Lilian Ngoyi, Rebecca Njeri Kairi, and Wambui Wagarama as well known as Julius Nyerere, Nelson Mandela, and Jomo Kenyatta. This role is best documented at present for Tanzania, Kenya, South Africa, and, to a lesser extent, the Sudan. The differing patterns of women's recruitment in each country suggest a more nuanced view of nationalism than the usual picture of Western-educated male elite leadership would suggest. Based on her analysis of women's life histories, Susan Geiger concludes that nationalism was as much "women's work" as the work of the men usually credited with its spread (Geiger 1996).

Widely different social and political networks drew Tanzanian and Sudanese women into nationalist politics. In the former case, women were often seen as the strongest supporters of TANU (the Tanganyika African National Union). These female activists were "traditional" Muslims with little or no formal education, rather than members of the small Christian-educated elite who at this time were retreating into domesticity. TANU women drew from their experience in women's *ngoma,* dance groups, the sense of a trans-ethnic, Swahili-speaking urban community that informed their nationalism. These associations, which provided an ingenious mechanism for politicization that escaped the attention of suspicious colonial officials, became critical vehicles for rousing and expressing nationalist sentiment. Women saw in TANU not only an opportunity to gain national independence, but also a means to struggle against male domination (Geiger 1998). In the Sudan, a similarly high level of women's participation was generated first through the local Communist Party, and later through the larger nationalist movement. Although it began among educated urban women, the Women's League (and its successor, the Women's Movement) spread to workers and peasants in the northern part of the country (Fluehr-Lobban 1977).

The South African women who led and took part in the demonstrations against passes for women worked in a more repressive context. While highlighting women's legal disabilities in the 1954 Women's Charter, they considered national liberation their primary goal. As urban dwellers struggling against proletarianization, these women were in many ways conservative. Fearful of being forced into live-in domestic work, they sought to protect the household and family relationships so devastated by the migrant labor system and to resist coming under the rigid controls that governed the lives of men. This campaign, most dramatically expressed in a moving demonstration of twenty thousand women in Pretoria on August 9, 1956, increased in militancy as it spread to the countryside. In the Bafarutshe reserve near the Botswana border, for example, women incited a virtual civil war against anyone who cooperated in the distribution of passes (Lodge 1983; J. Wells 1983).

The only guerrilla struggle for independence in East or southern Africa prior to the 1960s, the "Mau Mau" revolt in Kenya, inevitably drew Kikuyu women into the conflict. Governed by a clearly defined hierarchy of rural female leaders, many women took part in the oathing ceremonies that created bonds to the movement, and some joined the armed forces. But they played their most crucial role in helping to maintain the supply lines that funneled food, information, medicine, and weapons from the towns and reserves into the forests. Although these tasks were important, the Kenya insurgency differed from later liberation struggles in the lack of self-conscious reflection on women's mobilization or on the oppressive aspects of gender relationships. As a movement geared more to the recovery of Kikuyu land and to the attainment of political independence than to the broader transformation of social relationships, this lack of emphasis on women is not unexpected (Presley 1992).

For the women and men who became forest fighters, however, gender relations and the definition of gender became central issues. The more literate Kenya Parliament rebels, as they called themselves, enforced monogamous marriage and, after an initial period of experimentation, a traditional gender division of labor, under which women cooked and gathered firewood regardless of their rank. Less educated and less hierarchal, the Kenya Riigi men and women fought side by side, spurning marriage along with customary gendered tasks. Also reflecting struggles about gender, debates about whether loyalist women and children should be killed centered on defining the differences between women and men, particularly in relation to women's mothering and nurturing roles (Luise White 1990b).

### The Ambiguities of Change, 1965 to the Present

The struggle for independence involved many women in new forms of political activity. But its attainment no more solved the problems of African women than it did the other pressing dilemmas of poverty and economic dependency within a capitalist world order. Indeed, the articulation of women's issues was strongest in the movements still struggling for liberation, particularly in such countries as Mozambique, where high priority was given to social reconstruction within liberated zones during the course of the war. Throughout East and southern Africa, formal independence did lead to more widespread female education at all levels as governments responded to insistent demands for improved educational opportunities. But the tendency for development projects (when they address women's issues at all) to accept the existing sexual division of labor as unalterable, or to exacerbate this division, means that little transformation has occurred in the lives of most poor women. And the majority of independent African states, rhetoric to the contrary notwithstanding, continue to express ambivalence about women's equality.

## RURAL COMMUNITIES

Despite some exceptions, for many rural women, both peasant farmers and those laboring on large farms and plantations, the last three decades have brought little positive change from above. Many development programs have ignored the role of women in agricultural production; after the mid-1970s, however, the UN Decade for Women and the food crisis in many parts of the continent generated greater sensitivity to gender issues. Many would argue that without attention to the unequal distribution of resources and the unequal allocation of labor in rural households, overall economic success will not necessarily improve women's position. Meanwhile the consequences of "development" policies are striking: women control less land, their land is less fertile and produces lower crop yields, legal and political barriers to women's land ownership continue, women have little access to credit or to agricultural extension services, and new technology has often increased their workload without a tangible increase in benefits (Lewis 1984; Muntemba 1982; Nelson 1982; B. Rogers 1980; S. Rogers 1982).

Projects to register and consolidate land have been particularly detrimental to women; in several cases documented for Kenya, such projects have deprived all but a minute percentage of women of any independent access to land. In the Luo area, for example, by the late 1970s, women constituted only 5 percent of owners of individually held land titles, and the government planned no provisions to establish access rights for other women (Okeyo 1980). Similarly, in the initial post-independence Tanzanian settlement schemes, land and all its proceeds went to the husband, and calculation of labor time took no account of women's domestic responsibilities. Although officials who established the later collective *ujamaa* villages responded to criticism and provided for women's rights to land, women remain disadvantaged in access to labor and to decision-making power (Brain 1976; Fortmann 1982).

Women have faced the most extreme deprivation in the labor reserve areas of southern Africa and in other regions in time of famine, when relief camps are filled primarily with starving women and children. Extreme poverty and malnutrition, meager income-earning possibilities, and high rates of infant mortality have been amply documented within the borders of South Africa. In neighboring Lesotho, where 95 percent of wage earners work in South Africa and 70 percent of rural households are in effect managed by women, their agricultural activities yield little cash and insufficient food for subsistence. Women here survive on occasional remittances, bridewealth payments, cooperative agricultural arrangements, beer brewing, petty trade, and "concubinage." This system creates both material and emotional misery and places women in a situation more similar to that of poor urban women than to that of rural women in more prosperous situations. Refugee schemes in time of disaster have typically addressed women's maternal and housekeeping functions at the expense of their productive roles (Mueller 1977; Murray 1981).

Urban Communities

The situation of most urban women also has altered little since the 1960s, either economically (as industrial and commercial capital controlled by men continue to dominate the production process) or in terms of negative attitudes toward women that blame them for the "corruption" of family life and view them solely as mothers and wives whose sexuality should be controlled within the family. For most urban women, however, the need for independent sources of income remains the main fact of city life. Often single heads of households, they persist in independent, casual labor, perform multiple activities to survive, and continue rural patterns of growing food for their families wherever they find available land. They also become skilled at manipulating their relationships with men to their own advantage.

Furthermore, many changes affecting women have had ambiguous consequences. The expansion of schooling for girls combined with the Africanization of positions in government and industry has increased the number of educated professional women. Yet most women enter stereotypically female fields, and some, while claiming independence and an aversion to marriage, have adopted luxurious lifestyles heavily dependent on male resources. In some countries, the increase in wage labor for women has been largely in domestic service: a low-paying position characterized particularly in South Africa by extreme vulnerability and powerlessness, weak bargaining rights, and time demands that create tremendous tension between women's roles as mothers and as wage earners. Though industrialization is relatively limited in the region outside of South Africa, increasing numbers of women in several other countries are now working in factories. Their jobs, however, are low-paying and semi-skilled (most acutely so in the rural factories of South Africa); they usually work with clothing or food, and they are likely to be replaced by men when mechanization occurs (Berger 1992; Cock 1980; Sheldon 1991).

As the most vulnerable members of the urban community, poor women throughout East and Central Africa have become easy targets for overzealous campaigns against prostitution, vagrancy, unlicensed trading, and beer-brewing. Women and children also were among the main victims of South African laws to clear the cities of those whose labor was not needed by whites; the apartheid state deemed them "superfluous appendages."

## RELIGION, FAMILY, AND IDEOLOGY

Independence has brought to East and southern Africa conflicting demands for "modernization" and for the preservation of "tradition." With the patriarchal vision of tradition constructed in many areas during the colonial period as a model, subordinate and domesticated women have at times come to symbolize "African custom." This tendency is apparent both in family policy and in religious practice and ideology.

The ambiguities of family policy are clear in attitudes toward family planning. Pressures to bear children remain strong, and most women continue to consider large families central to their emotional and economic well-being. Therefore, options are often limited for those who wish to restrict the number of children they bear. Abortion is illegal in most East and southern African countries, and contraception remains a contentious subject. The exception is South Africa, where the new government voted to legalize abortion after heated debate on the issue. Large numbers of children continue to be born out of wedlock, and many girls drop out of school because of pregnancy. One of the few governments to encourage birth control, the apartheid state in South Africa did so for purely cynical motives, endangering women's health by offering them injections of Depo Provera, a drug then banned in the United States and a number of other countries (Bradford 1991; B. Brown 1987).

Marriage reforms and attitudes toward marriage are complex, often combining efforts at increasing women's rights with a reluctance to upset customs perceived as "traditional," such as bridewealth, polygyny, and clitoridectomy. Some studies suggest that the resulting contradictions in legislation may increase the tendency of some women to prefer single motherhood to the constraints of marriage. In Tanzania, the Marriage Act of 1971 (which enhanced women's security in certain respects) has led some women to eschew marriage in order to maintain custody of older children in case of divorce (Bryceson 1985). In a distinctly different context, the marriage rate in South Africa has been steadily declining, with a recently studied group of women explaining that they wanted to have more certain rights over their children than the law provided (van der Vliet 1984). While Mozambican legal changes consciously sought to improve women's situation (Isaacman and Stephen 1980), the all-male National Assembly of Kenya voted in 1969 to repeal an act that required men to contribute to the support of illegitimate children (Wipper 1971). The Ethiopian Civil Code, although affirming that spouses owe each other respect, support, and assistance, recognizes the husband as head of the family, meriting obedience from his wife (Haile 1980).

Legal constraints aside, women display a wide range of attitudes toward marriage and family. Most continue to marry and to value children as a central focus of their lives. But in urban Zambia, many educated women tend to avoid marriage, while relying heavily on male contributions to their lifestyle. Poor market women there continue to raise their daughters in a "traditional" manner, insisting that they undergo initiation and instructing them to be subordinate to their husbands. These women also maintain, however, that marriage requires drastic change (Schuster 1979). In the Sudan, sustained pressure from women's groups led to legal reforms in women's economic and family position after independence, although the Women's Union took care not to attack strongly held "traditions," such as pharaonic circumcision, the most extreme form of genital mutilation (Fluehr-Lobban 1977). Yet the Somali Women's Democratic Organization, formed in 1977, gained the support of many women and, for a time, of the government in its campaign against excision (McLean and Graham 1985).

Religious movements, showing much the same ambivalent mixture of attitudes by and toward women, often perceive them as the sustainers of custom. In the Bapostolo (or Vapostori) Church, widespread in East and Central Africa, the majority of members are female. Although a few women may attain exceptional respect as prophetesses, healers, midwives, or judges, however, they are generally excluded from political leadership. In a related group in Zimbabwe, which prides itself on self-sufficiency and detachment from European culture, women are considered the symbolic retainers of custom (Jules-Rosette 1979; Kileff and Kileff 1979).

Indeed, in some contexts, the religious justification of emerging patriarchy has become quite blatant. In the once matrilineal Malawi village of Magomero, as women's economic power in the village declined, women began to follow their husbands' religious affiliation, and church leaders unanimously supported the transition to patrilineal inheritance (Landeg White 1987).

Some of the most stringent regulation of women prevails in the Sudan. In Muslim urban areas of the north, where an ideology of female seclusion and sex segregation continues, *zaar* spirit-possession ceremonies offer women participation in multi-ethnic groups that meet frequently for dances and healing rituals. These rituals also provide important forms of emotional release and expression, as well as a wide range of contacts in the urban environment. Yet, while providing meaningful social contacts for women who would otherwise be isolated, they in no way challenge the ethos that has made seclusion and genital mutilation the marks of middle-class status over the course of the twentieth century; only a few highly educated career women and those too old and poor to conform have been able to escape the increasing rigor of Islamic practice. Under the Islamist military government that has ruled the country since 1989, legal sanctions reinforce social norms. Women who disobey the decree that compels them to wear black veils and black ankle-length dresses face punishment by whipping (Constantinides 1982; Hale 1996; Jules-Rosette 1979; Kileff and Kileff 1979).

## ASSOCIATIONS AND STRATEGIES

Their often marginalized situation notwithstanding, many women have struggled both individually and collectively against poverty, an ambivalent social position, and the expectation of subservience to men. Individual strategies vary enormously, of course. Urban Zambian women seeking protection against marital and economic insecurity have increased their use of love medicines. Maasai women in Kenya, while lacking control over livestock, implicitly assert their equality with men by uniting in solidarity to protect women who commit adultery. Also responding collectively to their situation, Kenyan women have publicly attacked "traditional" women's roles, objecting in particular to the deference toward men and the arduous physical labor demanded of them. During constitutional negotiations in South Africa, some rural women threatened to boycott the elections if the right to practice customary law was included in the bill of rights.

In a tendency best documented for Kenya, rural women have reacted to their declining economic position by forming a variety of groups in an effort to regain control over critical resources. Responding to their husbands' control of the surplus from both subsistence crops and cash crops, women in Kiambu District have formed self-help associations that allow them to channel their cash proceeds into organizations under their own direction (Stamp 1986). In the cattle-keeping Tugen area, where men have come to see women as property and to expect obedience from them, women retain a bold and self-confident air in the presence of men and have begun to take charge of their own health, seeking information on family planning and beginning to question the practice of excising their daughters (Kettel 1986). As in Kenya, Zimbabwean women, also generally excluded from land-distribution programs, have remained politically active in rural areas, forming clubs and cooperatives and establishing irrigation systems, marketing schemes, and revolving credit associations (Jacobs and Howard 1987; Seidman 1984).

Urban women in East and southern Africa are generally less highly organized than their West African counterparts and often rely mainly on their own individual strategies. Yet market women and beer brewers in Nairobi and Kampala have formed organizations and informal networks to assist their activities and, occasionally, to invest their funds collectively. Their solidarity is based partly on their sense of marginalization, arising from the illegal nature of their activities and from suspicions about their economic independence. With varying degrees of success, women in Nakuru, a smaller Kenyan town, have formed cooperative groups to purchase farmland (Nelson 1982; Robertson 1997b; Wachtel 1975/76).

Some urban women, such as the female traders of Lusaka, have joined more formalized groups to express their economic grievances (Hansen 1984). Most significant, however, are the female industrial workers in South Africa, many of them household heads, who were fully involved in labor protests during the period of intensive organizing that followed the Durban strikes in 1973. By the 1980s, a few active trade unionists were demanding that the independent black unions address such issues as sexual harassment, paternity leave, and the unequal division of labor in working-class households (Berger 1992). In addition, as rent strikers, members of women's organizations, parents of schoolchildren and detainees, guerrilla fighters, and political prisoners, women also contributed strongly to the rising voice of liberation during that turbulent decade.

The Tugen experience with land distribution in Kenya, where land titles went only to the most vulnerable women (widows, unmarried mothers, divorcées, second wives) and the most powerful (the wives or daughters of influential men), points to another trend of recent years: increasing differentiation among women (Kettel 1986). As education increases the ranks of teachers, nurses, and secretaries, while others rise through well-chosen marriages, class divisions have widened. In Uganda in the 1970s, for example, tension was quite open between elite women and their female domestic workers. Reflecting this trend, many women's organizations, purporting to speak for all women, have in fact articulated goals that define the roles of lower-class women to suit elite interests (Obbo 1986). The leadership of Maendeleo ya Wanawake, the main national women's organization in Kenya, had changed by the 1970s from a militant group concerned about the rights of all women to an exclusive, politically connected urban elite alienated from its rural members (Wipper 1972).

Yet from among these educated women have come a prominent minority of writers, artists, and other professionals, some of whom have taken considerable risks on behalf of poor women. They include physicians and health workers who have organized locally against genital mutilation and other forms of anti-female violence; women who have identified with the goals of a global women's movement, working to define and create specifically African forms of feminism; environmentalists (such as Wangari Maathai in Kenya) who have led grassroots women to protect the land on which their livelihood depends; and the writers and artists who have articulated the conflicts that many women feel (*Gender Violence* 1994; Meena 1992; Oduol and Kabira 1995).

Highlighting the accomplishments and struggles of two prominent women conveys the challenges that many have faced. Maathai, as founder of the Greenbelt movement and head of the National Council of Women of Kenya in the 1980s, expanded the agenda of the women's movement to include both the environment and human rights. In 1992, joining a protest by mothers of political prisoners, she suffered detention without trial and a brutal beating by the police. Although women delegates endorsed her as a presidential candidate later that year, she declined the offer, believing she could contribute more to women as an environmentalist and activist (Maathai 1988; Oduol and Kabira 1995; Stamp 1995). Similarly trained in science and honed on political activism is Mamphela Ramphele. Drawn into the Black Consciousness Movement in South Africa while a medical student at the University of Natal, she became the close associate and lover of the movement's leader, Steve Biko. In the remote rural area to which she was banished for her political activities in the aftermath of the 1976 student uprising in Soweto, she established a community health center that served the needs of an impoverished homeland population. After her banning order expired, Ramphele returned to university. She earned a Ph.D. in anthropology and turned her organizing skills to academic administration. In 1996 she was appointed vice chancellor of the University of Cape Town, the first African, male or female, to assume the leadership of a formerly white elite institution. Reflecting on her experience, she wrote,

> The double jeopardy of being black and female in a racist and sexist society may well make one less afraid of the sanctions against success. A non-subservient black woman is by definition a transgressive—she is the ultimate outsider. But political activism, with its infusion of a purpose higher than oneself, and the steeling effect of having had to break most of the rules in a society desperately in need of transformation, have added an important depth to my adult life. (Ramphele 1996, p. 181)

Bessie Head and Grace Ogot stand out among the best-known female writers in East and southern Africa, although the work of others also has attracted attention: Barbara Kimenyi (Uganda), Noemia de Sousa (Mozambique), Martha Mvungi (Tanzania), Rebeka Njau and Charity Waciuma (Kenya), Tsitsi Dangarembga (Zimbabwe), and Miriam Tlali, Amelia House, and Lauretta Ngcobo (South Africa), and the South African autobiographies of Ellen Kuzwayo, Emma Mashinini, Phyllis Ntantala, and Sindiwe Magona. Ogot, in her novel *The Promised Land* and in some of her short stories, addresses the conflict between the limiting effects of traditional attitudes toward women, including submissiveness to men, and the positive attributes of a spiritual and communal heritage. Perhaps reflecting her own ambivalence and that of her characters, her writing never resolves these issues. Head, a more complex novelist (*When Rain Clouds Gather, A Question of Power*), addressed questions of gender and race as an outsider. Of racially mixed background and living in exile in Botswana, she never experienced the positive attractions of ethnic community. But in seeking to re-create collective and individual attachments on a new basis, she adopted as a central theme of her work the ambiguity and difficulty inherent in the effort to construct a "new world" of equality between women and men.

The protagonist of Tsitsi Dangarembga's novel *Nervous Conditions* confronts the conflicting demands on women directly. When her uncle, who has financed her education, raises the issue of how much schooling she should have before she thinks about marrying "a decent man" and setting up "a decent home," she reflects, "Marriage. I had nothing against it in principle. In an abstract way I thought it was a very good idea. But it was irritating the way it always cropped up in one form or another, stretching its tentacles back to bind me before I had even begun to think about it seriously, threatening to disrupt my life before I could even call it my own" (p. 180).

## POLITICAL LIFE AND THE POLITICS OF LIBERATION

The attainment of national independence failed to bring the benefits many women had anticipated. Few national constitutions specifically outlaw gender discrimination, and many exempt family and customary law from constitutional regulation. In most countries, women's participation in the political process has been restricted, except on a local level, and many male politicians have found women to be convenient scapegoats for their own shortcomings. At various times women have been blamed for divorce, illegitimacy, and the "loss of African customs," leaving young urban women in particular open to verbal and physical abuse for wearing mini-skirts, makeup, or foreign hairstyles. Women have attained a political voice, most often where men are absent, as in the Pare district of Tanzania (O'Barr 1975/76) or in Lesotho (Mueller 1977). Yet in the latter case, village political leaders have so little power that women feel they stand a greater chance of access to valued resources through effective domestic management than through the public life of the community (Obbo 1980; Wipper 1972).

Even where national politicians have made efforts to increase women's participation in nation-building and development, they have too often conceptualized women as domestic rather than economic beings and guided their assistance under the aegis of community development and social welfare agencies. This has been particularly true in Tanzania, where the ruling party supported the development of a women's organization at the time of independence. Although women participants in the UWT (Umoja wa Wanawake wa Tanzania) have gradually included economic as well as domestic activities and goals, women remained peripheral to conceptions of public policy. Significantly, the Third Five Year Development Plan, adopted in 1976, included no specifically women-focused projects, despite its primary goal of creating self-sufficiency in the provision of food. Furthermore, the female activists so critical to the success of TANU in the 1950s have nearly all disappeared from the political process. Ill-educated, most were unsuited to assume positions in the new government and have returned to the menial, casual pursuits of other urban women of their class (Geiger 1987). Just as the UWT's dependence on TANU has muted women's independent voice, since the 1974 revolution rural women's groups in Ethiopia have been subordinated to larger peasant associations with little interest in women's perspectives (Haile 1980).

In the national liberation movements that brought independence to Mozambique and Zimbabwe, Frelimo (the Front for the Liberation of Mozambique) and ZANU (the Zimbabwe African National Union) respectively voiced strong support for liberating women from what they characterized as the degrading and inhibiting aspects of both "customary" practices (such as polygyny and bridewealth) and the colonial heritage. In both movements, women (mainly young and educated at least through primary school) took full part in the military struggle and engaged in fighting and other support activities in significant numbers. "Without the women," in the words of one recent study of Zimbabwe, "the war could not have been won" (Staunton 1990, p. xii). Yet following the struggle, party leaders returned to older perceptions of women's place, seeing the goal of government programs as assisting them to be better mothers within the existing family structure. When a rural woman in 1994 suggested that land permits in resettled areas be registered jointly in the names of both spouses, President Robert Mugabe retorted, "If women want property, then they should not get married" (Cheater and Gaidzanwa 1996, p. 200). Many women remain politicized, however, and continue to be involved in the lower ranks of ZANU and in spontaneous political activity such as rent strikes, strikes over food prices, and demonstrations over licenses for petty traders (Seidman 1984; Urdang 1995).

In Mozambique, more attuned after independence to the continuing struggle for gender equality, many women remained active in party affairs and in political and economic projects at the village level; yet, because the division of household labor remained unchanged, the new situation burdened them with a triple weight of work in production, home, and politics. Nonetheless, sustained pressure from Frelimo and from the Organization of Mozambican Women created a favorable environment for change until the war and famine of the 1980s and early 1990s made continuing social transformation impossible (Sheldon 1991, 1992, 1994; Urdang 1983, 1989).

In the recently concluded struggles in South Africa, Namibia, and Eritrea, women were incorporated into armed units, and their concerns entered public political discourse, although they generally remained underrepresented in leadership positions. Women's community groups in South Africa, central to grassroots struggle, provided the impetus for a succession of political organizations, including the Black Women's Federation, formed and banned in the mid-1970s; the regional women's groups of the 1980s; and the Women's League of the African National Congress (ANC), newly relaunched in 1990 after the ANC was unbanned. Women in the Eritrean People's Liberation Front (EPLF), struggling for autonomy from Ethiopia, were particularly successful in promoting gender-balanced land reform, education for Muslim girls and women, and more egalitarian marriage relationships in the areas under the movement's control (Cowan 1983; Hassim 1991; Hubbard and Solomon 1995; Seidman 1993; A. Wilson 1991).

The 1990s have brought both new challenges and new opportunities. While the continuing spread of AIDS, the mandates of structural adjustment programs, and periodic crises (as in Somalia and Rwanda) threaten women's economic position, and often their lives, the continent-wide push for democratization opens up new possibilities for political action. In the 1994 elections in South Africa, for example, women won 106 of 400 seats in the first democratic National Assembly in the country's history. When Kenya restored multi-party politics in 1991, women's organizations immediately launched campaigns to educate women on democratic participation and to strategize for the election of women candidates on both the local and the national level (Stamp 1995). With a variety of dynamic women's groups in many countries, issues such as sexual harassment, rape, and domestic violence now take their place alongside political participation, clean water and sanitation, and access to land as issues that prompt women's organizing (Cowan 1983; Hassim 1991; Hubbard and Solomon 1995; Kemp et al. 1995; Murray-Hudson 1983; Oduol and Kabira 1995; Seidman 1993; Stamp 1995; A. Wilson 1991).

While some of these groups have begun to claim the designation of "feminist," others would eschew the label and evidence a consciousness different from that of many women's organizations in the West (Strobel 1995). The United Nations Fourth World Conference on Women, held in Beijing in 1995, afforded African participants the opportunity to formulate and voice a strong political agenda on behalf of women and girls. The appointment of a Tanzanian, Gertrude Mongella, as secretary general of the gathering heightened its importance to gender awareness on the continent. Yet all African delegates (except those from South Africa) were vocal against including sexual and reproductive rights in the final declaration.

Thus, as the twentieth century closes, African women have become active participants in international dialogues on women's issues. While certain questions such as violence against women have sparked new forms of activism and organizing, along with political and economic access, family issues and sexuality remain contested topics. This balance of opinion points to the variety of women's voices. It also highlights the efforts of some women to respond to the disruptive influences of the last hundred years by seeking to define and preserve distinctive features of African family life and to involve men as well as women in efforts to eradicate gender inequality.*

The rapid changes of the twentieth century have dramatically transformed the situation of women in East and southern Africa. With Africa's intensified involvement in a worldwide economic system, African women have been divided from each other in new ways: by class, by religion, and by residence in cities or in the countryside. Their economic place has contracted, and their former political authority has gone unrecognized. Women have maintained their centrality to many aspects of religion, but sometimes in subordinate positions. Despite shifts in family structure and in the ideological context of domestic life, they remain closely attached to their children; yet limited control over resources can make this responsibility difficult to fulfill.

The negative aspects of these changes notwithstanding, the results for women have been ambiguous and contradictory. Left behind in most of the formal shifts in economic and educational opportunities, women have struggled independently in both urban and rural settings to support themselves and their children. Shut out from political power under colonialism and under most independent governments, they have formed associations (secular and religious), organized protests, and taken part in nationalist and revolutionary struggles. The economic position of many women is precarious, particularly in countries devastated by war and famine and in the impoverished rural areas of South Africa. But African women have shown a remarkable ability throughout the twentieth century both to adapt and to struggle in response to difficult conditions. This individual and collective resilience will be critical to reconstructing gender relations in the future.

*In addition to the works cited within this section, see Basu 1995; Nelson and Chowdhury 1994; Seager 1997.

# Part II

## WOMEN IN WEST AND WEST-CENTRAL AFRICA

### E. Frances White

### PREHISTORIC WEST AND WEST CENTRAL AFRICA

The history of women before the rise of the Sudanese* kingdoms of
Ghana, Mali, and Songhay appears to be barely penetrable from our
present-day vantage point. We know that women and children collected much of the food consumed by gathering fruit, nuts, edible
leaves, and roots, while sometime during the Stone Age (2,000,000–
10,000 B.C.E.) men began to hunt in bands (Shaw 1981). Rock paintings, a major source of information for this early period, tell us little
beyond the facts gleaned from archaeology. Paintings from around
6000 B.C.E. show women in a bent position, as if they were winnow-
ing cereal crops, but corroborating evidence is incomplete (Ki-Zerbo
1981). Such depictions tell us little about the history of women and

*Note that "Sudan" here refers to a region of West Africa, not the country.

gender relations. They certainly do not help us understand why archaeological digs at Ahaggar in the Sahara have revealed a socio-political system which, by the fourth century of our era, was controlled by a woman. Salama (1981) points out that "there were several examples of authority being attributed to a holy woman" among the Berbers. The ruler of Ahaggar was buried in a tomb that revealed her wealth, obtained from control of the social system and the lucrative trans-Saharan trade. Items buried with her included seven gold bracelets, eight silver bracelets, and several precious jewels.

A number of sources conjecture about what led to the emergence of settled agriculture from gathering societies (Porteres and Barrau 1981; Shaw 1981). But despite the speculation that gatherers easily figured out the relationship between planting seeds and producing food, and the obvious role that women have played in farming, we have little information on the important transition that took place in women's labor. Archaeological sources have not problematized the control over women's labor required by agricultural societies to produce the kind of Iron Age splendor that has been revealed about such cultures as Nok in present-day Nigeria. Indeed, the eight-volume *General History of Africa,* published by UNESCO, which summarizes the current significant knowledge on African history, appears to bend over backwards to avoid saying anything that takes into account gender and the socially constructed, gender division of labor. Such sources tend to take input into agriculture as natural. There are no discussions of what it must have meant to organize and coordinate women's productive activities. Nok society could not have reproduced itself without a system of control over women's labor, and we need to know more about how this system evolved in order to more fully understand social reproduction during the Iron Age.

## WESTERN SUDAN TO 1800

When it comes to studying the early history of women in the western Sudan, many roadblocks prevent historians from producing a coherent narrative. The lack of both evidence and appropriate questions posed by scholars hampers such efforts. Many of the travelers' accounts that describe trade, state formation, and warfare in detail give biased accounts of women. A survey of many Arabic texts in translation reveals reports on West African women that tell us little about their lives. In general, the Sudanese women's behavior and comportment are held up against a standard that makes them appear to be uncivilized; in particular, these early accounts seem most concerned with whether women were appropriately dressed. For example, the famous Moroccan traveler Ibn Battuta reports on Mali:

> One of their disapproved acts is that their female servants and slave girls . . . and little girls appear before men naked, with their privy parts uncovered. . . . Another is that their women go into the sultan's presence naked and uncovered, and that his daughters go naked. On the night of 25 Ramadan I saw about 200 slave girls bringing food from his palace naked, having with them two of his daughters with rounded breasts having no covering upon them. (Levtzion and Hopkins 1981, pp. 296–97)

Such accounts share much with the biased and sexist accounts by Europeans in later centuries. These shallow and frustrating reports on women prevent us from achieving a fuller understanding of social reproduction in the Sudan. Instead of a clear picture of how the early Sudanese states, such as Ghana, Mali, Songhay, and the Hausa city-states, reproduced their societies, we have to rely on a general sketch that obscures the changing nature of gender relations and the inter-action between states and kinship systems. General sources indicate that most people living in Ghana, Mali, Songhay, and the Hausa city-states were agriculturalists who farmed using the hoe (Adamu 1984; Cissoko 1984; Ly-Tall 1984; Niane 1984). A strict gender division of labor characterized these societies. Women cared for the children, gathered firewood and water, cooked, collected tree crops, and tended to small stock, while men prepared the land for planting (Callaway 1987). Both men and women planted, but usually they each had pri-mary responsibility for different crops. Unfortunately, many sources tell us what crops were produced but fail to mention by whom and under what conditions. In some areas, women took part in other pro-ductive activities such as making salt (Lovejoy 1986). In much of the Sudan, weaving was an important task that women performed. Many women sold processed foods and cotton goods in local markets (Cal-laway 1987).

In the larger Hausa towns, as well as in other urban areas such as Timbuktu, Jenne, and Gao, stratification among women was greater than in rural areas. In general, women were either royal, free com-moners, or slaves. The division between royal women and slave women could be obscured by the position of concubines in powerful lineages. All of the kings, or *askias*, of Songhay were children of con-cubines. Such a position as mother of the ruler must have given con-cubines far more power than most free women held (Kirk-Greene and Hogben 1966). Hausaland provides the clearest picture of royal women in the Sudan. A number of the Hausa city-states (including Zaria, Katsina, and Daura) have traditions that begin with an original female ruler and a series of successful ruling queens. A dispute has emerged among scholars about whether these traditions should be taken literally. Smith argues that although some women played important political roles, the traditions actually recognize the transition from matrilineal to patrilineal descent (Smith 1978). Callaway counters that the traditions signify more than this transition. She argues that the existence of female offices and titles, combined with evidence of actual female rulers and the central role of women in pre-Islamic religion, would suggest that these early female rulers were real, not fictional, people (Callaway 1987). While it is difficult to draw definite conclusions about the extent of ruling-class women's power as the Hausa city-states were forming, scholars speak with more certainty for the periods after the thirteenth century. By this time, Islam had already begun to compete with the *bori* cult, or indigenous state religion, which was led and controlled by ruling-class women. It would seem that women lost much of their political power as the city-states used Islam to rationalize their power (Callaway 1987). The impact of Islam on Hausa women's lives was far from uniform. Royal women may have lost political power, but many common women benefited from the changes accompanying Islamization, since the conversion to Islam saved some women from enslavement and led to improved standards for their treatment in their families.

Although patrilineal descent had replaced matrilineal descent by 1200, certain key positions continued to be reserved for women. Smith (1978) has provided a detailed account of offices held by royal women in Daura. There the most powerful woman was the *magajiya,* or queen mother. As the senior woman of royal descent, she acted as an important check on the power of the male ruler, or *sarki.* Although the *sarki* was the supreme ruler, the *magajiya* had the power to depose a *sarki* if she received the permission of the senior council of male officeholders. She could also intercede on behalf of people whom the *sarki* intended to punish for personally offending him. Not surprisingly, she would be sought out by both men and women as a patron and could develop an extensive network of clients around the country. The *magajiya* ruled with the assistance of a titled administrative staff known as the *lawanai.*

The *magajiya* was chosen by the next most powerful woman in Daura, the *iya.* Holding the senior title reserved for women of the royal lineage, the *iya* selected the *magajiya* after consulting with other royal women in her state compound, which served as an important political space. It was from her compound that the *iya* presided over the ritual washing and instruction of princes before their first weddings. Perhaps more important, it was from her compound that she directed the *bori* possession cult in conjunction with the *lawanai* (Smith 1978). Until the nineteenth century, the *bori* cult remained an essential vehicle for the hegemonic control of Hausa people by the elite, since it was believed to be responsible for the health of the state. Many of the most important participants in the cult were divorced women or *karuwai*. The *karuwai* were considered under the jurisdiction of the *iya*. Women easily obtained divorces and were thus able to maintain an unusual amount of control over their own sexuality (Callaway 1987).

The most famous Hausa woman from this period was Queen Aminatu or Amina of Zazzau. She ruled during the late sixteenth century, having become *magajiya* when she was sixteen, and her father ruled as Zazzau's *sarki*. In 1576, she succeeded her father's successor as supreme ruler. She continued a tradition she had begun earlier of taking part in military expeditions. As a successful soldier, she extended the boundaries of Zazzau to the Niger River, conquering Kano and Katsina in the process. She is credited with introducing eunuchs and kola nuts to her kingdom. Her power extended beyond the military to the economy as, under her rule, Zazzau came to dominate both the region's trans-Saharan trade and the east–west Sudanese trade. Therefore, it was during Aminatu's reign that Hausaland's first major economic expansion occurred (Callaway 1987; Coquery-Vidrovitch 1997; Sweetman 1984).

Such economic expansion contributed to increasing stratification. In particular, the numbers of slave women grew as the Sudanese states' involvement in the trans-Saharan trade expanded. Men were often sold off into the trans-Saharan trade, while slave women played an important role in increasing the number of dependents among the elite. In societies in which large numbers of dependents were crucial for reproduction of elite social status, slavery proved to be an important avenue for creating these dependents. As Meillassoux (1997) points out, women were preferred to men as slaves, and the fact that they were priced one-third to two-thirds higher than male slaves reflected this preference. Both Klein and Meillassoux dispute suggestions that women were valued for their reproductive attributes; they argue instead that slave owners valued slave women's labor. Klein adds that these women were valued because they could be integrated into families as concubines, forced to produce food and supplies for armies, and married to slave men to keep them invested in the system. Slave wives and concubines were particularly valued by men in ruling lineages, maraboutic (Islamic holy men's) households, and merchant families, because they had no families to interfere with their treatment or to make claims on their children. Unlike free women, they could not divorce. Elite women desired female slaves to free them from household and agricultural tasks that were assigned to women according to the gender division of labor. In addition, for elite women, who typically could not command the labor of free individuals (wives or kin) as could free men, owning slaves provided significant access to labor that could be mobilized for wealth (R. Roberts 1984).

In general, the picture that emerges of the western Sudan is of societies with a rigid gender division of labor, especially among the free commoners. Free men and women planted different crops. Slaves freed royal women from agricultural and other tasks. Stratification in the Sudan increased as the states expanded their roles in the trans-Saharan trade. The number of slave women increased as the elite, both female and male, sought them for their labor power and their usefulness in expanding the number of dependents. Men sometimes preferred to marry slave wives because no affinal ties were established in such marriages that would create obligations for these men.

## THE WEST COAST AND ITS HINTERLAND, 1400–1800

The most significant developments for women during this era included the introduction of new crops, the growth in interregional and Afro-European trade, and the development of relatively powerful states. Women influenced and were influenced by these developments in a number of ways. Perhaps most significant, the region witnessed increasing stratification among women as states imposed themselves over kin-ordered societies. In no case did women collectively have as much access as men had to state power and the most lucrative trade items. Nonetheless, some women profited from the increasing trade and captured portions of state power.

### Trade and Production

Agriculture and both long-distance and local trade were central to the developments in this region, and women's labor contributed to their expansion. On the Gold Coast, for example, early European travelers reported on women's important roles in marketing. Most women were restricted to selling foodstuffs and handicrafts (McCall 1961). Nonetheless, their trading roles were essential for the development of the Gold Coast port towns and growing inland towns. Agriculture and trade formed the basis of urbanization beginning in the eleventh century; by the eighteenth century, towns with populations as large as 10,000 to 20,000 could support artisans, traders, religious people, nobles, and beggars (Kea 1982). Women's trade in foodstuffs was essential for this urban expansion.

The history of Oyo in Yorubaland also helps illustrate the impact of women's trading and productive roles in state formation. Oyo began to develop into an empire by the fifteenth century, basing its wealth on long-distance trade with the north that had roots as far back as 100 B.C.E., and a series of periodic markets that linked its growing urban areas. These markets were essential for supporting the craft producers and long-distance traders who congregated in the towns. While men dominated the trade in luxury items, and the ruling aristocracy monopolized profits from this trade, women controlled the sale of foodstuffs, cloth, and such locally manufactured goods as mats. This division of labor in the marketplace reflected the Yoruba gender hierarchy, in which men headed families and controlled land and women's labor. Unlike many male traders, women tended to exchange their goods for use value rather than manufacturing profit. The low volume of their trade limited the power that they received from participation in the internal trade.

Despite these disadvantages, women's participation in local trade was central to Oyo's urbanized economy. By the eighteenth century, each town had a female ruler known as the *iyalode*, who, among other things, looked after the women's trading interests (Awe 1977; Denzer 1994; Matory 1994). Trading was only one of a number of roles women played in Oyo. They also participated in planting, harvesting, and processing agricultural products. As Simi Afonja points out, most writers have tended to underestimate the role of women in agriculture before the nineteenth century (Afonja 1981).

Oyo's king, known as the *alafin*, used his wives, *ayabas*, to acquire much of his wealth. Most were palace slaves who produced cloth, natron, and salt. Others traded these products for the benefit of the *alafin*. The Oyo royal palace housed titled women of high rank, including a queen mother, eight priestesses, dozens of lower officials, and the king's wives. The queen mother advised the *alafin* on important decisions and controlled direct access to him (Awe 1977).

Like other Yoruba towns, Oyo had a women's representative, called the *iyalode*, who had her own special insignia of office. This position was usually held by a woman elected by the other women in recognition of her leadership qualities and achieved wealth. She held a court that settled quarrels among women and helped decide women's opinions on such issues as war and the establishment of new markets (Awe 1977).

Participation in Afro-European trade had little effect on most Yoruba women until the eighteenth century, when Oyo became more involved in the Atlantic slave trade. Prior to this time, the aristocracy had dominated long-distance trade, and thus trade with Europeans had little impact on most Yoruba lives (Ajayi 1972; Akinjogbin 1972). The women who benefited most from this trade were elite women who were relieved from domestic and farming chores by slaves (Afonja 1981).

In the mid-eighteenth century, conditions began to change as military chiefs entered the slave trade by raiding small neighboring kingdoms. The ruling class began to lose control over the slave trade, and the number of slaves in Oyo rose dramatically. In the nineteenth century, women began to concentrate more on trade instead of dividing their time between trading and farming. These changes resulted from a number of factors that began in the eighteenth century, including the further growth of towns and cities, the introduction of new foodstuffs, and the decline in the number of farmers (Afonja 1981).

### The Atlantic Slave Trade

The arrival of the Portuguese on the West African coast in 1444 portended significant changes in the lives of many West African women. To fully understand how the slave trade developed, it is necessary to examine the systems of inequality based on age and gender that existed before 1400. These systems preceded the slave trade and were a precondition for its success. Slaves had to be obtained in as orderly a fashion as possible; the cooperation of some Africans in this process was invaluable. Nonetheless, as Walter Rodney (1970) argued, the Afro-European trade led to increased inequality, particularly in those social relations where inequality already existed.

The slave trade was built on an ideological and economic system based on kinship, which allowed West Africans to recruit outsiders into their communities through processes such as marriage, pawning, kidnapping, and slave raiding. Prior to the Atlantic slave trade, violent means of acquiring outsiders were seldom used, but the possible profits from the trade led to an increase in violence. The slaves' experiences were often influenced by their gender. Slave traders most often sold men away into the Atlantic slave trade, while they kept women for the domestic trade. Owners preferred women as slaves, because females were more easily incorporated into kin-ordered societies than men. Women slaves essentially became wives, because families could treat these women, unprotected by kin, any way they wished. The children slave women produced for a lineage had no obligations to another kin group. These wives could be viewed as inferior, because they did not link two families together. Women slaves were also important because they did the bulk of the agricultural labor in most coastal societies, and thus their presence augmented the ability of a lineage to produce, often leaving free women the time to turn to trade and other pursuits.

Rather than forming a subordinate caste of permanent workers as slaves did in Europe and North America, African slaves increased the population of the community. They were essentially people without kin, and therefore without protectors, in societies in which kinship relations were dominant. Most slaves became incorporated into a kin group as subordinate members; often the children or grandchildren they produced for their new lineage became full-fledged kin members. It is important to note that even without slaves incorporated into lineages, these kinship corporations were generally hierarchically structured by age and gender (Miers and Kopytoff 1977).

The slave trade became an important means by which more fortunate women recruited labor. Although men in patrilineal societies were able to obtain labor through the lineage system, most women found this avenue unavailable to them. (Men in matrilineal societies also used slave wives to obtain dependents.) Slavery became an important way for women to acquire dependents and to gain the free time to trade. Moreover, women enjoyed control over both their slaves' labor and their slaves' children's labor (Robertson and Klein 1997).

The first major base for the Atlantic slave trade was the Senegambian region. The impact of this trade on the region was to increase stratification. The rulers of the numerous small states and their followers benefited from the control of the slave trade, contributing to the differentiation of the elite of warriors and nobles from the more numerous free peasants (Klein 1977). Many of those slaves not sold off into the Atlantic trade were incorporated into the lineages of the ruling elite as domestic slaves. These slaves, most of whom were women, worked for their owners five days a week from sunrise until two P.M., and then were free to farm for themselves. A few male slaves ended up as slave soldiers, who did most of the slave raiding for the elite owners (Klein 1977).

Before the nineteenth century, participation in the slave trade required resources that were unavailable to most Senegambians, for the slave soldiers had to be outfitted and fed. Men were most likely to be able to afford direct participation in the trade, but a surprising number of women also gained from it. Thus the simple notion that women were only victims of the slave trade has to be put aside.

Several contemporary observers and historians have noted the presence of a highly visible but small group of women who acted as cultural and commercial intermediaries between European and African traders (Brooks 1976, 1993). Before the beginning of the Afro-European trade, women in the Senegambian region often held high political positions and were involved in trade. Through marriage, women often served as a link between European traders and the coastal communities of Gambia and Sierra Leone. This gave them the additional advantage of having ties to both communities. During the height of the slave trade, some of these African and Afro-European women became wealthy traders; they possessed property and influence, and they expected and received respect from the male traders. Wealth translated into possession of domestic slaves, trading ships, houses, gold, silver, jewelry, and fashionable clothes. Collectively, the successful among these intermediaries were known as *signares* or *senhora*. Some of the more famous included Senhora Philippa, who controlled the trading center at Rufisque in the mid-1630s, and Senhora Catti, who became a commercial agent for the ruler of Cayor, a Wolof state, in 1685. Bibiana Vaz built up an extensive trading empire between the Gambia and Sierra Leone rivers in the 1670s and 1680s, even establishing a short-lived Afro-European republic. Her rise to power represented the beginnings of mulatto influence in the area, as Afro-European children took advantage of connections to both African and European trading networks to set themselves up as important intermediaries and power brokers (Rodney 1970).

European men recognized several potential advantages of their relationships with the *signares*. The *signares* provided them with access to African trading networks and stable households with skilled domestic slaves to take care of them, assisted them in their trading ventures, and offered invaluable instruction in the local language and customs. In return, Europeans offered the *signares* access to European networks and merchandise. Thus the *signares* were important in easing the trading and social relations between cultures that barely understood each other at the beginning of the slave-trade era (Brooks 1976).

*State Formation*

The growth of states accompanied the increasing interregional and Afro-European trade. Women took part in the process of state formation on many different levels. For example, female slaves on the Gold Coast provided much of the farm produce that supported the growth of the ruling classes during the sixteenth and seventeenth centuries. These women's labor was so crucial to economic and political development that the important port town of Winneba specialized as a slave market that sold only female slaves (Kea 1982). Women at the other end of the spectrum at times even controlled small states. As mentioned, Bibiana Vaz turned her success in the Atlantic slave trade into a short-lived republic.

Aidoo (1981) argues that militarization of the Asante region in the late seventeenth and eighteenth centuries worked against women's achievement of political power, since premenopausal women could not participate in military service. Thus, as the state became increasingly dominated by military men, there was less room for women's involvement in government. Nonetheless, some ruling-class women were able to turn their positions as queen mothers, or *asantehemaas*, into political power.

Perhaps the most significant factor for women in the process of state formation was the relationship between these increasingly powerful states and kinship relations. Women were able to carry various degrees of power from these kinship relations into the state apparatus. Dahomey, founded in the era of the Afro-European trade, which greatly influenced its development, exemplifies this complex history. Migrants from Ajaland founded Dahomey around 1625, but it developed significantly differently than its Aja sister states to the south, including Allada and Whyday. Whereas the earlier Aja states used kinship ideology to hold their states together, Dahomey based its hegemonic ideology on a strong king whose office inspired loyalty. The Dahomean kingdom likened the state to a perforated pot, and the king to the water that all his subjects had to help keep in the pot. Citizenship was no longer based on kinship ties; rather, it was based on willingness to belong to the state and to serve the king. Similarly, a kind of meritocratic ideology based on service to the king replaced lineage connections (Akinjogbin 1972).

Kinship ideology was not abandoned completely, however. Instead, the state built on the lineage structures found in the villages. In fact, the Dahomean palace, which became the center of power in the kingdom, developed gradually out of the polygynous household structure. The royal palace reflected both the extraordinary power of some Dahomean women and the limitations faced by most women. While the king was clearly the ruler there, the queen mother also wielded great power (Bay 1995). Indeed, the palace was largely a hierarchically structured, female institution, housing as many as eight thousand women by the nineteenth century. Many of these women were the king's wives or dependents, known as *ahosi*. Some eight hundred to a thousand were said to be actual physical wives in the late eighteenth century; most were captured in warfare. In addition, every lineage was required to place a daughter in the palace. By the early eighteenth century, the king sent agents around the kingdom seeking slave wives (Bay 1997). This practice helped build the interests of each lineage into the center of the kingdom's power. Wealthy and powerful families who could afford to lose the labor and bridewealth from a daughter gave the king more daughters than was required as a way of building a power base within the palace (Bay 1997).

The *ahosi* provided a number of services to the king, including acting as a kind of police force. A European traveler to Dahomey in the 1720s reported, "The King's Wives are the Executors of his Sentences, and 'tis merry enough when a Grandee has offended the King, 3 to 400 of them are sent to the Offender's House, which they immediately strip and level with the Ground" (quoted in Bay 1997, p. 347). The women of such an unfortunate household often ended up as *ahosi* themselves. It was during the 1720s, a period of expansion under King Agaja, that Dahomey first used women as soldiers. King Gezo (1819–1858) institutionalized women soldiers into what nineteenth-century European travelers called Amazons (Bay 1997).

As Akinjogbin has noted, eighteenth-century Dahomey witnessed "the growing absolutism of the king and the increasing efficiency of the internal administration" (Akinjogbin 1972, p. 334). Women in the palace played a major role in this process. The most powerful of the eighteenth-century kings, Tegbesu (1740–1774), was responsible for much of this centralization; but he could not have been successful without his powerful queen mother, Hwanjile (Bay 1995). Like most queen mothers, Hwanjile was a captive from an area in which Dahomey was attempting to expand. During the mid-eighteenth century, Dahomey's attention was focused on Aja country to the south and west, an area that included Hwanjile's natal village, Home. Tegbesu made Home an important administrative center and built a palace for Hwanjile there (Bay 1997). This practice of choosing a queen mother from newly acquired territory helped cement control over this conquered land and paralleled the practice of demanding a daughter from each lineage in the kingdom. The queen mothers acted as informants on the captured territory, but they also offered a stake in the government to the new subjects (Bay 1995).

When Tegbesu ascended to the throne, he faced a state weakened by assault from the more powerful state to the east, Oyo, and was threatened by other claimants to the throne. Hwanjile was instrumental in consolidating his power. Together, Hwanjile and Tegbesu worked to wipe out the power of the local priests who supported the dissidents in their attempt to overthrow him. In place of the indigenous religion, Hwanjile introduced deities from her home. This major effort at reorganizing religious beliefs was so successful that a number of the gods who are still worshiped in Dahomey (present-day Benin)* are attributed to Hwanjile (Bay 1997). Queen mothers such as Hwanjile not only helped to cement the power of a king; they also helped bring kings to power in the first place. As many Europeans remarked, no one could reach a king without securing the approval of the powerful palace women. It was they who spoke directly to him. And only they knew when a king died, which gave them time to position themselves so as to have an influence on who would be chosen king next.

In nearby Benin, the title of *iyoba* was established as the empire expanded dramatically. This expansion was linked to the arrival of Portuguese mercenaries, who gave the empire clear advantages in weaponry. The most powerful woman in the kingdom of Benin (in present-day Nigeria) also never spoke directly to the *oba*, or king. A queen mother rose to prominence by producing the ruling *oba*'s first son, who was destined to succeed his father. As queen mother, she was rewarded for her role as the quintessential mother by being awarded the rank of a powerful male. Acting on behalf of her son, Oba Esigie, Queen Mother Idia is remembered for contributing to Benin's growth (F. Kaplan 1993). Perhaps to check the power of the queen mother over the *oba*, she communicated with him only through emissaries.

Recognized as the woman who had given birth to the next *oba*, the queen mother rose from the powerful but highly competitive, secluded group of the *oba*'s wives. In the kingdom of Benin, the queen had an important state function. Women from all over the kingdom could be found among these wives. These women played a major role in tying the kingdom together. The queens were attended by female slaves and male eunuchs. The only others allowed to communicate directly with them were members of the *oba*'s family and fe-

*The country Dahomey changed its name to Benin in 1976. It is not to be confused with Benin state within Nigeria.

male members of the queen's families chosen to serve the queens. While the queens kept property in villages and especially their birth-places, they maintained these ties through emissaries (Kaplan 1993). This growing sector of the Benin royal family represented successful empire-building in southern Nigeria. The power of the queen mother represented women's unique role in this expansion.

During the nineteenth century, as Yoruba and European notions of authority grew more prominent, the role of royal wives declined (Bay 1995). The Yoruba placed a much greater emphasis on royal and male authority.

The processes of trade and state formation had a tremendous impact on gender roles and gender relations. Overall, the period witnessed increasing stratification among women as trade expanded and states became more powerful. Women were essential to these developments. As petty traders, they supported craft producers, long-distance traders, and religious specialists in the newly developing urban areas. Urbanization would not have been possible without these petty traders. But the gender division of labor, which reserved trading in luxury items for men, reflected the gender hierarchy that favored men over women.

Part of the increasing stratification among women resulted from the increase in slavery. Most local slaves were women, while men were sold off into the Atlantic slave trade. At the same time, free women, especially those from the elite classes, benefited from the growth in slavery, as slaves freed them from agricultural and domestic duties.

State formation depended on kinship ideology and had important consequences for women. Central to this ideology were the greater labor obligations that women had toward men. Nonetheless, the states during this era reserved important roles for elite women. Some women, such as the *iyalode* among the Yoruba, gained power through collective women's political activities. Others, such as the queen mother among the Dahomey, were chosen by male rulers. Although it is difficult to say precisely how gender, trade, and state formation shaped women's lives, it is clear that men had more access to power than did women everywhere. Women's political and economic power varied across the region because of a number of factors, including the nature of stratification among women, the strength of women's networks, and the character of women's obligations to their kin.*

*In addition to the works cited within this section, see Robertson and Klein 1997.

## WEST-CENTRAL AFRICA TO 1800
*written with Cathy Skidmore-Hess*

During this period, women in West-Central Africa shared a number of common historical themes with women along the West African coast, including the experience of expanding trade with Europe and the growth of small states attempting to dominate that trade. Like women in West Africa, those in West-Central Africa had varying degrees of success responding to these changes. Some women were able to emerge as important leaders from the confusion created by the slave trade and Portuguese intrusion.

It should not be surprising that the regions share similar histories, because West-Central Africa is populated in large part by Bantu-speaking peoples. Bantu is one of the major language groups in Africa. In the sixth century B.C.E., groups of people began migrating from the Benue and Cross Rivers region of present-day Nigeria, aided by iron hoe technology that enabled them to cultivate in the forested regions. Secondary sources reveal very little about the part that women played in the massive Bantu population expansion (Vansina 1983). We can speculate that women's role in agriculture was crucial for the spread of cereals and root crops as most Bantu speakers in West-Central Africa colonized most of Central, southern, and East Africa. Most Bantu-speaking societies practiced patrilocality, whether they were patrilineal or matrilineal. It is likely, therefore, that women acted as cultural brokers, spreading ideas and agricultural techniques between their natal village and their husband's village.

With the arrival of the Portuguese at the end of the fifteenth century, the lives of many women in the coastal region became dominated by the slave trade. As in West Africa, most of the slaves sold from the West-Central region into the Afro-European trade were male. Women were kept for the internal slave trade, increasing the power of the nobility vis-à-vis the lineages. In the Kongo, slaves became an increasingly important alternate source of dependents for the king, or *mani,* and his nobility, as the Mwissikongo aristocracy created a more centralized monarchy. This aristocracy, whose distinct culture included literacy in Portuguese and a Christian sect, developed a town-based lifestyle supported by slave-worked plantations and a tribute system from surplus rural production (Broadhead 1997). It is unclear what impact Christianity as an elite sect had on women.

During the seventeenth century, agriculture increasingly relied on new crops introduced from the New World, often changing productive relations. Cassava, for example, demanded more labor from women, shifting the division of labor to their disadvantage. This heavier workload, which must have been carried in part by slave women, caused higher rates of miscarriage and perhaps even increased abortions (Vansina 1983).

Women took an active role in the process of centralization of state power. The Kongo kingdom was divided into small units of approximately twelve villages, which paid rent to a titleholder, called a *marquis*. The ruling elite often relied on women to hold these offices (Thornton 1983). Such control over an important source of income indicates that some women wielded substantial authority, even though women were generally subordinate to men of the same age. Other powerful women included the head wife of a nobleman, who might control several hundred junior wives and slaves. During the sixteenth and seventeenth centuries, it was not unusual for women to become chiefs of the matrilineal descent groups that were the basic units in Kongo (Hilton 1985). Finally, women played an important role on the *ne mbanda,* the council that balanced the king's power at the center of the kingdom. Four out of the twelve council members were female, often widowed queen mothers and the king's aunts and sisters. Little is known about the actual roles of these councilors. The only known title, *nzimbu mpungu* or female chief, was invested with powers of the otherworld (Hilton 1985)

States such as Kongo were unable to maintain control of the region for very long, as smaller states competed successfully for the Portuguese trade, internal local lineages undermined elite control over their rural-based tribute system, and ecological disasters threatened their agricultural program. The instability of the region allowed an extraordinary woman, Njinga, to step out of the role that most women played to gain control over her own state. Njinga effectively used diplomatic ties and her own status as a royal woman to gain positions of political and religious authority. Beginning in the 1620s, when it became clear that her half-brother Ngola, a Kiluanje, could not cope with her kingdom's deepening economic problems, she and her sisters seized power. After realizing that Njinga would not move her court closer to areas of Portuguese control, the Portuguese joined with Imbangala mercenaries and discontented nobles within the kingdom in an effort to place someone else on the throne. Facing drought, civil war, and invasion, Njinga moved eastward. She then attempted to negotiate several settlements with the Portuguese. After they proved to be unwilling or unable to come to terms with her, Njinga adopted a more mobile authority structure that allowed her to evade her enemies and gain the loyalty of certain bands of Imbangala mercenaries. With the help of these mercenaries and a large number of refu-

gees from her former kingdom of Ndongo, Njinga reestablished herself in the region of Matamba, where she built a slave-trading and
textile exchange network that kept her soldiers occupied and increased
her own economic base of authority.

In the 1650s, as Njinga remained in power, her personal reputa-
tion grew. Initially forced to play many roles that were symbolically
male, Njinga gradually began to associate more feminine symbols with
royal authority. Before her death, she named her sister Kambo as her
successor. Although Kambo lacked the personal authority and charisma to prevent a civil war from breaking out between members of
the elite and the leaders of the Imbangala army, Njinga's legacy continued. During the next century, a number of women would hold the
throne of Matamba, and numerous local traditions would commemo-
rate Njinga's resistance to the Portuguese (Heintze 1981; Parreira 1990;
Skidmore-Hess 1995; Thornton 1991).

Just as Njinga successfully used religious ideology to augment
her position as a royal woman during a period of political upheaval,
Kimpa Vita (known by the Portuguese as Doña Beatrice) combined
various religious ideologies to try to create stability in her region.
Initially she drew upon her power in an organization that frequently
dealt with problems of infertility among women. Over time, however, her movement focused on Catholic images of fecundity and abun-
dance. In particular, she emphasized St. Anthony, who was often
portrayed holding the baby Jesus.

Kimpa Vita's movement represented the attempt by nobility to
end the disintegration of elite control over the Kongo kingdom in the
eighteenth century. Born into the nobility in 1686, she had few of the
advantages that a noblewoman in the sixteenth century would have
enjoyed. As the Mwissikongo were forced to abandon their capital
and disperse to provincial bases, elite women lost power because they
were no longer able to influence events as sisters and daughters in
powerful elite families (Broadhead 1997). Kimpa Vita created a movement that appealed both to the elite, who desired a return to centralized government, and to commoners, who desperately wanted peace.

In 1702, Kimpa Vita declared that St. Anthony had entered her
body as she was dying. The St. Antonine movement that she developed was deeply rooted in Kongolese religious beliefs about death,
and it also appealed to many elite who were part of the Christian sect.
In the early days of the movement, Kimpa Vita encouraged direct
religious experience, thus challenging the influence of the Capuchin
missionaries, priestly chiefs, and the kings. Later, she established a
hierarchical structure that included "little Antonines" who traveled
throughout Kongo, preaching reunification of the kingdom and act-

ing as priests. Eventually, however, she took on many of the characteristics of the priestly chiefs and Capuchins whom she criticized. She
settled in São Salvador, demanding that the nobility return to the
capital and follow a new king of Kongo, whom she would choose
(Hilton 1985). Ultimately, her claiming the power to enthrone the
Kongo king created hostility among many of the rival claimants to
the throne. Although she incorporated many elements of Christianity into her doctrine, the Capuchin priests considered her a serious
threat to their power and plotted against her.

Many of the Kongolese peasants found her calls for peace and
restoration of the kingdom irresistible, allowing her to successfully
repopulate São Salvador in 1705 (Thornton 1983). Bernardo da Gallo,
an Italian Capuchin missionary, commented with displeasure on the
peasants who heeded Kimpa Vita's plea to resettle the capital:

> Therefore it happened that there were those who went to wor-
> ship the supposed Saint, to see their homeland reborn, to see their
> friends: some to recover their health miraculously, and others to be
> first to reoccupy the place; São Salvador was rapidly repopulated.
> In this way the false saint became the restorer, ruler and lord of the
> Congo, and was acclaimed adored and esteemed as such by every-
> one. (Quoted in Thornton 1983, p. 109)

Unfortunately for Kimpa Vita, she was captured by a rival faction
and convicted of treason and heresy. As punishment, she was put to
death.

Clearly her quest for power was far from a legitimate one in a
system in which men generally ruled. Nonetheless, she was only one
of many illegitimate claimants to power in a time of crisis over hegemonic control. This turmoil grew out of the increasing Afro-European
trade, the intrusion of the Portuguese into internal political affairs,
and the attempts to build states that would control the area. Her attempts to reestablish elite control over Kongo reflected the opportunities that a few extraordinary women had in this confusing time.
Most women, however, found their workload increased as Europeans introduced new crops and the ruling elite attempted to exact increasingly large amounts of tribute from slaves and commoners.

## WESTERN SUDAN DURING THE
## NINETEENTH CENTURY

Hausaland's political landscape was dramatically changed during the
early part of the nineteenth century by a *jihad* (war against unbelievers) led by Uthman dan Fodio. Waged largely by an educated Fulani

class, this *jihad* replaced the city-states with Islamic emirates. Uthman dan Fodio was concerned about the position of women, often writing about their appropriate treatment. He argued that women should be secluded and controlled by their husbands. At the same time he advocated educating women, even suggesting that they had the right to disobey husbands who did not educate their wives or who did not follow Allah appropriately (Ogunbiyi 1969). He acted on his views on women's education within his own family, considering it his duty to educate his wives and daughters. The Fodio family produced at least five generations of women intellectuals, who generated a body of work in Fula, Arabic, and Hausa that is still extant. Their writings focused on a number of the important issues faced by their contemporaries, as they defended the ideals of newly emerging emirates. Jean Boyd argues,

> They wrote deliberately, purposefully, often with burning zeal. They taught and lectured, scolded, warned, exhorted, ridiculed; they marshaled recorded events and set them down; they wrote elegies which praised the dead for such qualities as modesty, piety, scholarship, humility, generosity, kindliness, but without mention of beauty, wealth, elegance of dress, strength, physical prowess, or feats of arms. (1986, p. 130)

The *jihad* influenced women's lives in a number of ways that dan Fodio never envisioned. For example, many free women found themselves exposed to the possibility of enslavement during the unrest created by the *jihad*. Once peace was restored, many women appreciated the order that left them less vulnerable to slave raiding. Internal slavery increased dramatically, however, as slaves were imported into the emirates. Most of these slaves were women who worked on small farms alongside their owners, or on plantations that ranged in size from a dozen to a thousand slaves, many of whom were women (Lovejoy 1988). Throughout the western Sudan, slave plantation production grew, affecting free women's work (Klein 1997). Slaves replaced free women in salt production during the nineteenth century, expanding production to meet increased demand in the region (Lovejoy 1986). Slaves relieved noble Maraka women from agricultural labor during this period also, allowing the elite women to expand the indigo-dyed cloth production that they controlled. These women welcomed the increase in slave labor, because it allowed many to increase their profits dramatically. They preferred female slaves to replace them in their work, but they used male slaves to weave cotton. It was not unusual in the region for male slaves to cross the normally rigid gender division of labor and take on female tasks (Olivier de Sardan 1997; Roberts 1984).

Unfortunately for noble Maraka women, slave production for male owners began to compete with free women's production, threatening their economic resources (Roberts 1984). Unlike slave women, elite women were secluded and could go out only after dark, veiled. The differences between most slave and free women were summed up by a poem written in 1865 by the imam of Chediya, a town between Kano and Bauchi: "Farm-work is not becoming for a wife, you know; she is free, you may not put her to hoe grass [like a slave]" (Lovejoy 1981, p. 220).

Not all slave women worked in agricultural production; some wealthy male traders and scholars had concubines that numbered in the hundreds (Klein 1997). These slave women found that Islam gave them some protection, including a rule that they should be manumitted after giving birth to their owner's child. Of course, not all masters followed this law (Olivier de Sardan 1997).

The Hausa *jihad* also led to the enforcement of seclusion among Hausa women and a resulting change in women's work in urban areas. Unable to work in the fields, women developed crafts and cooking skills that they marketed through an extended network of children and kin. The income generated from these activities often led to an increase in individual wealth (Coles and Mack, 1991). However, the conditions of seclusion also hindered women in developing large-scale enterprises. Prominent in almost all aspects of textile manufacturing, women could not organize and mobilize labor as effectively as their male counterparts. While women textile manufacturers remained concentrated in southern portions of the Sokoto Caliphate (Nupe and Ilorin), men developed large-scale enterprises in the north-central sections of the state (Kriger 1993).

The nineteenth-century political changes greatly affected elite women's access to state power. As new polities developed, women found themselves virtually shut out of the new governing structures. For example, as Baure formed, the ruling *sarki* became determined to protect himself by eliminating checks on his power by the *magajiya* (queen mother). Therefore, the office of the *magajiya* remained vacant for sixty years after the rise of the Fulani. The result for ruling-class women was that their most powerful position in the town government was undermined. Even after the position was filled, the *magajiya* no longer had the right to veto decisions made by the *sarki*. Her principal role was limited to directing the rituals of royal women at first marriages and childbirths. The *iya* continued to supervise divorced women in the *bori* cult, but the cult itself lost power because of the increased influence of Islam as the state religion (M. G. Smith 1978).

Overall, therefore, as the Sokoto Caliphate established itself as the major regional power, the impact of the Fulani-led *jihad* on women was both uneven and contradictory. Ruling-class women lost much of their political and religious clout, a change that had roots in the changing state structure over the previous six centuries. They were also increasingly likely to be secluded. At the same time, Uthman dan Fodio urged men to treat their wives fairly and educate their daughters. The end of the *jihad* brought peaceful conditions that left women in Hausaland less vulnerable to enslavement but increased the numbers of female slaves from wars outside the caliphate. As the economy of the region expanded, these women were more likely to serve on plantations than in the past.

## THE COAST AND ITS HINTERLAND
## DURING THE NINETEENTH CENTURY

For many who lived along the coast of West Africa, the nineteenth century was a time of turmoil. Most important, the transition from slaves to vegetable products as the major trade items of Afro-European trade combined with internal developments to create an increase in slave raiding. Before this era, slave traders had sold most captive men to Europeans and kept women for domestic slavery. With the decline of the Atlantic slave trade, the sex ratio among slaves became more even. But women were still most likely to be enslaved; many men were simply killed during the raids. While women faced increased vulnerability, many were able to turn the rise in petty commodity production to their advantage. Patterns began to emerge during the nineteenth century that became clear during the colonial period. In particular, petty trading offered many women independence they ordinarily would not have had. Its limitations as a static economic sphere for women with few alternatives did not become obvious until the twentieth century.

### Trade and Production

Women responded to increasing levels of trade during the nineteenth century by turning to marketing, in part because of their role in the subsistence economy. Their family obligations made the acquisition of marketing profits appealing, allowing them to provide more to their kin than they might simply from farming. Once women met their obligations to feed their families, their profits could be disposed of as they pleased. Among the Igbo in what is now Nigeria, successful women used their profits to buy achievement-based titles. Both women and men could take titles, but men found it easier to participate in this system than women, because they generally had greater access to wealth. As Amadiume argued for the Nnobi Igbo, "there was a direct link between the accumulation of wives, the acquisition of wealth and the exercise of power and authority" (1987, p. 42). Men were able to increase their number of dependent laborers by marrying women. Wives worked on their land and produced daughters, from whom men received bridewealth payments. Successful women, however, could also marry wives, whose labor and children they controlled. Since the Igbo had a flexible gender system in which women could become "males"—that is, they could play roles normally reserved for men—woman-to-woman marriage did not disrupt their gender ideology or the gender division of labor. In her discussion of female husbands, Amadiume cautions her readers against confusing biological sex and socially constructed gender. Although a gender division of labor characterized Igbo society, women sometimes took on male identities.

Another example of the flexibility of the gender system is what Amadiume calls male daughters. Some lucky women could head lineages and inherit land and other property usually reserved for men if they were particularly favored by their fathers or if there were no appropriate male heirs. In addition, these daughters of a patrilineage acted like males toward the wives in that lineage. The bond between fathers, daughters, and sons set up the daughters of a lineage in a position of authority toward wives. Amadiume gives no examples of men who became women, an indication of the advantage that men have in a system that values them over women.

The number of women able to marry wives and take titles increased during the nineteenth century as the region became more stratified. Similar transformations occurred in Yorubaland, where trade began to replace agriculture as many free women's primary occupation; slaves, both male and female, took their place. In part, this change was brought about by increased urbanization and a modification of the agricultural sector that included the introduction of new crops. The increase in the numbers of slaves also liberated free women from household and farming tasks. As Afonja (1981) notes, this withdrawal of women from agriculture occurred more rapidly in urban than in rural areas, where women were most likely to combine farming and marketing.

Overall, however, the scale of women's trade increased during the nineteenth century as women entered the trade in cash crops.

The increasing importance of cash crops reflected changes in the Afro-European trade, as the British, in particular, demanded vegetable goods and tree crops instead of slaves from coastal traders. The region responded by increasing the production of palm products, a response that would greatly affect the social structure. As Afonja argues, cash crop production changes the values associated with the means of production—that is, with land, labor, and capital. These changes, which became more pronounced during the colonial era, began to emerge in the nineteenth century as lineages started to lose control over land and family labor. As individual ownership replaced control of land by male lineage members, the value of land became central to capital accumulation, and subsistence needs no longer dominated agriculture. Many women found themselves at a disadvantage in this new competition over land, because men were more likely to inherit land, resulting in an increased asymmetry between male and female power.

*Women's Organizations*

Although gender ideology often worked against their interests, women did have organizations that represented them. Among the Nnobi Igbo, patrilineage daughters were organized into the *unu okpu*, led by the oldest daughter. The *unu okpu* helped settle disputes in the lineage and also ensured that they were treated with the proper respect. Lineage wives joined the *inyom di*, which helped organize women to meet their responsibilities toward the patrilineage into which they had married. At the same time, it stressed the need for cooperation and solidarity among women. All women, as wives and daughters, were under the jurisdiction of the women's council, *inyom nnobi*. In contrast to the *unu okpu* and *inyom di*, leadership in the women's council was based on achievement and personality rather than seniority. The council was responsible for looking after women's welfare at the same time that it ensured their good behavior by levying fines. The council could protect women from abusive husbands and from decisions by the male elders that worked against women's interests. If necessary, it could call a strike, in which women refused to provide their normal services. Taken together, the three women's organizations worked both for and against women's interests. The daughters and wives of the patrilineage had conflicting interests that the women's council could only hope to mediate. In addition, the women's council was responsible as much for ensuring women's appropriate behavior as for defending women from men.

The Bundu secret society in Sierra Leone had a similar double-edged impact. Some authors have tried to determine whether Bundu was a positive force in women's lives. Hoffer (1972; MacCormack

1975) describes how Bundu gave women political power, while Bledsoe (1980) argues that it gave only older women power while contributing to the oppression of younger women. In fact, as an institution that virtually all women joined and that related to most areas of their life, it is not surprising that Bundu could work for all women's interests at the same time that it contributed to the control that men and older women had over young women.

Bundu was clearly a powerful political and social force among the Mende of Sierra Leone. Sixteenth-century Portuguese travelers reported the existence of female solidarities. It is likely that the original Mende migrants to the area, the Mane, brought Bundu-like initiation societies with them, which became intertwined with the indigenous societies during the eighteenth and nineteenth centuries (Boone 1986). Similar to its male equivalent, Poro, Bundu was open to all free-born female community members, but it was structured hierarchically. At the top of the structure were women who had demonstrated their leadership abilities and passed a series of tests about their knowledge of philosophy and medicine. At the bottom were the new initiates, who underwent difficult rites of passage that tested their courage, strength, and knowledge of village history. Initiation into Bundu included a test of young girls' virginity and certification through clitoridectomy for those who passed this test. Only those who joined these societies could expect to participate fully in village life. Surely no young woman could expect to marry without the approval of her Bundu elders, for it was they who arranged marriages with suitable men (Boone 1986). A study of Bundu demonstrates that women's interests were not uniformly served. Clearly, the successful elders reaped more advantages than young, relatively powerless wives.

## Women and Nineteenth-Century States

Throughout the nineteenth century, attempts to control and participate in the slave trade led to the increasing militarization of much of the region. With some notable exceptions, the growing importance of the military in the state apparatus disadvantaged women vis-à-vis men. Many women lost out because of heightened insecurity that resulted from greater slave raiding. Some women from the ruling elite lost access to state power. As we shall see, a few exceptional women were able to use military and economic crises faced by male rulers to gain political power.

For example, the Asante developed a centralized, expansionist state that left little room for women to participate in political power. The major exception was the *asantehemaa*, or queen mother, of the

Asante Union, who shared power with the *asantehene* (male ruler). Aidoo describes the *asantehemaa*'s office:

> As a full member and co-chairman of the governing council or assembly of state, the queen mother's presence was required whenever important matters of state were to be decided. She also had to hear all judicial cases involving the sacred oaths of the state. She was entitled to, and did have, her own separate court where she was assisted by female counselors and functionaries. Her independent jurisdiction covered all domestic matters affecting women and members of the royal family. In certain cases, however, male litigants could apply to have their civil cases transferred from the chief's court to the queen mother's where fees and fines were generally lower. (Aidoo 1981, p. 66)

Although the *asantehene* clearly exercised more power than the queen mother, the *asantehemaa* had the right to nominate a candidate to rule as *asantehene*. She could make three attempts to gain the approval of the chiefs of the states making up the Asante Union. Aidoo argues that the power of able queen mothers increased during times of state crisis, when male leadership was in trouble. Under normal circumstances, the queen mother's power was limited by a number of factors. First, it was not supported by her relationship to other women. She had authority over women, but she did not represent their interests and therefore could not build on women's collective power. Second, the *asantehemaa* exercised power in a culture where aggressive men were valued but aggressiveness in premenopausal women was denigrated. Thus there was no place for premenopausal women in the all-important military. Third, despite the fact that women in this matrilineal society were treated with respect as mothers and sisters, Akan culture feared menstruating women and greatly restricted their public activities. As Aidoo points out, all of the nineteenth-century Akan queen mothers who participated in warfare were beyond menopause. Thus, the *asantehemaa* exercised authority as exceptional women and had to work around many limitations on their power.

Despite these limitations, a number of the *asantehemaa* during the nineteenth century played important roles in the challenges to Asante power by British imperialism. One influential queen mother was Yaa Kyaa, affectionately called Akyaawa. In the 1820s, she accompanied Asantehene Osei Yaw on his military campaigns to the south. Already in her fifties, she was described in 1824 by C. C. Reindorf, a missionary at the Basle Mission in Accra, as "a woman of masculine spirit" who did not approve of a tactical retreat from British forces undertaken by Osei Yaw's army (Wilks 1988). Akyaawa took the license granted to postmenopausal women to openly criticize Osei Yaw's conduct of this military campaign, a role that may have been religiously sanctioned for her as well. She eventually became an important mediator between the Asante and the British, with whom she arranged an important peace treaty. In part, her influence reflected the troubled times Asante was experiencing as it began losing control over trade on the coast.

By the 1880s, Asante's capital, Kumase, was suffering from a serious internal political crisis, partially brought on by Asante's inability to deal with British imperialism. Into these troubled times of military defeat and palace coups stepped another *asantehemaa*, Yaa Akyaa, who tried to assert control over the disintegrating kingdom. As a leading entrepreneur in Kumase, she was able to bribe politicians, wage war, and direct the campaigns to take over control of the *asantehemaa* and *asantehene* throne. She became *asantehemaa* by deposing her mother, placing her minor-age son, Prempe I, on the throne despite opposition from her brothers that cost many of their supporters their lives (Aidoo 1981).

Although Yaa Akyaa had established herself as the de facto ruler in Asante, she could not withstand the power of the British. They had always looked askance at her "strong will and resolution" (Aidoo 1981, p. 74). For her part, she often treated the British agents in Kumase with contempt. When the British took the opportunity to dethrone Asantehene Prempe I in 1896, they recognized that Yaa Akyaa was the real power and exiled them both to the Seychelles Islands. This act of direct imperialism ended the career of the powerful and shrewd *asantehemaa*, who died in exile at 75 in 1917 (Aidoo 1981). Like her predecessor Akyaawa, Yaa Akyaa inserted herself into troubled times. Although elite Asante women generally lost political power during the nineteenth century, a few were able to gain power when the male elite's grasp on the state began to slip

Madame Yoko, a Mende chief in the Sierra Leone hinterland from 1885 to 1905, was unusually successful at capturing state power in the context of slave raiding and military offenses. She gained control of a large section of the Mende, the Kpaa Mende, after her husband's death. Her skillful manipulation of the British based in the Sierra Leone colony on the coast contributed to her rise to power. In part because of the British role in helping her secure power, the legitimacy of Yoko's rule is in dispute by scholars. Abraham (1978) argues that Yoko, like other women rulers among the Mende, owed her power almost entirely to British colonial rule. But Hoffer (1972) points out that Mende women had a long history of political activity, which included becoming chiefs of towns. According to Hoffer, this unusual political power was based in the female solidarity, Bundu. Therefore, Yoko's rise to power should be distinguished from the power held by Asante queen mothers, who ruled without the support of collective women's power.

Madame Yoko increased Bundu's popularity among the Kpaa Mende, starting her own Bundu initiation school. Her ability to form alliances by controlling the marriages of the young girls whom she initiated clearly worked to her political advantage. Many powerful Kpaa Mende families sent their daughters to her for initiation, and even to live as wards in her households. Therefore, although she was unable to use polygynous marriage directly, as would a powerful man in recruiting dependents, she exploited Bundu as an alternative source. As Hoffer (1972) suggests, "Madame Yoko did what a male paramount chief could not do: she made politically significant alliances in two directions, both in taking the girls into her Bundu bush and wardship, and again in sending them out to husbands" (162). It would appear, then, that there was internal structural support for Yoko's power.

Nonetheless, the British influence radiating from the coast must have been crucial for Yoko as she enlarged the territory controlled by the Kpaa Mende. This influence needs to be viewed in the context of a century in which the British expanded an informal empire into the Sierra Leone hinterland. Clearly, many rulers brought the British into their disputes and came to depend on their military support and to anticipate their financial stipends (Skinner 1980).

Military expansion and civil strife interacted with gender ideology to influence women's lives among the Yoruba also. Women were called upon to provision armies during the Yoruba civil wars, often setting up their markets just behind the army lines (Ajayi and Smith 1964). Madame Tinubu played a crucial role in providing provisions for the Egba during the 1864 Dahomey–Egba war. She had established herself as an influential trader and politician during the 1850s at Lagos but was expelled for her opposition to British influence. She reestablished herself at Abeokuta during the Ijaye war in the early 1860s. She received the *iyalode* title for her efforts and continued to be an important economic and political force until her death in 1887 (Mba 1982).

Two of the new towns established during the wars, New Oyo and Ibadan, represented the variety of changes that women's power underwent as these two new urban areas developed. The *alafin* (king) of

New Oyo was able to establish a more centralized state that could succeed better in warfare than the one he had left behind in Old Oyo. Unfortunately for women, the power of the *iyalode* to represent women's interests was undercut by his increased, centralized control over the government. The royal mothers and priestesses in the palace came to dominate decisions on women's interests, but the royal women had fewer contacts with most women than had the *iyalode* in Old Oyo. Thus the interests of women as a group suffered, and the *iyalode* became more like the *asantehemaa* than she had in the past, cut off from collective women's power (Awe 1977).

In newly established Ibadan, however, the *iyalode* came to play an important role in the government's functioning. There the Yoruba fugitives established a new form of government that depended more on merit than on heredity. Thus the *iyalode,* like the other officers, gained office through contributions to the town's military efforts. One would think that military expansion would uniformly undermine women's access to state power, as it did in New Oyo and Asante. But women's experiences in Ibadan and the Sierra Leone hinterland suggest that some women participated in and gained from regional military conflict.

## Women in the Emerging Comprador Class

While many of the changes faced by the women of this region stemmed from internal developments, such as the fragmentary tendencies in state governments, external factors were evident as well. Particularly important were European attempts to suppress the Atlantic slave trade, the expansion of trade in cash crops, and the establishment of European coastal enclaves. These changes brought about direct contact between some coastal peoples and European merchants, missionaries, and officials that led to the development of a new comprador class (entrepreneurs who collaborated with and benefited from European presence). Women played an important role in the formation of this class.

Sierra Leone produced one of the most complex and developed comprador classes. The British had established the colony with the hope that they could produce a society much like their own. They were especially concerned with encouraging African women to accept the kinds of roles that were developing in industrializing Britain. Much to their surprise, many of the women whom they settled in the colony turned to trade for their livelihood. This active participation in the economic domain was of great concern to many of the colonists and missionaries, whose own society was increasingly sex-segregated.

But the women used their ties to European firms and established connections with the people living in the hinterland to develop a flourishing trade early in the nineteenth century. Settler women brought in by the British took advantage of Freetown's growing population to expand the rice, garden vegetable, and fish trade with the hinterland. By mid-century, many established trading posts upcountry both competed against and cooperated with settler men traders. Others established themselves as far northwest as Senegambia and as far southeast as Fernando Po in a loose-knit trading diaspora that was centered on Freetown. By the end of the century, the settler women had come to dominate the coastal kola nut trade between Sierra Leone and the Gambia.

As the settler women created their trading network, they drew on Western and indigenous cultural elements to give their diaspora cohesion. A sizable number of the women traders were Muslim and were able to build trading connections to other Muslims. Some women married men in the interior to establish their legitimacy. Membership in the women's secret societies gave some traders indispensable connections and protection in the absence of kinship ties. Bundu could certify that these stranger-traders could be trusted in commercial relations at the same time that it held the traders to certain standards of local behavior (E. White 1987).

Although Bundu and marriage alliances facilitated trading relations for settler women, conflict sometimes erupted between these traders and their hosts. The traders had to watch out for looting and arson that was sanctioned by local authorities, and even for enslavement during the conflicts that plagued the region. At least two factors contributed to problems faced by the women traders. First, they shared with settler men problematic ties to the British. As the century wore on and Afro-British trading relations became increasingly weighted toward European interests, the people in the colony's hinterland became increasingly hostile toward the British and their local representatives, the comprador settlers and the missionaries.

Second, the presence of settler women in the hinterland created conflict because they implicitly challenged gender relations. They traded and traveled about with a kind of independence denied most other women. Local male authorities worried that the traders' lifestyles would appeal to their women. In fact, some indigenous women fled their homes and joined the settler women's trading diaspora.

Although the women traders were an important element in the expanding flow of natural products from the colony's hinterland to Europe, British traders, government officials, and missionaries seemed uncomfortable with these women's roles. As a comprador class, the settler traders had helped to establish a colony that competed with the Atlantic slave trade, demonstrating that Afro-European relations did not have to be based on European enslavement of Africans. But the colony did not look like the mirror of British society that its founders desired. Many settlers did convert to Christianity and become missionaries in the hinterland, and literacy became an important part of settler society. But with the exception of a few elite women, most settler women did not emulate their European role models. Rather than staying at home to preside over a domestic sphere that served as a refuge from the public world of men, most women joined in the brisk trade that characterized the colony. Some of these women traveled far and wide as they extended their diaspora from Senegambia to Fernando Po.

Settler women were able to establish such independence in part because they took advantage of dislocations created by the slave trade. As settler society developed during the nineteenth century, men were unable to re-create the patriarchal controls over women that they had had throughout most of West Africa. Consequently, family ties were relatively flexible, and women took the opportunity to move about freely.

By contrast, in nearby Cape Palmas of present-day southeastern Liberia, women who converted to Christianity tried to distance themselves from the local population and did not engage in trading or farming. Repatriated African-American settlers, Christian missionaries, and local populations all agreed on a distinction between "civilized," a Westernized Christian prestigious category, and "native," an indigenous, less privileged category. The specific content and meaning of those categories varied considerably, depending on one's position in the hierarchy. The norms for "civilized" culture and society were first set by men known as Krumen, who traded with and worked on European ships. These standards were established by early African-American settlers, who, in large part, came from "a middle-class, business oriented, urban culture rather than an African American background characterized by rural plantation slavery and a strong core of modified West African cultural element," as characterized Sierra Leone's early settlers (Moran 1990, p. 58). Gender constructions played a major role in the establishment and reproduction of this prestige system. "Civilized" women were held more stringently to restrictive standards of behavior than "civilized" men; and women were more likely to experience downward mobility. Even upward mobility came at a cost for women, as they found themselves much more dependent on men for economic survival. In this case, the rise of a comprador class brought contradictory changes for women.

The development of a Western-educated, Christianized elite in Lagos and Abeokuta reflected the growth of a comprador class among the Yoruba as well. This newly emerging class recruited most of its members from the recaptives of Sierra Leone and became known as the Saro. The disruptions of the slave experience and the missionary efforts of the British created conditions for the lives of the women in this class that differed significantly from other Yoruba women's experiences. The Saro women shared much with the elite settler women down the coast in Sierra Leone. As in Freetown, the close ties with the British exposed the Saro to Christianity and its European marriage institution. At first, many elite women found Christian-style marriage appealing, as they abandoned polygyny and bridewealth for British promises of a better life. In particular, married women initially found attractive British inheritance laws that gave Christian wives and their children the right to their husbands' property. The policy, however, adversely affected others, such as plural customary or outside wives and their children (Mann 1985).

Christian marriage, however, did not develop as either these elite Yoruba women or the British missionaries expected. Marriage bonds proved to be very flexible, and men and women moved in and out of marriage with relative ease compared to most Yoruba. Early on, elite men were ambivalent about monogamy, often simply ignoring this requirement of Christian marriage by taking concubines and customary wives. Indeed, even some women began to turn against European-style marriage when they found it left them overly dependent on husbands who frequently failed to follow through on their obligations to support them. Abandoned wives and women whose husbands spent their resources on outside women had nowhere to turn for support. The conjugal relationship that failed many women in England proved especially fragile in Yorubaland, since the ideology that supported this relationship had to compete with the dominant Yoruba culture, which included polygyny, strong affinal ties created by the exchange of bridewealth, and women's autonomous economic activity. Moreover, throughout much of the century, social standards set up by those Saro attempting to establish a distinct class position required that women forgo participation in trading, the occupation that helped so many other Yoruba women to survive. Toward the end of the century, women began to demand greater economic independence to respond to their vulnerable positions (Mann 1985). These elite women became involved in class formation, both by the development of distinct cultural markers and by promoting their economic interests. Many of them opened schools for girls to promote elite culture as well as to give themselves some economic independence. Others found ways to trade that did not involve sitting in the marketplace or publicly hawking.

The growth of the comprador classes along the west coast and in the hinterland reflected the increasing stratification of the region. Women had never been a uniform group with identical interests, but the differences among women increased over the nineteenth century. The expansion of petty trading and cash crops offered some women greater opportunities than others. Among the Igbo, an increasing number of women were able to buy titles and to marry women as female husbands. But far from becoming wealthier, many women suffered through the era as domestic slavery increased. Most slaves continued to be female, although the sex ratio began to become more balanced.

At the same time, many elite women, like the *iyalode* of New Oyo, lost political power as they were pushed aside by the development of more centralized and militaristic states that ignored women's collective power. A few women, such as Akyaawa and Yaa Akyaa of Asante, were able to take advantage of the disintegration of elite male power and to gain control of the state apparatus.

Throughout the period, women formed organizations that represented their interests and established female-controlled networks. Such organizations as the women's councils among the Igbo and Bundu among the Mende reflected the double-edged impact of these groups. These organizations represented women's interests to the more powerful men, but they also drew women into a system that ultimately was to their disadvantage as a group. Finally, since women's interests were not uniform, these organizations represented the interests of the older, more successful women rather than younger women.

## WEST-CENTRAL AFRICA IN THE NINETEENTH CENTURY

West-Central Africa entered the nineteenth century with its coastal region still dominated by the Afro-European slave trade. Many areas of the region that had escaped the disruptions created by this trade fell under its influence during the nineteenth century, with the major area for slave raiding shifting northward. These changes had particular significance for women. Trade became increasingly dominated by men, who lived in single-sex coastal commercial centers where they could purchase their necessary goods rather than get them from their wives. Social mobility in the Kongo region became increasingly based on business success and connections, to which men had greatest access. Under these circumstances, elite women lost power and influence. Women often lived in separate quarters in the merchant houses and were segregated at public events. Rather than marry free women, many men preferred to purchase wives so that they could avoid obligations to affinal kin (Broadhead 1997).

Some new opportunities did open up for women. As food producers, they supplied the large-scale, clandestine slave-trade businesses during the first part of the nineteenth century. After cash crops replaced slaves in the Afro-European trade, many women turned to them. This shift away from subsistence agriculture to cash crops led to food shortages in some areas (Broadhead 1997).

Overall stratification among women declined during the nineteenth century. European observers noticed few differences between slave and free women as elite women lost power. Most women farmed, few having as much time for a leisure lifestyle as many women had in previous centuries (Broadhead 1997). Although a few women traders, such as Dona Ana da Sousa, rose to great prominence, political life became dominated by male traders, while women were confined to the subsistence sector.

As the northeast part of West-Central Africa entered this era of Afro-European trade, women found their lives affected in a variety of ways. Overall, women along the Congo River continued to work almost as they had in former times, despite an increase in cassava production. Trade along the river was organized in accordance with the existing gender division of labor. Men worked as paddlers on slave-raiding boats that could take up to sixty paddlers, and they fished during their spare time. Women had few chances to amass wealth in this trade, but they sustained the expanding trading system by increasing their production of cassava. One important offshoot of participation in slave-raiding was the dramatic rise in domestic slaves in the area, a rise that was particularly noticeable after the European-run markets for slaves shut down. The slave-raiding system continued to produce slaves, forcing their prices down and making them available even for some slaves to buy. A complex social structure emerged in which slaves and owners overlapped (Harms 1997). As in much of West Africa, many of these slaves were female.

In this matrilineal society, men found that marrying slave wives offered them an alternative to marriage with affines who might interfere in their lives. Thus men developed patrilineal, endogamous trading firms that recruited wives through the slaving system. Consequently, many women had no natal kin to watch over their interests. The patrilineal companies that wealthy men formed did not naturally self-reproduce, and European observers noted the skewed ratio between adults and the far less numerous children (Harms 1997).

Most owners and slaves had an interest in controlling the number of children. The time that it took to turn children, especially boys, into productive family members made reproduction by cheap slave imports more cost-effective for both owners and slaves. Slave women were mainly interested in having people in their working group who could help them produce a surplus and make their lives easier. Moreover, slave women had little control over their children, since their offspring belonged to their owners and could not take care of their mothers in their later years. In addition, slave women responded to their forced marriages by limiting the number of children they produced (Coquery-Vidrovitch 1997; Miller 1983).

Most of the material available on women for this period in West-Central Africa focuses on the impact of the slave trade on their lives (Robertson and Klein 1997). As the Afro-European trade expanded to include new parts of the region, women were marginalized in state power and large-scale business. Stratification among women decreased as elite women's status declined. The enormous increase in slave-raiding increased the number of slave women in the region. Men turned away from the older, patriarchal kinship system, under which they waited for older men to help them obtain wives by providing bridewealth. Instead, they preferred to recruit wives through the slave-raiding system. Slave wives were very vulnerable, since they had no relatives to look after their interests. Free men with access to wealth preferred to avoid the ties to affines that came with older forms of marriage.

## EARLY COLONIAL RULE, 1880–1920

At the turn of the twentieth century, colonial rulers were still in the process of establishing their hegemony over their recently acquired territories. Generally, colonial states were weak and could be maintained only by the use of force. For many women, the imposition of colonial rule initially led to unstable times. In Sierra Leone, for example, many settler women suffered great losses as the Mende rebelled in 1898 against the extension of a British protectorate to the hinterland in 1898. The settler women's kola trade, based in Mende and Sherbro territory, dropped off precipitously as a result of this revolt. Priscilla A. Jones reported to the commissioner responsible for investigating the rebellion that she had lost her husband and her trade goods:

> I trade in kola nuts, taking them in exchange for cotton, tobacco, spirits, etc. The chief of Tombay town is commonly called Beah Boy; he used to visit my husband, and my husband read a letter to the chief from the District Commissioners about the hut tax if he could be given three months' grace. Sammuel Cole [her boat captain] told me that my husband had been killed and the property plundered. (E. White 1987, p. 57)

The records do not reveal whether Priscilla Jones found the commissioner to be a sympathetic listener. Ironically, the British ignored the legitimate grievances of people coming face to face with the loss of their independence and blamed the settlers for fomenting this rebellion (E. White 1987). Many coastal traders faced similar difficulties. Omu Okwei of Ossomari, near Onitsha, lost her husband to British competition as the Royal Niger Company forced him and most of the other traders from the town of Brass out of the upper Niger with stiff and restricted competition. The British set the stage for this competition by bombarding the riverine towns into submission between 1892 and 1910. In an autobiography produced for missionaries, the ex-slave Bwanikwa reported that the coming of the Congo Free State in the 1890s destroyed the state in which she had been a slave, leaving her much more vulnerable to physical violence, for she was not always guaranteed the protection of an owner with a vested interest in her well-being (M. Wright 1997).

As the Europeans gained control over their colonies, they attempted to abolish slavery. The end of the internal slave trade and slavery itself eventually made life safer for many women and gave them more control over their own lives. Yet abolition offered less to women ex-slaves than to male ex-slaves. Men were more likely to leave their former owners than women because they had an easier time establishing economic security on their own (Miers and Roberts 1988; Northrup 1988; M. F. Smith 1981).

Colonial officials used confusion over the distinctions between wives and female slaves, especially concubines, to discourage women ex-slaves from leaving their masters. Europeans argued that wives belonged to their husbands. In areas where slavery was large-scale and most of the slaves were female, decisions by liberated slaves to leave their masters could have disrupted the economic and social relations that the colonizers needed to make their enterprises work

(Miers and Roberts 1988). Following the conquest of northern Nigeria, the British watched concubines flee from their former owners, which forced the owners to work in their own fields and surprised the British, who had thought the concubines were content (Hogendorn and Lovejoy 1988).

In the Maradi region of Niger, elite men and women used marriage to retain control of their former slaves. After emancipation, junior wives and concubines performed agricultural duties. These women responded by asserting the importance of marriage rituals, veiling, and purdah. In so doing, they both asserted their own worth and found a means of evading certain demands on their labor (Cooper 1994, 1997).

In some cases, as in the French Sudan, women joined men in forming new agricultural villages of ex-slaves. They often worked side by side in the fields, ignoring the gender division of labor that characterized the societies that surrounded them. Richard Roberts interviewed a freed slave descendant, who explained how hardship forced ex-slaves to ignore appropriate gender roles, a practice forced on them during slavery:

> At the start of liberation former slaves who installed themselves in a new village had to create a new life. For that end, effort was necessary. During this period the organization [i.e., division of labor under slavery] was observed. That is to say, that men and women did the same work. But with time, prosperity arrived. Women undertook food preparation and domestic chores. However, each [woman] retained the right to the "field of the night," just as the slaves had the right to their own fields. (Roberts 1988, p. 295)

To maintain their workforce, many masters offered former slaves new incentives, such as new clothes, more food, and better working conditions (Hogendorn and Lovejoy 1988). Many of the owners who lost most with the advent of abolition were women. Abolition wiped out a major source of labor for free and elite-class women who relied on slaves to increase their agricultural output. Both free men and women were now forced to turn to lineage ties as their major source for recruiting dependents, and men had greater access to lineage-based labor and wives' labor than did women (Robertson 1997a; M. Wright 1983).

This desire by elders to depend increasingly on kin ties to gain laboring dependents was resisted by many young women, for this era was also characterized by a loosening of patriarchal control over some women's lives. Many women took the opportunities offered by urbanization to flee unpleasant family restrictions, which may have become tighter because of the demise of slavery. For example, in Abeokuta, young women found that the extension of British power led to the relaxation of marriage laws. Women often selected younger men with more disposable income (Byfield 1996). Urban life, however, had only limited options to offer women. Many had to live outside the law, illegally working as prostitutes. Most turned to petty trade for subsistence. Nonetheless, these new options did represent a decline in control over women's labor and in decision-making by the lineage. This early stage of colonial rule began to undermine the hegemony of men and older women over young women by offering the latter avenues of escape from the control of their lineages, particularly important during a time when elders could no longer use slavery for recruiting dependents and therefore wanted tighter control over young women.

As men turned to wage labor and cash crops to pay taxes, buy consumer goods, and fill labor quotas, women found themselves left with a growing workload as they compensated for the increasingly absent men. The expansion of cash crops had the added effect of greater male interest in creating privately owned land. Since men in most West and Central African societies had more access to land ownership, women lost access to land when privately owned property increased in importance.

As in the last century before the expansion of colonial rule, stratification among women in West Africa increased as commodification led to more trading opportunities. Omu Okwei's life illustrates a number of issues faced by women in the early colonial era. First, her early successes highlight the economic possibilities for some women in an era of commercial expansion. But whereas Okwei succeeded, many women failed. It is not difficult to imagine the plight of unnamed women whose husbands were forced out of the upper Niger River area by British traders, and who did not have Okwei's luck and perseverance. Moreover, Okwei's success depended in part on her control over other women. She managed to disguise slavery by adopting and receiving pawned girls, whom she used to forge marriage alliances with European and African traders, including a bank manager in Onitsha and a Royal Niger Company trader in Atani. These alliances helped earn most favored treatment for her in many business transactions. In addition, she acquired domestic servants whom she used as agents in most of the Niger delta ports, including Brass, Port Harcourt, and Warri (Ekejiuba 1967).

Her business interests were not always synonymous with those of other women traders. She developed important ties to the men on the Onitsha town council, who could look after her interests after the Council of Women lost their regulation of the waterside market to the town council. Women as a group lost significant regulatory power as the town government responded to expanding commerce. Okwei, however, stood to gain from the transfer of control over the main market from the Council of Women to the male-dominated town council.

Okwei was taking part in the process of class formation. Nonetheless, the European companies and the power of the externally controlled state to intervene in the market combined with a dramatic expansion in trade to increase the process of this class formation (Sacks 1982). Okwei became a wealthy and powerful petty bourgeois trader, whose mobility beyond this class was severely limited during the era of colonialism. Moreover, although she did relatively well during this era, the changes brought about by colonial rule did have consequences for her as a woman. Ossomari appointed her as *omu* of the Council of Women during an era when the *omu*'s power had been undermined by economic changes and the hostile British colonial state. Certain British traders could respect her abilities, but the colonial state looked askance at women wielding political power. The transfer of waterside market control from the Council of Women to the Town Council symbolizes this hostility toward women. It is not surprising, therefore, that the position of *omu* has been vacant in Ossomari since Okwei's death. Her economic successes brought her to political power in an era when the office was less influential.

In part, the office of *omu* lost power because of a successful attack on it by Christian missionaries. Christianity and Western education, often indistinguishable, interacted in very complex ways with precolonial cultures to affect women's lives. For example, missionaries began to influence notions of appropriate gender roles for women by holding up as a model the most conservative of Western family ideologies (Amadiume 1987). In the Congo Free State, missionaries combined with lineage elders to attack the growing independence of young women (M. Wright 1983). At the same time, missionaries often criticized the practice of pawning young girls, a practice that gave elite women access to labor.

Economically successful women appeared to lose out to economically successful men. For example, women in Lagos had less access to land ownership than their male counterparts. As land became commodified in the late nineteenth century, women's restricted abilities to accumulate property made it difficult for them to keep abreast of economic changes. As Lagos's population grew dramatically and commercial land development took off, women's subordinate roles in family networks often prevented them from alienating family property. Thus they were unable to use land to secure loans just as land was becoming an important private commodity.

Kristin Mann aptly summarized many women's expectations:

> The penetration of European merchant capital in early colonial Lagos introduced new forms of land tenure and property rights that disadvantaged women. Many fewer women than men obtained alienable, individually owned land and houses in the scramble for landed property that followed the annexation. This loss was significant in itself because land was becoming an increasingly scarce and valuable resource. But it also limited women's access to credit and hence to the capital needed to trade. Women's disability in land acquisition put them at yet another disadvantage relative to men. (Mann 1991, p. 705)

The impact of the early colonial period depended a great deal on the place of women in the economy and lineage structure. Of course, all women and men suffered because of the loss of power to the European overlords, but the actual effect on women's lives varied. Many women found themselves freed from slavery, while other, more elite women experienced a decline in their ability to recruit labor because of the abolition of slavery. All women suffered because the Europeans imported a conservative Western family ideology against which their lives were judged; some suffered more than others as missionaries attacked their sources of power. Overall, the period was one of greater stratification among women as commodification spread, and some women, such as Omu Okwei, succeeded in the competitive business world at the turn of the century.

## THE HIGH COLONIAL ERA, 1920–1960

By 1920, the Europeans had gained formal control over virtually all of continental Africa. More than in the early colonial era, the expansion of cash crops as primarily a male domain and male migration to towns and mining areas left women without the assistance of young men in subsistence farming. In order to feed their families and to make up for the low wages paid to men, women increased their agricultural input and turned to petty trading to supplement their farming.

Whereas the earlier period had been characterized by a trend toward the loosening of patriarchal control over women, this period witnessed a partial reversal of this trend. Several factors worked against women's independence, including the attitudes of colonial rulers who felt that women should be under the control of men; the economic interests of the colonial state and foreign businesses, who recognized that helping heads of lineages and chiefs to maintain patriarchal control would increase agricultural production; and the interests of lineage heads, who wished to curtail the development of female independence (M. Wright 1997). Neither the colonial rulers nor the lineage elders were able completely to control changes in kinship relations, however. In many cases, young men used their newly acquired wages to secure wives at an earlier age than in the past. Polygynous unions, however, were often delayed until men grew older, because they could not afford the expense of several wives. More men than women settled in urban areas. For those women who did migrate to towns, economic opportunities continued to be limited to prostitution and petty trading (Luise White 1984).

In general, colonial rulers came from societies that did not recognize women's collective political power as legitimate. Once in control of West and Central Africa, they simply ignored the institutionalized power that women held in many precolonial societies. This attitude contributed to the erosion of women's political power, which was further undermined by missionaries who attacked its religious underpinning. Women did not always accept this situation without protest. They both joined men in anticolonial activities and organized as women to protest their situation.

## Erosion of Women's Economic and Political Power

Among the Baule of Ivory Coast, colonial penetration resulted in a loss of autonomy and power for women (Etienne 1980). The commodification of cloth was especially disruptive to the more egalitarian gender relations of the precolonial era. The Baule lived away from the centers of precolonial trade and coastal state formation. Although they developed little centralized state authority, they did participate in interregional trade. A key trade item was cloth, which men and women produced cooperatively. Women generally grew cotton on land that men had cleared for their use. The women then cleaned and carded this cotton, spun it into thread, and produced indigo dye to color it. Once these processes were completed, they turned the cotton over to men, who wove it and sewed it into strips. Although men played an important role in the production process, the Baule considered women to be the owners of this cloth. At times the cooperative relationship between wives and husbands was altered by men who acquired cotton from women other than their wives, and by women who appropriated the labor of male dependents. These alterations left room for ruptures in the reciprocal and interdependent relations that characterized most wife–husband relations.

In effect, colonial penetration built on these ruptures in the precolonial era to disrupt relatively egalitarian conjugal relations. The stage for this disruption was set by a desire on the part of the French to increase cotton production, and by the 1923 opening of the Gonfreville textile factory near Bouak. These changes caused women's role in cloth production to be obscured as their new roles became mediated by cash and the growing capitalist commodity economy. The French demanded that Baule men produce cotton as a cash crop, and agricultural agents focused on men when they provided assistance in this production. As Boserup (1970) has argued, colonial rulers often failed to recognize women's precolonial roles in production, as the foreigners took to Africa their Western belief that men should farm and women should remain at home. This cash crop production in Ivory Coast required that women help men with the crops; but men owned the final products. Thus women lost control of one of the most important Baule products. Moreover, men could now purchase thread from the Gonfreville textile factory and no longer had to rely on wives as their main source for cotton. As the economy became increasingly commodified, factory-made cotton replaced handmade cloth. The latter became relegated to the ritual and prestige sector, while the Baule turned to factory-made cloth for everyday subsistence use. Competition from the factory-produced cloth undermined women's control of the textile market.

Women's control over cloth production was eroded still further in 1950, when Gonfreville began employing Baule women. As workers in the textile factory, women had virtually no control over their products; rather, their labor was alienated by the production process. At the same time, they became consumers whose role in production went unacknowledged.

Not surprisingly, Baule women protested their deteriorating circumstances by joining the anticolonial struggle. In confronting the colonial rulers, they turned to a precolonial form of protest when they angrily used a symbolic ritual, *adjanu,* that relied on verbal and visual insults, including nudity. This demonstration in 1949 was intended to liberate political prisoners in Grand-Bassam. The French responded violently, injuring a number of women. Nonetheless, these women had clearly recognized the relationship between their declining conditions and the political prisoners at Grand-Bassam.

Many women in West and Central Africa were able to face the

changes brought by colonial penetration with more room to ma-
neuver. In particular, the expansion of the petty commodity market
brought women new opportunities to trade. These opportunities,
however, had a complex impact. For example, in many parts of West
and Central Africa, commodification brought with it an unexpected
crisis in gender relations. Much to the colonial rulers' surprise, changes
in the economy began to threaten patriarchal control over women.
Commodification and a preexisting permissive attitude toward sex
led to a dramatic increase in prostitution in the Cross River Basin of
Nigeria (Naanen 1991). In many places, divorce increased as some
women, especially those with successful trading ventures, gained access to the material resources needed to survive outside of marriage.
As they earned enough money to exist without the institution that
had formerly bound them to men, they inadvertently gained more
control over their sexuality. Some women, then, were able to break
away from unfulfilling sexual, productive, and reproductive obligations to their husbands. This independence worked against the interests of lineage elders and the colonial and local states. Women's retreat from marriage threatened the production of cash crops and wage
labor, since they no longer provided their husbands with the subsistence that freed them to devote time to the other activities.

A growing amount of literature recognizes that colonial control
of the domestic sphere was also important to maintaining control of
the male workforce. In Katanga, women's ability to produce food and
children ensured a stable workforce for the local mines (Gondola
1997). In offering regular prenatal consultations, supplementary food
rations, and baby gifts, Union Minière of Katanga recognized that the
workers' wives were central to their enterprise (Dibwe 1993). In the
Zambian copperbelt, male colonial officials and traditional male authorities struggled to direct women's labor and sexuality by defining
and redefining the institution of marriage (Parpart 1994). Similarly,
when the black soldiers of the French colonial army were posted away
from their homes, the French authorities recruited local women to
act as cooks, mistresses, and wives, believing that these women would
stabilize the forces and prevent desertion among their ranks. However, although this policy was initially successful, it ultimately undermined the authorities' intent when these same soldiers developed a
stake in the local community through their families (Thompson 1990).

Within Belgian Central Africa, where colonial authorities sought
to categorize and tax women according to their marital status, changes in the definition of a single woman provoked a rebellion within
Bujumbura. In an effort to end "camouflaged" or hidden polygyny

among "Christian, colonial-educated, évolue men," the authorities passed an anti-polygamy law in 1950. It redefined polygynous unions as business relationships and did not recognize the right of polygynous wives to remain in urban areas. Outraged that wives of polygynous unions, widows, and prostitutes were all defined as *femme libre* (single women) and taxed accordingly by the Belgian authorities, Muslim women petitioned the vice governor-general and threw letters of protest into the cars of the entourage of the visiting Belgian king (Hunt 1991). Both local and state authorities worked to restrict women's mobility and independence by strengthening marriage institutions.

In West Africa, such an effort on the part of the colonial authorities is well illustrated by the Sefwi Wiawso state in western Gold Coast (P. Roberts 1987). In this region, the state council moved to address a crisis in gender relations by passing a series of amendments to customary law between 1925 and 1932. Changes in the economy had led to this crisis. Before the widespread introduction of cocoa into the area during the 1920s, husbands and wives lived in complementary but independent economic spheres. Men cleared land for their wives and supplied them with meat and fish. Women farmed the land provided by their husbands and fed them and the husbands' dependents who were assigned to the wives' houses. Divorces were relatively easy to obtain, and women often retired to their natal family's farm after they had children to avoid any further labor and reproductive obligations to their husbands.

Cocoa production disrupted this complementary relationship as men turned to their wives to work on their cocoa farms in the face of the collapse of slave labor as an alternative. But many women did not feel that they were adequately compensated for their labor, while they worked on crops that they did not control. Divorce often followed, as women complained that their husbands refused to give them their own cocoa farms or to divide property evenly among their wives.

The situation was further complicated by the collapse of the cocoa market at the end of the 1920s and the growth of mining and transportation towns in Sefwi Wiawso. Women responded to these changes by increasing their marketing in food crops to male wage laborers. For many women, this trade offered an alternative to remaining in marriage. From the viewpoint of local authorities, women without male guardians posed a threat to patriarchal families. In particular, they worried that men no longer controlled the allocation of women's labor through marriage. These "free women," as they were called, even interfered with the exchange of women by arranging their daughters' marriages and divorces. The increase in the number of independent women was accompanied by venereal disease and an anti-witchcraft campaign to counter the disease's spread.

To intervene in what male elders considered a crisis, the state council enacted laws designed to contain prostitution, to stabilize marriage through decreased divorce, and to stem the rising costs of acquiring a wife. These developments, however, were not within the state council's control. The growth of commodity production ultimately undermined attempts to control women, because trade offered them the opportunity to gain more control over their lives.

While commodification opened up new opportunities for women, especially female elders, the expansion of the world economy ultimately spelled disaster for most women. As women left farming for trading, they found that trade was becoming increasingly less important in the overall economy than it had been at the beginning of the colonial era. This process has been illustrated by novelist Buchi Emecheta (1979) in *The Joys of Motherhood*. Nnu Ego, the focus of the novel, follows her new husband to Lagos, where he works as a domestic servant. When he is forced to join the British colonial army during World War II, she is left with the responsibilities of supporting herself and her children. Petty trading opportunities do not seem to be sufficient for feeding her family and paying her children's school fees. Prostitution appears to offer her a better standard of living, but Nnu Ego's values do not make this a viable option. At several points she is reduced to scavenging for firewood to sell. Emecheta movingly portrays the plight of women at the very bottom of the petty trading hierarchy, as Nnu Ego tries to meet her obligations to her children with very few resources. Her daughters, however, look toward a future less constrained by traditional kinship ties, which their economic opportunities will not allow them to maintain.

Ga women traders in Accra experienced a new freedom to arrange their own marriages and to move in and out of marriage bonds, but trade was the only option for subsistence that some women had. Many men were able to convert their control over dependents to control over resources, monopolizing private land ownership. Moreover, women faced discrimination in the labor market, as men turned to wage labor and even participated in the state administration (Robertson 1990).

Both colonialism and the capitalism that accompanied it entwined with already existing social formations in a variety of ways. Colonial rulers had sometimes conflicting interests in stability that would make their colonies governable and changes that would facilitate capitalist penetration. As Sara Berry argues in her discussion of the Yoruba experience, colonial rulers attempted to co-opt established institutions and authorities in their efforts to consolidate their financial and political position. "In the process," she suggests, "capitalist penetration and colonial rule neither destroyed nor subsumed intact precolonial Yoruba social units but operated both to reproduce and to transform them" (1985, p. 12).

Perhaps the social units of greatest concern to the colonial rulers when they thought of controlling women were kinship organizations. The colonizers both built on existing kinship relations and sought to transform them when these relations did not ensure that women fit the gender roles that Europeans felt were appropriate. As shown above in the discussion of the Sefwi Wiawso, male elders and colonial rulers passed customary laws that attempted to keep women under the control of their lineages.

Western-style education was also used to set boundaries on women's behavior. Colonial rulers designed schools to teach girls how to be good wives to elite men. Jules de Coppet, the governor-general of French West Africa, sent a circular, "The Instruction of Native Girls," to his lieutenant governors. As Diane Barthel suggests, he made it clear that the goals of female education were "the inculcation of European ideas on health and child care, the training of suitable wives for the French-trained male elite, and also the socialization of future generations in French mores and culture" (1985, pp. 145–46). He stated,

> The practical girls' school aiming toward the domestic and hygienic education of women is the natural complement of rural popular school. It is based on the same principles, it claims the same organization, it proposes the same goal. The education of the native woman permits the evolution of the family and does not limit to the individual level the action of education received. It will consolidate, finally, in successive generations, the new habits acquired by education and will permanently install our action within the indigenous society. (Barthel 1985, p. 146)

Most girls exposed to Western-style education were the daughters of the newly educated elite. In fact, Western-educated fathers, concerned that colonial rulers were not providing enough schooling for girls, demanded that their daughters be educated. The newly educated male elite wanted wives for their sons who were skilled in Western-style gender roles so that they could raise their children to maintain their class position. After 1920, colonial rulers also began to see the importance of producing suitable wives for elite colonized men. But the administrators were further worried about the development of rebellious women who lacked the access to education that men had. For example, in 1921, George Hardy, once inspector general of education for French West Africa, worried about the development of a "Lysistrata under the coconut trees" if only boys were educated and girls remained shut out of schools (Barthel 1985, p. 145).

The disadvantages faced by Ga women are highlighted by their educational experiences. Men had more educational opportunities than women, a factor that was to the latter's disadvantage in the newly evolving economy. Women in the Congo faced similar problems. Most Western-style education there was offered by missionaries who shared the colonial rulers' concerns that schools instill in their colonial subjects conservative Western values that centered on the family and work. Before World War II, both women and men were given limited education that attempted to Christianize them without Westernization. The Belgians feared the creation of an assertive Westernized class such as had developed in Sierra Leone. With hopes that women would introduce Christian values into their cultures through proper mothering, missionaries trained them to become Christian wives and mothers and gave them few skills that would help them compete in the colonial economy. In so doing, they also attempted not just to draw distinctions between whites and blacks, but to assert class differences among Africans (Hunt 1990). After World War II, education for boys became much more geared to preparing them for wage labor and administrative tasks. By the time of independence, however, women could rarely become anything but Catholic sisters or elementary school teachers. Throughout the colonial period, few women gained access to even this limited education; less than 4 percent of secondary school pupils were female on the eve of independence in 1960 (Yates 1982).

Education was obviously a major tool used to spread imperialist culture. Western ideology was embedded in the process of education; it was the "hidden curriculum" in the structure of the school day (Masemann 1974). All students were exposed to Western ideologies about time and bureaucracy. Of course, missionaries and European teachers did not have complete control over what girls learned. Some of these students went on to enter male-dominated professional fields despite their training as homemakers (Barthel 1985). Others, such as Adelaide Smith Casely Hayford, joined nationalist movements as part of an educated elite demanding control over their own nation-states (Cromwell 1986).

Indeed, the spread of European imperial culture was complex and contradictory in a number of ways, as can be demonstrated by examining the roles played by European women in the colonizing effort. As Helen Callaway points out, European administrators first saw the colonial service primarily as a male domain, and Africa as an unsuitable place for proper European women. Yet European women did go to the colonies. While they faced much hostility, they played an important role in stabilizing the colonial hierarchies established by male administrators. Europeans in West and West-Central African colonies both supported Victorian ideas of women's place in the world and undermined these ideas by actively participating in the colonial venture, first as missionaries, then increasingly as nurses and educational officers, and eventually as administrators. This contradiction was explored by Margaret Strobel. She suggests that "even missionary women, whose commitment to career and calling was a challenge to those very [Victorian] notions [of domesticity and female dependence], accepted the patriarchal ideology and bureaucracy of the Church and promoted conventional European gender roles to African and Asian women" (Strobel 1998, p. 390). This contradiction represented the tension between sexism and imperialism, which on the surface seemed to work so well together. While colonialism and patriarchy may appear to be inextricable, European women's participation in the imperialist endeavor caused disruptions and contradictions between the two systems of domination.

World War II was a watershed, ushering in an era of increased participation by European women in the colonies as the war effort occupied men. In her study of European women in colonial Nigeria, Helen Callaway describes World War II and the succeeding decolonization phase as an era of the feminization of colonial culture. As Europeans began to lose control over their colonies, men began to retreat and allow women to take their places. No longer was Africa a place for young men to prove their masculinity. The new women officers

> thus formed an interim "buffer" group between two separate structures of male prestige, the departing British Colonial Service and the advancing cadres of Nigerian politicians and civil servants. . . . In this setting, the meaning of [European women's] presence in Nigeria as administrators cannot be interpreted in terms of "equal opportunity for women" so much as providing the Colonial Office with a temporary and non-threatening group aiding the graceful exit of the Raj. (Callaway 1987, p. 144)

Callaway argues that colonial women are often unfairly accused of having "lost" the empire or having created greater distance between the races, when they should be acknowledged for the roles they played in ending the era of direct imperialism. It is possible that they also helped disguise the meaning of the neo-colonial relations that replaced direct colonialism.

While some European women benefited from their participation in colonial rule, for many African women it meant the loss of political power and new restrictions on participating in government. Often the British and French in West Africa ignored precolonial women's offices and directed everything through men. Thus, for example, the *omu* or "mother" of the Igbo, who was responsible for controlling markets and settling disputes among women, lost power to the male ruler, the *obi*. The British legitimized the *obi*'s rule by giving him a salary to which the *omu* had no similar access (Okonjo 1983). By independence, the office of *omu* in many Igbo towns lay vacant. This kind of deterioration in women's position led women to protest.

*Resistance*

Many West and West-Central African women responded to colonial rule with open hostility and even rebellion, often struggling to defend their economic interest as traders. Others protested their loss of political power during the colonial era. Many turned to their precolonial gender-based solidarities to organize themselves. Igbo and Ibibio women rebelled against the colonial rulers and their local collaborators during the Women's War of 1929, revealingly called the "Aba Riots" by the British. These women used women's networks to organize thousands of women to confront the Native Administration throughout the region. They used a mechanism known as "sitting on a man" to insult the local authorities and protest what they believed was a plan to tax women. Their hostility also was fueled by fears that both their land and their bodies were losing fertility. This rebellion, however, was more than symbolic; women attacked the sixteen Native Courts, destroying several. The British responded to these tens of thousands of women by killing more than fifty and wounding at least that many (Amadiume 1987; Ifeka-Moller 1975; Mba 1982; Van Allen 1976).

A similar rebellion occurred in Cameroon between 1958 and 1959. As early as the late 1920s, women had institutionalized a precolonial tool, *anlu*, for punishing men who offended the women's community. They developed a hierarchical structure with local chapters that looked after women's interests. The *anlu* was able to call together up to seven thousand Kom women in a series of mass demonstrations at the end of the 1950s. As in the Igbo case, women felt that their economic interests were threatened. In particular, these women feared that the colonial government would give their land to the Igbo. In addition, they complained that the local chiefs would not protect their crops from the cattle of Fulani herders. In contrast to the reaction to the Igbo Women's War, the colonial rulers elected not to respond with physical force, and none of the protesters was hurt (Ardener 1975).

In Lagos, eight to ten thousand women joined together in the Lagos Market Women's Association, led by Alimotu Pelewura. Most of these women were illiterate and poor. They protested taxation of women and opposed a price-control scheme imposed during World War II. This organization was explicitly anticolonial, joining a general strike called during 1945. During the same period, middle-class women began to organize under the leadership of Oyinkan Abayomi. Married to the leader of the Nigerian Youth Movement, Abayomi founded the British West African Girls' Club, later the Ladies' Progressive Club, in 1927. This organization had a limited constituency of Westernized Christian middle-class women; estimations of its membership range from five hundred to two thousand (Johnson 1981, 1986; Mba 1982).

Both Susan Geiger and Jane Turrittin have examined women's influence on anticolonial struggles. Geiger points out that it was "in [the African nationalist leaders'] interest to present themselves as enlightened proponents of Western democracy and equality, including full political rights for women" (Geiger 1990, p. 227). However, Turrittin also notes that the male modernizing elite associated femaleness with backwardness and therefore had difficulty addressing women's double oppression (Turrittin 1993).

Within this context, more of the literature has begun to focus on a broader array of protest actions, specifically on forms of resistance unique to women such as "shaming" and "obscene" behavior. The growing literature available on individual women participants has also begun to reshape historians' views of the nationalist movements (Geiger 1990).

Perhaps one of the most successful cross-class organizations, the Abeokuta Women's Union, was founded by Funmilayo Ransome-Kuti. In the 1920s and 1930s, she was active in girls' and women's education, including teaching illiterate market women to read. In the 1940s, she became radicalized as she engaged with market women in struggles against taxation and for suffrage and political representation. Ransome-Kuti later became principal of the Abeokuta Girls' School. She was careful to wear Yoruba clothes and to speak in Yoruba during meetings so that she would be identified with her fellow union members rather than with the ruling British. The Women's Union worked against indirect rule, clearly exhibiting both a nationalist bent and a concern for women's economic interests (Johnson-Odim and Mba 1997).

A fictionalized account of a post–World War II railroad strike in Senegal in which women participated appears in Ousmane Sembene's *God's Bits of Wood* (1982). This novel brings out the important role that women played in supporting men who worked for low wages. Because of women's role in subsistence, the French were able to deny their workers a living wage. The strike could not have been successful without their support. Indeed, the most dramatic moment of the book comes when the women march from Thiès to Dakar to press the strikers' demands. Likewise, women played an important role in the Watchtower movement in Katanga, which was of great importance to the Manono miners' strike of 1941 (Higginson 1992).

One of the most dramatic cases of women's resistance took place in Guinea-Bissau during the 1960s and early 1970s. The people in this colony watched all the states in West and West-Central Africa except Angola gain their independence, while they had to resort to armed struggle to end Portuguese rule. Led by the African Party for the Independence of Guinea and Cape Verde (PAIGC), the independence movement saw the expulsion of the Portuguese as only a stage in the transition to a socialist society. Integral to their struggle was the transformation of internal social relations, including gender relations. To this end, the PAIGC leadership argued that women had to take the lead in ending male domination. As party leaders expressed it, women must "fight against two colonialisms—one of the Portuguese and the other of men" (Urdang 1979, p. 15). This two-sided battle was responsible for attracting many women to the independence struggle as they saw the possibilities for ending their oppression as women (Urdang 1979).

PAIGC recognized the contributions that women could make to the independence struggle. And women did come to play important political roles within the party structure, although they served in defensive military positions rather than in offensive combat. Most important, however, was the feminism articulated by PAIGC members that gave depth to the liberation struggle. Stephanie Urdang, who was largely responsible for introducing the English-speaking West to the ideology of "fighting two colonialisms," quotes one of the leading women party members on the new woman emerging during the revolution:

By a liberated woman I mean a woman who has a clear consciousness about her responsibility in the society and who is economically independent. By a liberated woman I mean one who is able to do all the jobs in the society without being discriminated against, a woman who can go to school to learn, who can become a leader. . . . While women are fighting for their freedom at present, a new system is evolving which is preparing the young people of the next generation. And this new system is trying to change their idea of liberty, their idea of freedom and their idea of coexistence between the elements of the family and within the society in general. . . .

If we build a society without exploitation of one human being by another, then of course women will have to be free in that society. Our struggle for national liberation is one way of assuring the liberation of women because, by doing the same work as men, or by doing work that ensures the liberation of our country, women convince themselves that they are able to do the same work as men. In the process women will learn that they are able to do many things that they could not have conceived of before. They will learn that in our party there are women in the highest level of leadership and that women are working in all different sectors of our lives. It is important because it convinces women that they have potential and shows men what that potential is. (1979, pp. 258–59)

Such clearly articulated goals became an inspiration for women in liberation movements around the world.

Perhaps the greatest irony of the colonial era was that Europeans used an ideology suggesting that they would improve African women's lives as part of their justification for imposing colonial rule. In reality, the changes set in motion by colonial rule and capitalist penetration impoverished many women. For example, commodification undermined the control that Baule women had over the cloth market in their region of Ivory Coast. Many women found themselves, like Emecheta's Nnu Ego, responsible for kinship obligations without the resources to meet them in new colonial towns. Moreover, the colonial rulers joined with lineage elders in attempting to limit women's independence and autonomy, for fear that women would not continue to subsidize the colonial economy by providing subsistence with very few resources. Rather than support women's traditional avenues to political power, the colonizers often actively undermined the political power of elite women. Finally, when women did gain greater economic or social independence, they did so despite the attitudes and policies of the Europeans. Women sometimes resisted their deterioration in status directly through strikes, nationalist activity, and, in the case of the Igbo and Guinea-Bissau, even actual rebellion. More commonly, individual women set out to gain independence for themselves by migrating to towns without their families' approval and turning the commodification of the economy to their benefit when possible.

## THE POSTCOLONIAL PERIOD

Many people living in West and West-Central Africa entered the postcolonial era with very high expectations. Indeed, most governments attempted to meet promises made during the decolonization period by improving education, creating jobs, and facilitating Western-style development. Unfortunately, the independent states have not met the expectations raised by independence for a variety of reasons. Internal conflict caused by competition to control limited resources and these states' weak positions in the international economy figured importantly among the factors that dashed people's expectations. Corrupt governments, sometimes supported by the West, have been another major factor.

Much of the literature on women during the contemporary period has examined these developments and asked the question, Have women gained or lost status since independence? Unfortunately, this question is too simplistic and ignores the realities of increasing class stratification among women. Some authors have begun to ask, How does gender interact with postcolonial changes to influence women's lives? Such a question recognizes that women as a group are stratified by class, age, and status, and that the possibility exists for women to gain and lose at the same time.

### Women in the Rural Economy

The life of most rural women is characterized by what Jane Guyer has described as "enterprise and autonomy on the one hand, and poverty and overwork on the other" (1995b, p. 19). This paradoxical situation results from the complex interaction between increased commodity production and local cultural systems that has dominated many women's lives. Guyer's review of the literature on rural African women has led her to suggest three ways that commodity production has affected rural women. First, production for international markets has expanded through the growth of export crop production by smallholder farmers. Second, internal, interregional trade has expanded. Third, wage labor for industry and large-scale agricultural enterprises has developed outside of the small-farming sector (Guyer 1995b).

This commodification has meant that many, though not all, rural women have been forced to feed their families on increasingly marginal land, and with less help from male relatives. Some women have responded to this situation by increasing their market activities and have added to the dramatic expansion of petty trading. In the cocoa-growing regions of southern Ghana, women often helped their husbands on their cocoa farms but continued to provide subsistence food for their families (Okali 1983). Some women have been able to move into cocoa farming themselves, but generally on a small scale; they collectively own less than 5 percent of all cocoa farms (Guyer 1995b). When the cocoa boom began to go bust in the 1960s, men started migrating to towns, leaving women to feed themselves and their dependents. Thus, the trend begun during the colonial era of leaving women solely in charge of subsistence continued in the postcolonial period. Since cocoa farmers monopolized the best land even during this depressed era, women have been responsible for feeding their families on increasingly infertile land. Many have met the challenge by combining farming with petty trade, food processing, and wage labor (Guyer 1995b).

The growth of cocoa production has adversely affected many Yoruba women in similar ways. As in southern Ghana, some women have been able to gain ownership of cocoa farms, often through inheritance. Nonetheless, the commercialization of land has worked against most women, who generally have less control over land and family labor than men have. Women are more likely to work on their husbands' farms than their own. As in the colonial era, Yoruba women have responded to these changes by increasing their participation in petty trading. They continue to dominate open markets; an increasing number have been able to move into the male-dominated domain of small retail shops, which require more capital than most women have (Afonja 1981, 1986). Commodification, therefore, has contributed to the increasingly complex stratification of rural women.

Many recent agricultural studies have given greater nuance and historical depth to the study of the gender division of labor. They have demonstrated that rural women often actively resisted new claims on their labor and sought ways to assert their economic independence. For example, Jane Guyer notes that among the Beti of Cameroon, the precolonial African crops tend to follow an activity-specific division of labor, while the newer cash crops tend to follow a system based on products or field types. This differentiation in patterns of production reflects both the growth of export crop production and women's reactions to the process. When women lost access to land and certain "male" crops as a result of men's increasing involvement with cash crops, women responded by "extending those farming activities that relied the least on male participation." They also attempted to gain access to male income generated by cash crops through other activities, such as selling cooked food, distilling liquor, and importing beer (Guyer 1991).

Studies of Gambian rice production have emphasized that the gendering of crops remains an ongoing process embedded in distribution of labor and power within the household itself. According to Judith Carney and Michael Watts, colonial officials' efforts to increase Gambia's rice output faltered as a result of the gender division of labor. These officials found that when men refused to cultivate a "woman's crop," women were unwilling and unable to extend the number of days they devoted to rice farming. Similarly, certain 1980s development projects encountered problems when women again reacted to the loss of access to rice land and property by withdrawing their labor (Carney and Watts 1991). More recently, a rise in the value of fruits and vegetables has altered rural labor patterns once again. As women's proceeds from these "cash crops" have begun to exceed men's, women have gained greater autonomy. Many have begun to challenge male authority and fail to perform certain kinds of domestic labor. In this way, gender relations have begun to shift, and many aspects of marriage have been renegotiated (Schroeder 1996).

Indeed, it is important to point out that developments in rural West and West-Central Africa have not affected all women the same way. Lucy Creevey (1986) has noted that women in Mali break with the common notion that rural women have declined in status in relation to men. This stereotypical view argues that men have either received tools and advice from colonial rulers and postcolonial development experts and turned to cash crops or migrated to plantations or towns to the south. Creevey found that most Malians, male and female, are still rural. There has been little migration by men, and women head only 14 percent of all households. She suggests that this stability has been maintained despite the difficult conditions created by periodic droughts and increasing desertification in the region. Creevey highlights the continuing interdependence of men and women in Malian agriculture:

> Bambara men clear the fields, young boys fertilize them with animal manure, and men build storage huts and supervise the storage of grain, except for the family surplus which women control. Bambara women receive rewards in cash for their work on men's fields. Furthermore, Bambara men help women by clearing land in their fields. Bambara women's fields are not restricted to food crops; they

also grow cash crops such as peanuts on their plots and use the revenue thus obtained for family needs and personal purchases. (1986, p. 58)

She further argues that ethnic background, age, religion, and family wealth affect the roles played by women. Although she recognizes the many problems faced by women in rural Mali, she argues that increasing commodification and economic development alone cannot be held responsible for these problems. It is unclear whether this case is unusual or represents a different interpretation by Creevey of similar material used in other case studies.

## Women in the Urban Economy

The crisis in the rural economy of much of West and West-Central Africa, combined with the lure of opportunities in cities, has led to the migration of both women and men to urban areas. As Adepoju (1983) points out, migration is nothing new in Africa. Warfare, trade, evangelism, drought, the search for fertile lands, and the slave trade all contributed to a highly mobile population in the precolonial era; these migrations usually took the form of group migration. In contrast to the precolonial era, more men than women migrated during both the colonial and the postcolonial periods. Although the migration of greater numbers of unmarried childless women in the 1980s again caused a shift in colonial and postcolonial demographic patterns, men still have greater wage labor opportunities, while women continue to play an essential role in subsistence agriculture (Sheldon 1996).

Nonetheless, an increasing number of women have migrated to towns. Sudarkasa (1977) suggests that most of these women were seeking trade opportunities. Of the four groups who have dominated commercial migration in West Africa—the Hausa, Dyula, Igbo, and Yoruba—women are most numerous among the Yoruba migrants, even outnumbering Yoruba male migrants. Many other women accompany their husbands to towns or cities. An increasing number of women try to enter wage labor, but many of them are forced to turn to trading because of their limited education and the limited job opportunities for women. Some young women migrate to their relatives' homes in towns, often exchanging domestic service for school fees.

Like their rural sisters, women in urban areas are largely responsible for feeding their families, perhaps the most fundamental fact of their lives. As a consequence, virtually all women are economically active, whether or not they are counted among the labor force by census takers, who consistently under-enumerate them. Although increasing numbers are involved in wage labor, including factory work and white-collar service industries, most women have turned to self-employment to survive in the urban economy (Robertson 1997a). Within the informal sector, women have blurred the line between rural and urban by using urban land to grow the food that they then sell to local workers and residents for profit (Freeman 1993).

Self-employment in petty trade and food processing offers many women independence, but the sheer number of women who have turned to this economic alternative makes barriers to earning a comfortable living difficult to surmount. Alternatives to self-employment are more limited for women than they are for men. One major reason for the disparity between women and men's wage labor opportunities is women's limited educational opportunities. Although most postcolonial states provide education for a larger percentage of their populations than colonial governments did, illiteracy among West and West-Central Africans, both female and male, is widespread (Ware 1983).

Nonetheless, girls generally have less access to education than boys; and when they attend school, they are more likely to terminate their education at the primary level (Robertson 1997a). In both urban and rural areas, girls are more likely to be kept out of school because their mothers require their assistance at home, on the farm, or in the marketplace. Families generally do not hold similar expectations of young boys. It is not surprising, then, that when families find it difficult to obtain school fees, they are more likely to pay for boys than for girls (United Nations Economic Commission for Africa 1975). This preference is also supported by the reality that educated young men are more likely than educated young women to find jobs in the urban economy. Even with a primary or secondary education, women are often forced to turn to self-employment rather than being able to use their schooling to gain wage labor.

Enid Schildkrout (1983) points to additional factors that keep Hausa girls out of school. In northern Nigeria, many Hausa resist educating their daughters because they prefer to marry them at puberty to ensure that they are virgins at first marriage. In addition, many Hausa who are Muslims associate Western-style education with Christianity and moral laxity in schools. Such concerns are common in many West African countries.

The spread of Western-style education has had a profound affect on most urban women's lives, whether or not they actually have been able to attend school. The mere presence of these educational systems has affected the economic stratification in towns and cities as educational qualifications become an important determination of position in the occupational structure (Fapohunda 1983). But the impact on women is complex and various. The expansion of educational opportunities in the postcolonial era has brought more girls into the system and increased literacy rates. In Ivory Coast, for example, a small number of women have gained access to the most elite education provided, although most leave school before the secondary level. This elite education includes training for professions that have been dominated by men in the West. In other countries, such as Cameroon, women are more likely to obtain secondary and post-secondary education than in Ivory Coast, but they are generally limited to education for jobs that usually go to women in the West and offer limited economic opportunities (Clignet 1977). In no states are women significantly represented in agricultural or technical training. Several authors have pointed out the irony of this fact, given women's crucial role in farming (Boserup 1970; Ware 1983).

In Emecheta's novel *Double Yoke* (1982), Nko faces many of the problems confronted by highly educated women in Africa. Nko finds herself caught between conflicting expectations. On the one hand, her boyfriend expects her to fulfill the role of the idealized rural woman who quietly respects her husband's wishes. On the other hand, she is pulled by the expectations of the educated elite that she have an independent intellectual life. Most significant, she believes that she cannot succeed at the university without agreeing to sleep with her professor, whom she does not desire. Education offers Nko both new opportunities and new, very frightening dilemmas.

Many urban women try to educate their daughters in order to increase their economic security and to ensure that these daughters will be able to care for their mothers in old age. This tactic, however, has mixed results. While in school, girls often miss out on important potential apprenticeships with women traders and other self-employed women. This gap in their training has significant implications, since so many women have to turn to self-employment despite years spent in school. Furthermore, schooling rarely makes up for these lost years of training by teaching educational skills, such as accounting, that could help them later in life (Robertson 1997a). Finally, women who send their daughters to school are deprived of critical assistance while they trade, making their own workload heavier (Schildkrout 1983).

As educational systems help increase the occupational hierarchies found in urban areas, stratification among women intensifies, and a small number of women do well economically in this system. Most successful women gain a head start in life by being born into a privileged family (Barthel 1975). The small group of elite women found in the cities of West and West-Central Africa have received much attention, most of it focusing on their sexual and marital relations with men. They will be discussed further in the next section.

### Kinship, Marriage, and Religion

The controversy over whether recent changes in the structure of kinship and marriage have been positive for women has been central to much of the contemporary literature. Most women marry at some point in their lives. Many families marry their teenaged girls to much older men. For many women, therefore, early adulthood looks much like the ideal expressed during the precolonial and colonial eras by most West and West-Central African peoples. But there are an increasing number of women who wait to marry same-age men when they reach their twenties. This change represents greater freedom for junior women and men to choose their own partners than was permitted in precolonial societies. Marriage has become more an expression of personal preference than the alliance between kin groups that it was in the past (Luise White 1984).

Moreover, divorce seems to be fairly common throughout West and West-Central Africa. Relationships formed with men after a divorce often represent a break with customary or Western-style marriage. Instead, divorced women may choose what the Asante call a lover marriage: they enter long-term love relationships with men without the formality of a marriage ceremony (Abu 1983). Not all women choose to form such relationships, as the evidence of growing numbers of households headed by women would suggest. Indeed, Michel Verdon (1982) argues that traditional and Christian marriage rituals have virtually disappeared among the Ewe of southern Ghana since World War II. Even before this era, divorce was common, because women were able to rely on their matrikin ties to obtain land rights, and they were able to maintain custody of their children. The disappearance of marriage ceremonies, however, has resulted from declining control of parents over their daughters in the face of labor migration and increased school attendance. In addition, marriage contracts no longer serve the economic function of bridging male and female spheres. Marriage bonds have become increasingly fragile under increased mobility and urbanization.

The meaning of these fragile marriage bonds in women's lives is complex and contradictory. As Luise White suggests, "labor migration and rural poverty have increased women's workloads and anxieties, but have also increased the options and social relations available to them, and placed many of the latter under the women's control" (1984, p. 63). On the one hand, many women find themselves forced to take on economic responsibilities alone that would be more easily met with husbands or stronger kinship ties. At the same time, some of these women have been forced to turn to their lovers for economic support, even though there exist few culturally sanctioned, organized roles for these lovers to play in supporting women and their children. In towns, isolation from family and kinship ties often deprives women of the lineage support that would have existed in the past. Thus, for example, women find it more difficult to share childcare responsibilities with family members and co-wives. On the other hand, many women clearly choose the independence that comes with flexible heterosexual bonds and loosening kinship ties. Many of the responsibilities in decision-making that now accrue to women are welcomed even if these new responsibilities signify increased economic burdens.

Much of the contemporary literature and popular wisdom on African women has revealed a discomfort with the loosening of conjugal and kinship bonds. Women's ability to move in and out of marriage relations is often disparaged in part because the relationship between women and men is often based on economic interests. As Mann suggests,

> Many African women have come to view relationships with men instrumentally. Women use domestic and sexual relationships as a means of obtaining resources and access to opportunities and of furthering individual social and economic ambitions. If a particular relationship fails to fulfill a woman's goals, she may leave it and seek another more rewarding. (1985, p. 110)

In Africa, as elsewhere historically, heterosexual bonds have long had a central economic element. What is new is not that heterosexual bonds are a source of resources and opportunities, but rather that the bonds between kin groups that marriage represented have disappeared. In this situation, both women and men have more freedom to choose partners and to break relationships, a double-edged sword for women who want independence but lack the resources to survive without male support. In this context, the position of the PAIGC of Guinea-Bissau against forced marriage, polygynous marriage, and limited options for women to divorce is notable (Urdang 1979). Postcolonial states have been much more likely to support patriarchal control over women than to undermine it.

Flora Nwapa (1998) brings a feminist critique of marriage and family life to her novels about women in Nigeria. In *Efuru* (1966a), *Once Is Enough* (1981), and *Idu* (1966b), she emphasizes the negative effects of traditional constraints on women's lives. Many of her main characters are childless and are therefore mistreated by their families. But Nwapa is also a critic of modern society; society's expectations work against women's interests. Women are too often tied into unhappy marriages or left to fend for themselves if they should be unfortunate enough to be infertile.

As Vidal (1977) suggests for Abidjan, changes in heterosexual bonds have occurred across classes. Many professional women have chosen to remain unmarried rather than enter a marriage that they consider unsuitable (Dinan 1977). High-income, educated women tend to object to polygyny because they do not wish to share their husbands' resources. For most elite women, their model marriage includes a monogamous relationship in which they share responsibilities with their (faithful) husbands. More often than not, the reality does not meet their ideals. Men resist the demands made on them by nuclear families. Often they develop relationships with outside wives or mistresses (Luise White 1984). Oppong (1974) argues that elite women are more likely to live with their husbands than in the past and to suffer under their separation from matrikin. At the same time, their security in their conjugal relationship is undermined by outside wives and the demands made on their husband by his matrikin. Under such circumstances, many professional women choose to forgo or delay marriage, building pragmatic relationships with men that give them the necessary resources to survive and thrive in the urban economy (Dinan 1977).

As Nwapa shows in *Once Is Enough* (1981), the decision to remain single often leaves women open to charges of misconduct and immorality. Mariama Ba takes up a similar issue in *So Long a Letter* (1981). This novel focuses on two marriages, one between Modou and Ramatoulaye and the other between Mawdo and Aissatou. Ramatoulaye elects to remain a faithful wife despite desertion by her husband, while Aissatou decides to leave hers. Ramatoulaye faces the problems of raising her children on her own as she fights against the sexism that constrains women's lives in Senegal. Both Ba and Nwapa represent voices that have emerged in Africa's postcolonial era raising women's issues, although not all have explicitly declared themselves to be feminists, and some keep their distance from Western feminists. Some novelists have given voice to African feminist concerns about women's desire for more autonomy and independence in a system in which women are caught in what Emecheta portrays as the double yoke of traditional ideas and contemporary realities. Others, such as Nwapa and Ama Ata Aidoo (1970, 1977), place the source of African sexism in European imperialism and colonial rule. Most African women writers focus on the tension between women's individual freedom and the needs of their families and communities (Okhamafe 1990).

Not all women's protest voices are raised by novelists. Filomina Chioma Steady, a feminist anthropologist, writes of African feminism as the original form of feminism, and she argues for recognition of an indigenous form of women's political struggle that combines humanism with concern for women's welfare (1987, 1985). Without fear of expressing her anger, Awa Thiam (1996) has written a strong and provocative exposé of women's plight in West Africa. She includes a critique of clitoridectomy as it is practiced in much of contemporary West Africa. Olayinka Koso-Thomas (1987) joins Thiam in this critique. As a Western-trained doctor, Koso-Thomas attempts to place female circumcision in its cultural context and yet exposes the way it cripples so many women's lives. She writes with the passion of someone who has seen the damage that this practice can cause, with the authority of a doctor, and with the sensitivity of an insider.

Academic feminists have been gathering since at least 1977, when West African women intellectuals formed AAWORD, the Association of African Women for Research and Development (Awe and Mba 1991). The women in AAWORD came from anglophone and francophone West Africa: they attempted to stake out an independent feminist position that asked questions relevant to African women's lives. Building on such organizations, the Women's Research and Documentation Center (WORDOC) has been very active since its founding in 1985. Based at the institute of African Studies at Ibadan, WORDOC has conducted lively and informative research in West African and Nigerian historiography (Awe and Mba 1991).

Women's personal lives are also influenced by the variety of religious experiences to which women in West and West-Central Africa have been exposed. In West Africa, Christianity remains a minority religion in all states but Nigeria, where the southern part of the country remains Christian. Instead there has been a dramatic spread of Islam. Just as the cultures vary throughout the region, however, Islam's impact has depended on the host cultures and the timing of penetration. In Hausaland, for example, one finds many women veiled and secluded (Callaway and Creevey 1994). In other parts of West Africa, such as Senegambia and Sierra Leone, there are few physical restrictions on women's lives. It remains to be seen how the spread of political Islam, or Islamism, internationally will affect West Africa women's lives.

## Women, Development, and the State

While expressing much frustration over the lack of progress on women's issues, the literature has expanded to incorporate women's actions in shaping and resisting the postcolonial state. During Nigeria's Third Republic, women attempted to incorporate gender relations within society and the family into definitions of democracy. Unfortunately, the government rejected most of these efforts, leaving women with few real gains (Shettima 1995).

In general, during the transition from colonial rule to independent postcolonial states, few serious efforts were made to increase the level of women's participation in state politics. Instead, states continued the practice institutionalized during the colonial era of ignoring women's political interests. Okonjo (1983) argues that women in Nigeria have been able to recapture only a small share of the political power they had during the precolonial era, when women held culturally acknowledged authority in a dual-sex system. The continuing development of a unisex political system that favors men has put women at a disadvantage. No longer do women control a parallel political system that addresses their various interests, as they did among the Igbo and Yoruba. Few women are elected to office, and most women who hold high offices must depend on men to appoint them to their political positions.

The record for military regimes is mixed. On the one hand, military regimes occasionally create space outside of "tradition" in which women can act publicly in new ways (Mba 1989). Also, because such regimes can more easily do things by executive fiat, they can, without nodding to "custom" or even consulting women themselves, implement radical changes in women's lives. For instance, it was a military regime in Nigeria that in 1976 gave women in the Islamic north of the country the right to vote, more than a decade after women elsewhere in the country had gained that right. Similarly, in the early 1990s it was a Nigerian military regime that outlawed female genital mutilation (Shettima 1995). The more general rule, however, has been that military regimes manipulate gender in ways that are deleterious to women. For example, in some cases, men in power have set women up as scapegoats for the failures of their governments and capitalist development. Dennis (1987) argues that such was the case during the short-lived (1984–85) Federal Military Government (FGM) of Nigeria. The FMG took over in a coup during a period of extreme economic crisis for the Nigerian government and its people, a crisis brought on in part by declining revenue from oil, which had replaced cash crops as the main source of revenue during the early 1970s. In addition, the state was faced with paying for large-scale public expenditures on industrialization and public works that had been undertaken, with little return, during the oil boom years. Most important for women, the postcolonial Nigerian governments had continued the British practice of ignoring food farming, small-scale trading, and petty commodity production. Yet women, who dominated these sectors, still had the obligation to feed their families with little support and even some hostility from the state. Accompanying the economic crisis was what appeared to many to be a breakdown in social relations, as everyday life became increasingly capricious.

Underlying this socio-economic crisis was what Dennis has called "structural contradictions in Nigerian society and its external relationships" (Dennis 1987, p. 21). But the conflict between various groups of the national bourgeoisie to control the state and its resources was an issue that the Federal Military Government wished to ignore. Instead they charged that the crisis resulted from "indiscipline . . . failure of particular social groups to perform adequately their prescribed social role, preventing society from functioning as it should" (p. 19). Among the categories of women represented by "indisciplined" groups were working mothers and wives, who were seen as neglecting their children; single women, who were considered to be prostitutes who led men into undisciplined behavior; and petty traders, who were accused of hoarding goods and creating a crisis in consumer items. Taken together, these categories include most Nigerian women.

Complex factors led to this attack on women by the state. According to Toyin Falola, Yoruba women often gained authority through their control of the marketplace. This "women's space" was both a political arena and one of the central institutions of Yoruba society. Powerful market women used their control of this territory to manipulate prominent men wanting to gain from the market. In so doing, they hoped to extend their authority (Falola 1995). Nevertheless, petty traders were an easy target because consumers, suffering under extremely high inflation and even shortages of some food and household necessities, were willing to blame them for these problems. In general, however, market women were the most powerless link in the retail food chain; they could hardly be held responsible for such high prices. They were simply attempting to provide for their families in difficult times. Yet the government encouraged this unfair scapegoating by sending soldiers to the markets to beat traders and force them to lower their prices. Such activity was no long-term solution to deep structural problems.

This attack on petty traders also fit into the FMG's development ideology. The government accepted the idea developed during the colonial era that Nigeria was divided into traditional, or backward, and modern sectors. They looked forward to creating industrial societies with urban areas that mirrored those found in the West. This worldview had implications for women because it assumed that market women and subsistence farmers lived in the traditional sector, which was in need of modernization. Indeed, petty traders stood in the way of modernization in this view, since they crowded streets and kept the informal economic sector thriving. Influenced in part by Western education and the colonial experience, and also by the growth of conservative Islam in northern Nigeria, the military rulers felt that women's proper place was in the home, taking responsibility for the morality of their children and husbands.

Most unfortunate for women, this ideology ignored the realities of most women's lives. For many women the economic crisis meant increased marginalization, farming on infertile land, searching for employment, or trading in an economy in a downward spiral. Yet at the same time that it became increasingly difficult to find resources, most Nigerians still expected women to provide food for their families. The "War of Indiscipline" was based on a false notion of women's traditional roles that assumed that women were responsible only for their children's moral development, but not for their material well-being. The obligation and desire to feed dependents has forced many women into the informal sector, largely because the formal sector remains closed to them and farming is no longer productive. Ironically, this appeal to women as the guardians of morality and tradition contradicts the stress on modernization by the FMG, placing too many women in a no-win situation.

This appeal to mythical tradition that circumscribes women's behavior might well sound familiar to an audience in the West, where women are criticized for neglecting their children when they are forced into the work world to ensure their children's welfare. Other states in West and West-Central Africa have ignored such contradictions in turning to "traditional" values. In the 1970s, for example, Zaïre's president, Mobutu Sese Seko, articulated a return to traditional values in his policy, called *authenticité*. With roots in negritude and African nationalism, which appealed to many in Zaïre (now Congo), *authenticité* helped Mobutu to legitimize his power by making his autocratic rule appear to be based on African values (Wilson 1982). These "authentic" values included a male-dominated state under the complete control of its ruler. Wilson argues that under this ideology, all authentic women were mothers and housekeepers who obeyed the authority of their husbands, kinsmen, and, ultimately, the president.

Like Nigeria's Federal Military Government, *authenticité* held women solely responsible for the system of morality. Women who broke with their prescribed roles thus had to be reformed and policed. Once again, as in Nigeria, this appeal to tradition helped legitimize a state facing increased economic difficulties, which included a decline in the food-producing sector and a general economic downturn. In addition, the paradoxical contradictions in the state ideology characterized precolonial agriculture as backward and women farmers as beasts of burden. Needless to say, no efforts were made to improve the subsistence sector that women served. *Authenticité* also attempted to justify Mobutu's repression of women. By declaring that women had achieved full emancipation in 1970 under his rule, he characterized any criticism of his policies toward women and the struggles they had to endure as a direct challenge that he would not tolerate. Likewise, the critics of the Mobutu regime questioned women's sexual exploitation, but have left unexamined the larger context of unequal power relations within society (Mianda 1995).

The view held by so many states that women remain in a traditional sector has influenced the development projects undertaken by many governments and non-government organizations. As many critics of development strategies began to argue in the 1970s, too many government and international aid organizations paid little attention to women's roles in production. Modeling development plans on Western experiences, most planners favored cash crop production and industrialization at the expense of food production (Nelson 1981).

As Dey (1981) argues, this undervaluing of women's agricultural roles includes Chinese and Taiwanese experts. Dey compared three development projects in the Gambia: the Taiwanese Agricultural Mission (1966–74), the World Bank Agricultural Development Project (1973–76), and the Agro-Technical Team of the People's Republic of China (1975–80). All three projects assumed that the male household head controlled the forces of production, land, labor, crops, and finances, and would be responsible for redistributing any increases in his income as the result of technological assistance. But the stated goal of these projects and the Gambian government to reach self-sufficiency in food production remained unattainable. As Dey argues,

> By failing to take into account the complexities of the existing farming system and concentrating on men to the exclusion of women, the irrigated rice projects have lost in the technical sense that valuable available female expertise was wasted. Furthermore, investment was focused on relatively expensive capital-intensive irrigation schemes when striking results might have been obtained by a few simple improvements in women's rain-fed and swamp rice. Finally, by excluding women, the projects have increased women's economic dependence on men who now control an additional food and cash crop, and thereby heighten their vulnerability in an increasingly unstable and changing rural economy. (Dey 1981, p. 122)

Yet the effects of development projects on women have not been uniform. Venema (1986) found a more mixed result in nearby Senegal. He agrees with Dey that it is a mistake to assume that heads of households will equitably redistribute benefits from development plans. He stressed that the Wolof in Senegal do not live in unified production units. But unlike many others who have studied development plans in Africa, he argued that women engaged in cash crop production benefited from some of the changes brought on by state planning. In particular, Venema wished to refute Ester Boserup's argument that the introduction of plows and oxen always worked against women's interests (Boserup 1970). In addition, mechanization did not have a uniform impact on Wolof women. In one case, the introduction of the seed drill used by men did not negatively affect women, because it helped increase the area cultivated by them. In another case, however, the introduction of the grain mill decreased their income, because it undermined their millet-pounding work parties.

In response to the feminist movement and the current food crisis in Africa, development agencies and governments have increasingly turned their attention to women (Lewis 1984). Mbilinyi (1984) has attacked much of the "Women in Development" ideology designed by international development agencies to rectify their previous oversights of women's roles in farming. She points out that many of these projects aggravate divisions among women by supporting increased stratification. In particular, bourgeois women who participate in development projects and the few women who directly benefit from them develop material interests that conflict with those of poorer women. Mbilinyi reminds us that "women are not all the same, nor do they all share the same interest" (p. 14). Clearly, further studies on the various impacts of development schemes on African women's lives deserve attention.

Many women went into the postcolonial era with high expectations that their demands, which could be described as African feminist, would be met by the newly independent governments. Many of the new states attempted to meet some of these demands by offering more education and health care and expanding the economy. As economies began to stagnate, demands for improving women's lives were no longer a priority for those in state power. In addition, some of the new ruling elites found it convenient to blame women for the problems created by the states and an economy that they could not control.

Through most of this contemporary period, most women continue to live in the rural areas, meeting their obligations to their kinship relations by farming and trading. Those who live in urban areas also find that they carry a heavy burden in feeding their families. While most women struggle to survive, women have become increasingly stratified by class, a process that began several centuries ago. Some women have more access to education, employment, and/or capital than others. But even elite women suffer from an ideology that restricts women's options and sets up images of the ideal woman that few can emulate. Despite these problems, women have resisted their oppression as women and developed political movements that are sensitive to Africa's place in the world economy but also hold society responsible for the gender inequality that they face.

# SOURCES

For reasons of space, this listing is not comprehensive. It consists primarily of items available in U.S. libraries. It does not include many foreign-language publications or such primary sources as travel accounts, which remain to be explored more fully as a source for women's history. It also excludes the many African theses and working papers that are difficult to obtain in the United States. Titles marked with an asterisk are recommended for classroom use.

Abdalla, Raqiya Haji Dualeh. 1982. *Sisters in Affliction: Circumcision and the Infibulation of Women in Africa.* London: Zed Books.
Abu, Katharine. 1983. "The Separateness of Spouses: Conjugal Resources in an Ashanti Town." In Oppong, *Female and Male in West Africa.*
Adams, William Y. 1977. *Nubia: Corridor to Africa.* Princeton: Princeton University Press.
Adamu, M. 1984. "The Hausa and Their Neighbors in the Central Sudan." In Niane, *Africa from the Twelfth to the Sixteenth Century.*
Adamu, M., and A. H. M. Kirk-Greene, eds. 1986. *Pastoralists of the West African Savannah.* Manchester: Manchester University Press.
*Adepoju, Aderanti. 1983. "Patterns of Migration by Sex." In Oppong, *Female and Male in West Africa.*
Afonja, Simi. 1981. "Changing Modes of Production and the Sexual Division of Labor among the Yoruba." *Signs* 7, no. 2: 299–313.
———. 1986. "Land Control: A Critical Factor in Yoruba Gender Stratification." In Robertson and Berger, *Women and Class in Africa.*
Afshar, Haleh, ed. 1985. *Women, Work and Ideology in the Third World.* London and New York: Tavistock.
———. 1987. *Women, State and Ideology: Studies from Africa and Asia.* Albany: State University of New York Press.
Ahmed, Christine. 1991. "Not from a Rib: The Use of Gender and Gender Dynamics to Unlock Early African History." Paper presented at the African Studies Association meeting, St. Louis.
*Aidoo, Agnes Akosua. 1981. "Asante Queen Mothers in Government and Politics in the Nineteenth Century." In Steady, *The Black Woman Cross-Culturally.*

\*Aidoo, Ama Ata. 1970. *No Sweetness Here*. London: Longman.

\*———. 1977. *Our Sister Killjoy*. London: Longman.

Ajayi, J. F. A. 1972. "The Aftermath of the Fall of Old Oyo." In Ajayi and Crowder, *History of West Africa*.

Ajayi, J. F. A., and Michael Crowder, eds. 1972. *History of West Africa*. Vols. 1 and 2. New York: Columbia University Press.

Ajayi, J. F. A., and J. D. Y. Peel, eds. 1992. *People and Empire in African History: Essays in Memory of Michael Crowder*. London: Longman.

Ajayi, J. F. A., and Robert Smith. 1964. *Yoruba Warfare in the Nineteenth Century*. London: Cambridge University Press.

Akinjogbin, I. A. 1972. "The Expansion of Oyo and the Rise of Dahomey, 1600–1800." In Ajayi and Crowder, *History of West Africa*.

\*Akyeampong, Emmanuel. 1996. *Drink, Power, and Cultural Change*. Portsmouth, N.H.: Heinemann.

Allman, Jean. 1991. "Of 'Spinsters,' 'Concubines' and 'Wicked Women': Reflections on Gender and Social Change in Colonial Asante." *Gender and History* 3, no. 2: 176–89.

———. 1994. "Making Mothers: Missionaries, Medical Officers and Women's Work in Colonial Asante, 1924–1945." *History Workshop* 38: 25–48.

———. 1996. "Rounding Up Spinsters: Unmarried Women and Gender Chaos in Colonial Asante." *Journal of African History* 37, no. 2: 195–214.

———. 1997a. "Adultery and the State in Asante: Reflections on Gender, Class and Power from 1800–1950." In Hunwick and Wilkes, *The Cloth of Many Colored Silks*.

———. 1997b. "Fathering, Mothering and Making Sense of Ntamoba: Reflections on the Economy of Child-rearing in Colonial Asante." *Africa* 67, no. 2: 296–321.

Alpers, Edward A. 1984a. "'Ordinary Household Chores': Ritual and Power in a 19th-Century Swahili Women's Spirit Possession Cult." *International Journal of African Historical Studies* 17, no. 4: 677–702.

———. 1984b. "State, Merchant Capital, and Gender Relations in Southern Mozambique to the End of the Nineteenth Century: Some Tentative Hypotheses." *African Economic History* 13: 23–55.

———. 1986. "The Somali Community at Aden in the Nineteenth Century." *Northeast Africa Studies* 8, no. 2–3: 143–86.

\*———. 1997. "The Story of Swema: Female Vulnerability in Nineteenth-Century East Africa." In Robertson and Klein, *Women and Slavery in Africa*.

Amadiume, Ifi. 1987. *Male Daughters, Female Husbands: Gender and Sex in an African Society*. London: Zed Books.

\*Aman: The Story of a Somali Girl. 1994. As told to Virginia Lee Barnes and Janice Boddy. New York: Vintage Books.

Amory, Deborah P. 1998. "*Mashoga, Mabasha,* and *Magai:* 'Homosexuality' on the East Coast of Africa." In Murray and Roscoe, *Boy-Wives and Female Husbands*.

Anderson, David, and Douglas Johnson, eds. 1994. *Revealing Prophets: Prophecy in East African History*. London: James Currey.

Ardener, Shirley. 1975. "Sexual Insult and Female Militancy." In Ardener, *Perceiving Women*.

Ardener, Shirley, ed. 1975. *Perceiving Women*. London: J. M. Dent and Sons.

Arnold, Marion. 1997. *Women and Art in South Africa*. New York: St. Martin's Press.

Ault, James M., Jr. 1983. "Making 'Modern' Marriage 'Traditional.'" *Theory and Society* 12, no. 2: 181–210.

*Awe, Bolanle. 1977. "The Iyalode in the Traditional Yoruba Political System." In Schlegel, *Sexual Stratification.*

*———. 1991. "Writing Women into History: The Nigerian Experience." In Offen, Pierson, and Rendell, *Writing Women's History.*

*Awe Bolanle, ed. 1992. *Nigerian Women in Historical Perspective.* Lagos: Sankore Publishers.

*Awe, Bolanle, and Nina Mba. 1991. "Women's Research and Documentation Center (Nigeria)." *Signs* 16, no. 4: 859–64.

*Ba, Mariama. 1981. *So Long a Letter.* Portsmouth, N.H.: Heinemann.

Bankson, Barbro, and R. W. Niezen. 1995. "Women of the Jama'a Ansar al-Sunna: Female Participation in a West African Reform Movement." *Canadian Journal of African Studies* 29, no. 3: 375–402.

Barthel, Daniel L. 1975. "The Rise of a Female Professional Elite: The Case of Senegal." *African Studies Review* 13, no. 3: 1–17.

———. 1985. "Women's Educational Experience under Colonialism: Toward a Diachronic Model." *Signs* 7, no. 1: 137–54.

Basu, Amrita, ed., with the assistance of C. Elizabeth McGrory. 1995. *The Challenge of Local Feminisms: Women's Movements in Global Perspective.* Boulder, Colo.: Westview Press.

Bay, Edna. 1995. "Belief, Legitimacy and the Kpojito: An Institutional History of the Queen Mother in Precolonial Dahomey." *Journal of African History* 36, no. 1: 1–27.

———. 1997. "Servitude and Worldly Success in the Palace of Dahomey." In Robertson and Klein, *Women and Slavery in Africa.*

*Bay, Edna, ed. 1982. *Women and Work in Africa.* Boulder, Colo.: Westview Press.

Beach, D. N. 1980. *The Shona and Zimbabwe, 900–1850.* London: Heinemann.

Beinart, William. 1980. "Production and the Material Basis of Chieftainship: Pondoland, c. 1830–80." In Marks and Atmore, *Economy and Society in Pre-Industrial South Africa.*

Beinart, William, and Colin Bundy. 1987. *Hidden Struggles in Rural South Africa.* Berkeley and Los Angeles: University of California Press.

Beneria, Lourdes; ed. 1980. *Women and Development: The Sexual Division of Labor in Rural Societies.* New York: Praeger.

Berger, Iris. 1976. "Rebels or Status-Seekers? Women as Spirit Mediums in East Africa." In Hafkin and Bay, *Women in Africa.*

———. 1981. *Religion and Resistance: East African Kingdoms in the Precolonial Period.* Tervuren, Belgium: Musée Royal de l'Afrique Centrale.

———. 1986. "Sources of Class Consciousness: South African Women in Recent Labor Struggles." In Robertson and Berger, *Women and Class in Africa.*

———. 1987. "Solidarity Fragmented: Garment Workers of the Transvaal, 1930–1960." In Marks and Trapido, *Race, Class and Nationalism in Twentieth Century South Africa.*

———. 1989. "Gender and Working-Class History: South Africa in Comparative Perspective." *Journal of Women's History* 1, no. 2: 117–33.

———. 1990. "Gender, Race, and Political Empowerment: South African Canning Workers, 1940–1960." *Gender and Society* 4, no. 3: 398–420.

*———. 1992. *Threads of Solidarity: Women in South African Industry, 1900–1980.* Bloomington: Indiana University Press; London: James Currey.

————. 1994a. "'Beasts of Burden' Revisited: Interpretations of Women and Gender in Southern Africa." In Harms, *Paths toward the Past*.

————. 1994b. "Fertility as Power: Spirit Mediums, Priestesses and the State." In Anderson and Johnson, *Revealing Prophets*.

Berry, Sara. 1985. *Fathers Work for Their Sons: Accumulation, Mobility and Class Formation in an Extended Yoruba Community*. Berkeley and Los Angeles: University of California Press.

Biaya, T. K. 1993. "Femmes, possession et christianisme au Zaire. Analyse diachronique des production et pratiques de la spiritualité chrétienne africaine." Ph.D. diss., Université Laval (Canada).

Birmingham, David, and Phyllis M. Martin. 1983. *History of Central Africa*. Vol. 1. London: Longman.

Bledsoe, Caroline. 1980. *Women and Marriage in Kpelle Society*. Stanford: Stanford University Press.

Blier, Suzanne Preston. 1995. "The Path of the Leopard: Motherhood and Majesty in Early Danhomè." *Journal of African History* 36, no. 3: 391–417.

Bohannan, Paul, and G. Dalton, eds. 1982. *Markets in Africa*. Evanston, Ill.: Northwestern University Press.

*Boone, Sylvia Ardyn. 1986. *Radiance from the Waters: Ideals of Feminine Beauty in Mende Art*. New Haven: Yale University Press.

*Boserup, Ester. 1970. *Woman's Role in Economic Development*. London: Allen and Unwin; New York: St. Martin's Press, 1970.

Boyd, Jean. 1986. "The Fulani Women Poets." In Adamu and Kirke-Greene, *Pastoralists of the West African Savannah*.

————. 1989. *The Caliph's Sister*. London: Frank Cass.

*Bozzoli, Belinda. 1983. "Marxism, Feminism and South African Studies." *Journal of Southern African Studies* 9, no. 2: 139–71.

————, with the assistance of Mmantho Nkotsoe. 1991. *Women of Phokeng: Consciousness, Life Strategy, and Migrancy in South Africa, 1900–1983*. Portsmouth, N.H.: Heinemann.

Bradford, Helen. 1987. *A Taste of Freedom: The ICU in Rural South Africa*. New Haven: Yale University Press.

————. 1991. "Herbs, Knives and Plastic: 150 Years of Abortion in South Africa." In Meade and Walker, *Science, Medicine and Cultural Imperialism*.

————. 1996. "Women, Gender and Colonialism: Rethinking the History of the British Cape Colony in Its Frontier Zones, c. 1806–70." *Journal of African History* 37, no. 3: 351–70.

Brain, James L. 1976. "Less Than Second Class: Women in Rural Settlement Schemes." In Hafkin and Bay, *Women in Africa*.

Brantley, Cynthia. 1986. "Mekatalili and the Role of Women in Giriama Resistance." In Crummey, *Banditry*.

Bridenthal, Renate; Susan Mosher Stuard; and Merry E. Wiesner, eds. 1998. *Becoming Visible: Women in European History*. 3rd ed., revised. New York: Houghton Mifflin.

Broadhead, Susan Herlin. 1997. "Slave Wives, Free Sisters: Bakongo Women and Slavery, c. 1700–1850." In Robertson and Klein, *Women and Slavery in Africa*.

*Brooks, George E., Jr. 1976. "The Signares of Saint-Louis and Gorée: Women Entrepreneurs in Eighteenth-Century Senegal." In Hafkin and Bay, *Women in Africa*.

————. 1993. *Landlords and Strangers*. New York: Westview Press.

Brown, Barbara B. 1983. "The Impact of Male Labour Migration on Women in Botswana." *African Affairs*, no. 328: 367–88.

————. 1987. "Facing the 'Black Peril': The Politics of Population Control in South Africa." *Journal of Southern African Studies* 13, no. 3: 256–73.

Brown, Lloyd W. 1981. *Women Writers in Black Africa*. Westport, Conn.: Greenwood Press.

*Bruner, Charlotte H., ed. 1983. *Unwinding Threads: Writing by Women in Africa*. London: Heinemann.

Bryceson, Deborah Fahey. 1985. "Women's Proletarianization and the Family Wage in Tanzania." In Afshar, *Women, Work and Ideology in the Third World*.

Bujra, Janet. 1975. "Women 'Entrepreneurs' of Early Nairobi." *Canadian Journal of African Studies* 9, no. 2: 213–34.

————. 1986. "'Urging Women to Redouble Their Efforts . . .': Class, Gender, and Capitalist Transformation in Africa." In Robertson and Berger, *Women and Class in Africa*.

Bundy, Colin. 1980. "Peasants in Herschel: A Case Study of a South African Frontier District." In Marks and Atmore, *Economy and Society in Pre-Industrial South Africa*.

Burke, Timothy. 1996a. "'Fork Up and Smile': Marketing, Colonial Knowledge and the Female Subject in Zimbabwe." *Gender and History* 8, no. 3: 440–56. Also in Hunt, Liu, and Quataert, *Gendered Colonialisms in African History*.

————. 1996b. *Lifebuoy Men, Lux Women: Consumption, Commodification and Cleanliness in Modern Zimbabwe*. Durham, N.C.: Duke University Press.

Burness, Donald. 1977. "Nzinga Mbandi and Angolan Independence." *Luso-Brazilian Review* 14, no. 2: 25–29.

Burton, John W. 1982. "Nilotic Women: A Diachronic Perspective." *Journal of Modern African Studies* 20, no. 3: 467–91.

Byfield, Judith. 1994. "Pawns and Politics: The Pawnship Debate in Western Nigeria." In Falola and Lovejoy, *Pawnship in Africa*.

————. 1996. "Women, Marriage, Divorce and the Emerging Colonial State in Abeokuta (Nigeria), 1892–1904." *Canadian Journal of African Studies* 30, no. 1: 32–51.

Caldwell, John; Pat Caldwell; and I. O. Orubuloye. 1992. "The Destabilizing of the Traditional Yoruba Sexual System." *Population and Development Review* 17, no. 2: 229–62.

Callaway, Barbara. 1987. *Muslim Hausa Women in Nigeria: Tradition and Change*. Syracuse, N.Y.: Syracuse University Press.

————. 1994. *The Heritage of Islam: Women, Religion, and Politics in West Africa*. Boulder, Colo.: Lynne Rienner.

Callaway, Helen. 1987. *Gender, Culture and Empire: European Women in Colonial Nigeria*. Urbana and Chicago: University of Illinois Press.

Callaway, Helen, and Lucy Creevey. 1993. *The Heritage of Islam: Women, Religion, and Politics in West Africa*. Boulder, Colo.: Lynne Rienner.

Caplan, Patricia. 1982. "Gender, Ideology and Modes of Production on the Coast of East Africa." *Paideuma* 28: 29–43.

Caplan, Patricia, ed. 1987. *The Cultural Construction of Sexuality*. London: Tavistock.

Caplan, Patricia, and Janet Bujra, eds. 1982. *Women United, Women Divided*. Bloomington: Indiana University Press.

Carney, Judith, and Michael Watts. 1991. "Disciplining Women? Rice, Mechanization, and the Evolution of Mandinka Gender Relations in Senegambia." *Signs* 16, no. 4: 651–81.

Chanock, Martin. 1982. "Making Customary Law: Men, Women, and Courts in Colonial Northern Rhodesia." In Hay and Wright, *African Women and the Law.*

———. 1985. *Law, Custom and Social Order: The Colonial Experience in Malawi and Zambia.* Cambridge: Cambridge University Press.

Chaudhuri, Nupur, and Margaret Strobel, eds. 1992. *Western Women and Imperialism: Complicity and Resistance.* Bloomington: Indiana University Press.

Chauncey, George, Jr. 1981. "The Locus of Reproduction: Women's Labour in the Zambian Copperbelt, 1927–1953." *Journal of Southern African Studies* 7, no. 2: 135–64.

Cheater, A. P., and R. B. Gaidzanwa. 1996. "Citizenship in Neo-patrilineal States: Gender and Mobility in Southern Africa." *Journal of Southern African Studies* 22, no. 2: 189–200.

Chitere, Preston O. 1988. "The Women's Self-Help Movement in Kenya: A Historical Perspective, 1940–80." *Transafrican Journal of History* 17: 50–68.

Ciancanelli, Penelope. 1980. "Exchange, Reproduction and Sex Subordination among the Kikuyu of East Africa." *Review of African Political Economy* 12, no. 2: 25–36.

Cissoko, S. M. 1984. "The Songhay from the Twelfth to the Sixteenth Century." In Niane, *Africa from the Twelfth to the Sixteenth Century.*

Clark, Carolyn M. 1980. "Land and Food, Women and Power, in Nineteenth Century Kikuyu." *Africa* 50, no. 4: 357–69.

*Clark, Gracia. 1994. *Onions Are My Husband: Survival and Accumulation by West African Market Women.* Chicago: University of Chicago Press.

Cleaver, Tessa, and Marion Wallace. 1990. *Namibia: Women in War.* London: Zed Books.

Clignet, Remi. 1977. "Social Change and Sexual Differentiation in the Cameroon and the Ivory Coast." In Wellesley Editorial Committee, *Women and National Development.*

*Cock, Jacklyn. 1980. *Maids and Madams.* Johannesburg, South Africa: Ravan Press.

———. 1993. *Women and War in South Africa.* Cleveland, Ohio: The Pilgrim Press.

Coles, Catherine. 1996. "Three Generations of Hausa Women in Kaduna." In Sheldon, *Courtyards, Markets, City Streets.*

Coles, Catherine, and Beverly Mack, eds. 1991. *Hausa Women in the Twentieth Century.* Madison: University of Wisconsin Press.

Comaroff, Jean. 1985. *Body of Power, Spirit of Resistance: The Culture and History of a South African People.* Chicago: University of Chicago Press.

Constantinides, Pamela. 1982. "Women's Spirit Possession and Urban Adaptation in the Muslim Northern Sudan." In Caplan and Bujra, *Women United, Women Divided.*

Cooper, Barbara M. 1994. "Reflections on Slavery, Seclusion and Female Labor in the Maradi Region of Niger in the Nineteenth and Twentieth Centuries." *Journal of African History* 35: 61–78.

———. 1995a. "The Politics of Difference and Women's Associations in Niger: Of 'Prostitutes,' the Public, and Politics." *Signs* 20, no. 4: 851–881.

————. 1995b. "Women's Worth and Wedding Gift Exchange in Maradi, Niger, 1907–89." *Journal of African History* 36: 121–40.

*————. 1997. *Marriage in Maradi, 1900–1989*. Portsmouth, N.H.: Heinemann.

Cooper, Frederick, ed. *The Struggle for the City*. Beverly Hills, Calif.: Sage, 1983.

Coquery-Vidrovitch, Catherine. 1993. "Femmes et migrations urbaines en Afrique noir des débuts de la colonisation à l'independance." *L'Information Historique* 55, nos. 4–5: 150–57.

————. 1997. *African Women: A Modern History*. Trans. Beth Raps. Boulder, Colo.: Westview Press.

Cowan, Nicole. 1983. "Women in Eritrea: An Eye-witness Account." *Review of African Political Economy* 27/28: 143–52.

Creevey, Lucy E. 1986a. *Women Farmers in Africa: Rural Development in Mali and the Sahel*. Syracuse, N.Y.: Syracuse University Press.

————. 1986b. "The Role of Women in Malian Agriculture." In Creevey, *Women Farmers*.

Cromwell, Adelaide M. 1986. *An African Victorian Feminist: The Life and Times of Adelaide Smith Casely Hayford, 1868–1960*. Boston: Frank Cass.

Crummey, Donald. 1982. "Women, Property and Litigation among the Bagemder Amhara, 1750s to 1850s." In Hay and Wright, *African Women and the Law*.

Crummey, Donald, ed. 1986. *Banditry, Rebellion and Social Protest in Africa*. London: Heinemann.

Cummings-John, Constance Agatha. 1995. *Memoirs of a Krio Leader*. Edited, with introduction and annotation by LaRay Denzer. Ibadan, Nigeria: Sam Bookman for Humanities Research Centre.

Curtin, Patricia Romero. 1983. "Laboratory for the Oral History of Slavery: The Island of Lamu on the Kenya Coast." *American Historical Review* 88, no. 4: 858–82.

Dahlberg, Frances, ed. 1981. *Woman the Gatherer*. New Haven: Yale University Press.

Daly, M. W., ed. 1985. *Modernization in the Sudan*. New York: Lilian Barber Press.

*Dangarembga, Tsitsi. 1988. *Nervous Conditions*. Seattle: Seal Press.

Davison, Jean. 1997. *Gender, Lineage and Ethnicity in Southern Africa*. Boulder, Colo.: Westview Press.

Davison, Jean, with the women of Mutira. 1996. *Voices from Mutira: Change in the Lives of Rural Gikuyu Women, 1910–1995*. 2nd ed., revised. Boulder, Colo.: Lynne Rienner Publishers.

Day, Lynda. 1994. "The Evolution of Female Chiefship during the Late Nineteenth-Century Wars of the Mende." *International Journal of African Historical Studies* 27, no. 3: 481–503.

*Debroux, Catherine. 1987a. "La situation juridique de la femme Européene au Congo Belge de 1945 et 1960." *Enquêtes et Documents d'Histoire Africaine* 7: 14–23.

*————. 1987b. "La vie quotidienne de la femme Européene au Katanga entre 1945 et 1960." *Enquêtes et Documents d'Histoire Africaine* 7: 37–55.

*————. 1987c. "Les Activities Professionelles de la femme Européene au Congo Belge de 1945 à 1960." *Enquêtes et Documents d'Histoire Africaine* 7: 24–36.

Dei, George J. Sefa. 1994. "The Women of a Ghanian Village: A Study of Social Change." *African Studies Review* 37, no. 2: 121–45.

*Dennis, Carolyne. 1987. "Women and the State of Nigeria: The Case of the Federal Military Government, 1984–5." In Afshar, *Women, State and Ideology.*

Denzer, LaRay. 1992a. "Domestic Science Training in Colonial Yorubaland, Nigeria." In Hansen, *African Encounters with Domesticity.*

———. 1992b. "Gender and Decolonization: A Study of Three Women in West African Public Life." In Ajayi and Peel, *People and Empire in African History.*

———. 1994. "Yoruba Women: A Historiographical Study." *International Journal of African Historical Studies* 27, no. 1: 1–39.

des Forges, Alison. 1986. "'The Drum Is Greater Than the Shout': The 1912 Rebellion in Northern Rwanda." In Crummey, *Banditry.*

Devisch, Rene. 1993. *Weaving the Threads of Life: The "Khita" Gyn-Eco-Logical Healing Cult among the Yaka.* Chicago: University of Chicago Press.

Dey, Jennie. 1981. "Gambian Women: Unequal Partners in Gambian Rice Development Projects?" In Nelson, *African Women in the Development Process.*

Dibwe, dia Mwembu. 1993. "Les fonctions des femmes Africaines dans les camps Haut-Kantaga (1925–1960)." *Zaire-Afrique* 33, no. 272: 105–18.

di Leonardo, Micaela, ed. 1991. *Gender at the Crossroads of Knowledge: Feminist Anthropology in a Postmodern Era.* Berkeley and Los Angeles: University of California Press.

Dinan, Claudine. 1977. "Pragmatists or Feminists? The Professional Single Women of Accra, Ghana." *Cahiers d'Etudes Africaines* 65, no. 8: 155–76.

Draper, Patricia. 1975. "!Kung Women: Contrasts in Sexual Egalitarianism in Foraging and Sedentary Contexts." In Reiter, *Toward an Anthropology of Women.*

Duley, Margot I., and Mary I. Edwards, eds. 1986. *The Cross-Cultural Study of Women: A Comprehensive Guide.* New York: Feminist Press.

Ehret, C. 1984. "Between the Coast and the Great Lakes." In Niane, *Africa from the Twelfth to the Sixteenth Century.*

Ekechi, Felix, and Bessie House-Midamba. 1995. "Gender and Economic Power: The Case of Igbo Market Women of Eastern Nigeria." In House-Midamba and Ekechi, *African Market Women and Economic Power.*

Ekejiuba, Felicia. 1967. "Omu Okwei, the Merchant Queen of Ossomari: A Biographical Sketch." *Journal of the Historical Society of Nigeria* 3, no. 4: 633–46.

*El Dareer, Asma. 1982. *Woman, Why Do You Weep? Circumcision and Its Consequences.* London: Zed Books.

Eldredge, Elizabeth A. 1991. "Women in Production: The Economic Role of Women in Nineteenth-Century Lesotho." *Signs* 16, no. 4: 707–31.

El-Nadoury, R., with J. Vercoutter. 1981. "The Legacy of Pharaonic Egypt." In Mokhtar, *Ancient Civilizations of Africa.*

Elphick, Richard. 1985. *Khoikhoi and the Founding of White South Africa.* Johannesburg, South Africa: Ravan Press.

Emeagwali, Gloria T., ed. 1994. *Women Pay the Price: Structural Adjustment in Africa and the Caribbean.* Trenton, N.J.: Africa World Press.

*Emecheta, Buchi. 1979. *The Joys of Motherhood.* London: Allison and Busby; New York: G. Braziller.

*———. 1982. *Double Yoke*. London: Ogwuogwu Afor. Reprint, New York: G. Braziller, 1993.

Epprecht, Marc. 1993. "Domesticity and Piety in Colonial Lesotho: The Private Politics of Basotho Women's Pious Associations." *Journal of Southern African Studies* 19, no. 2: 202–24.

Epstein, A. L. 1981. *Urbanization and Kinship: The Domestic Domain on the Copperbelt of Zambia, 1950–1956*. London: Academic Press.

Etienne, Mona. 1980. "Women and Men, Cloth and Colonization: The Transformation of Production-Distribution Relations among the Baule (Ivory Coast)." In Etienne and Leacock, *Women and Colonization*.

Etienne, Mona, and Eleanor Leacock, eds. 1980. *Women and Colonization: Anthropological Perspectives*. New York: Praeger.

Fagan, B. M. 1984. "The Zambezi and Limpopo Basins, 1100–1500." In Niane, *Africa from the Twelfth to the Sixteenth Century*.

Fair, Laura. 1996. "Identity, Difference, and Dance: Female Initiation in Zanzibar, 1890–1930." *Frontiers* 17, no. 3: 146–72.

Falola, Toyin. 1995. "Gender, Business, and Space Control: Yoruba Market Women and Power." In House-Midamba and Ekechi, *African Market Women and Economic Power*.

Falola, Toyin, and Paul Lovejoy, eds. 1994. *Pawnship in Africa: Debt Bondage in Historical Perspective*. Boulder, Colo.: Westview Press.

*Fapohunda, Eleanor R. 1983. "Female and Male Work Profiles." In Oppong, *Female and Male in West Africa*.

Fluehr-Lobban, Carolyn. 1977. "Agitation for Change in the Sudan." In Schlegel, *Sexual Stratification*.

Fortmann, Louise. 1982. "Women and Work in a Communal Setting: The Tanzanian Policy of Ujamaa." In Bay, *Women and Work in Africa*.

Freedman, Jim. 1984. *Nyabingi: The Social History of an African Divinity*. Tervuren, Belgium: Musée Royal de l'Afrique Centrale.

Freeman, Donald. 1993. "Survival Strategy or Business Training Ground? The Significance of Urban Agriculture for the Advancement of Women in African Cities." *African Studies Review* 36, no. 3: 1–22.

Fyle, C. Magbaily. 1981. *The History of Sierra Leone: A Concise Introduction*. London: Evans Brothers.

Gaidzanwa, Rudo. 1992. "Bourgeois Theories of Gender and Feminism and Their Shortcomings with Reference to Southern African Countries." In Meena, *Gender in Southern Africa*.

Gaitskell, Deborah. 1979a. "'Christian Compounds for Girls': Church Hostels for African Women in Johannesburg, 1907–1970." *Journal of Southern African Studies* 6, no. 1: 44–69.

———. 1979b. "Laundry, Liquor and 'Playing Ladish.'" Paper presented to the South African Social History Workshop, Centre of International and Area Studies, University of London.

*———. 1982. "'Wailing for Purity': Prayer Unions, African Women and Adolescent Daughters, 1912–1940." In Marks and Rathbone, *Industrialisation and Social Change in South Africa*.

———. 1983. "Housewives, Maids or Mothers: Some Contradictions of Domesticity for Christian Women in Johannesburg, 1903–39." *Journal of African History* 24, no. 2: 241–56.

Gaitskell, Deborah; Judy Kimble; Moira Maconachie; and Elaine Unterhalter. 1983. "Class, Race and Gender: Domestic Workers in South Africa." *Review of African Political Economy* 27/28: 86–108.

Gardiner, Judith Kegan, ed. 1995. *Provoking Agents: Gender and Agency in Theory and Practice.* Urbana and Chicago: University of Illinois Press.

Gay, Judith. 1985. "'Mummies and Babies' and Friends and Lovers in Lesotho." *Journal of Homosexuality* 11, no. 3/4: 97–116.

Geiger, Susan. 1987. "Women in Nationalist Struggle: TANU Activists in Dar es Salaam." *International Journal of African Historical Studies* 20, no. 1: 1–26.

———. 1990. "Women and African Nationalism." *Journal of Women's History* 2, no. 1: 227–44.

———. 1996. "Tanganyikan Nationalism as 'Women's Work': Life Histories, Collective Biography and Changing Historiography." *Journal of African History* 37, no. 3: 465–78.

*———. 1998. *TANU Women: Gender and Culture in the Making of Tanganyikan Nationalism, 1955–1965.* Portsmouth, N.H.: Heinemann.

*Gender Violence and Women's Human Rights in Africa.* 1994. New Brunswick, N.J.: Center for Women's Global Leadership.

Gengenbach, Heidi. 1994. "Truth-Telling and the Politics of Women's Life Research in Africa: A Reply to Kirk Hoppe." *International Journal of African Historical Studies* 27, no. 3: 619–27.

Gevisser, Mark, and Edwin Cameron, eds. 1995. *Defiant Desire: Gay and Lesbian Lives in South Africa.* New York: Routledge.

Gold, Alice. 1981. "Women in Agricultural Change: The Nandi (Kenya) in the Nineteenth Century." Paper presented to the Conference on African Women in History, University of Santa Clara.

Gondola, Charles Didier. 1997. "Popular Music, Urban Society, and Changing Gender Relations in Kinshasa, Zaïre (1950–1990)." In Grosz-Ngate and Kokle, *Gendered Encounters.*

Goodwin, June. 1984. *Cry Amandla! South African Women and the Question of Power.* New York: Africana Publishing Co.

Gordon, April. 1995. "Gender, Ethnicity, and Class in Kenya: 'Burying Otieno' Revisited." *Signs* 20, no. 4: 883–912.

Gray, John. 1962. *History of Zanzibar from the Middle Ages to 1856.* London: Oxford University Press

*Greene, Sandra. 1996. *Gender, Ethnicity and Social Change on the Upper Slave Coast.* Portsmouth, N.H.: Heinemann.

Grier, Beverly, 1992. "Pawns, Porters and Petty Traders: Women in the Transition to Cash Crop Agriculture in Colonial Ghana." *Signs* 17, no. 2: 304–28.

Grosz-Ngate, Maria Luise, and Omari H. Kokle, eds. 1997. *Gendered Encounters: Challenging Cultural Boundaries and Social Hierarchies in Africa.* New York: Routledge.

Gunner, Elizabeth. 1979. "Songs of Innocence and Experience: Women as Composers and Performers of *Izibongo,* Zulu Praise Poetry." *Research in African Literatures* 10, no. 2: 239–67.

Guy, Jeff. 1980. "Ecological Factors in the Rise of Shaka and the Zulu Kingdom." In Marks and Atmore, *Economy and Society in Pre-Industrial South Africa.*

Guyer, Jane. 1991. "Female Farming in Anthropology and African History." In di Leonardo, *Gender at the Crossroads of Knowledge.*

*———. 1995a. "Women in the Rural Economy: Contemporary Variations." In Hay and Stichter, *African Women.*

*Guyer, Jane, ed. 1995b. *Money Matters: Instability, Values and Social Payments in the Modern History of West African Communities*. Portsmouth, N.H.: Heinemann.

*Hafkin, Nancy, and Edna Bay, eds. 1976. *Women in Africa: Studies in Social and Economic Change*. Stanford: Stanford University Press.

Haile, Daniel. 1980. *Law and the Status of Women in Ethiopia*. Addis Ababa, Ethiopia: United Nations Economic Commission for Africa.

Hakem, A. A., with the collaboration of I. Hrbek and J. Vercoutter. 1981. "The Civilization of Napata and Meroë." In Mokhtar, *Ancient Civilizations of Africa*.

Hale, Sondra. 1996. *Gender Politics in Sudan: Islamism, Socialism, and the State*. Boulder, Colo.: Westview Press.

Hanretta, Sean. 1998. "Women, Marginality and the Zulu State: Women's Institutions and Power in the Early Nineteenth Century." *Journal of African History* 39, no. 2: 389–415.

Hansen, Karen Tranberg. 1984. "Negotiating Sex and Gender in Urban Zambia." *Journal of Southern African Studies* 10, no. 2: 219–38.

———. 1989a. "The Black Market and Women Traders in Lusaka, Zambia." In Parpart and Staudt, *Women and the State in Africa*.

———. 1989b. *Distant Companions: Servants and Employers in Zambia, 1900–1985*. Ithaca, N.Y.: Cornell University Press.

———. 1990. "Body Politics: Sexuality, Gender, and Domestic Service in Zambia." *Journal of Women's History* 2, no. 1: 120–42.

Hansen, Karen Tranberg, ed. 1992. *African Encounters with Domesticity*. New Brunswick, N.J.: Rutgers University Press.

Harms, Robert W. 1997. "Sustaining the System: Trading Towns along the Middle Zaire." In Robertson and Klein, *Women and Slavery in Africa*.

Harms, Robert; Joseph Miller; David Newbury; and Michele Wagner, eds. 1994. *Paths toward the Past: African Historical Essays in Honor of Jan Vansina*. Atlanta: ASA Press.

Harries, Lyndon. 1962. *Swahili Poetry*. London: Oxford University Press.

Harries, Patrick. 1982. "Kinship, Ideology and the Nature of Pre-colonial Labour Migration." In Marks and Rathbone, *Industrialisation and Social Change in South Africa*.

———. 1994. *Work, Culture, and Identity: Migrant Laborers in Mozambique and South Africa, c. 1860–1910*. Portsmouth, N.H.: Heinemann.

Hassim, Shireen. 1991. "Gender, Social Location and Feminist Politics in South Africa." *Transformation* 15: 65–82.

Hawkes, K.; J. F. O'Connell; and N. G. Blurton Jones. 1997. "Hadza Women's Time Allocation, Offspring Provisioning, and the Evolution of Long Postmenopausal Life Spans." *Current Anthropology* 38, no. 4: 551–77.

Hay, Margaret Jean. 1976. "Luo Women and Economic Change during the Colonial Period." In Hafkin and Bay, *Women in Africa*.

———. 1988. "Queens, Prostitutes and Peasants: Historical Perspectives on African Women." *Canadian Journal of African Studies* 22, no. 3: 431–47.

Hay, Margaret Jean, and Sharon Stichter, eds. 1984. *African Women: South of the Sahara*. London: Longman.

*———. 1995. *African Women: South of the Sahara*. 2nd ed., revised. London: Longman.

*Hay, Margaret Jean, and Marcia Wright, eds. 1982. *African Women and the Law: Historical Perspectives.* Boston: Boston University Papers on Africa, No. 7.

*Head, Bessie. 1970. *When Rain Clouds Gather.* New York: Bantam.

*————. 1972. *Maru.* Portsmouth, N.H.: Heinemann.

*————. 1974. *A Question of Power.* Portsmouth, N.H.: Heinemann.

Heintze, Beatrix. 1981. "Das Ende Unabhangigen Staates Ndongo: Neue Chronologie und Reinterpretation (1617–1630)." *Paideuma* 27: 197–273.

————. 1984. "Angola nas garras do trafico de escravos: as guerra do Ndongo (1611–1630)." *Revista internacional de estudos africanos* 1: 11–59.

Hendrickson, Hildi, ed. 1996. *Clothing and Difference: Embodied Identities in Colonial and Postcolonial Africa.* Durham, N.C.: Duke University Press.

Herbert, Eugenia. 1993. *Iron, Gender, and Power: Rituals of Transformation in African Societies.* Bloomington: Indiana University Press.

Higginson, John. 1992. "Liberating the Captives: Independent Watchtower as an Avatar of Colonial Revolt in Southern Africa and Katanga, 1908–1941." *Journal of Social History* 26, no. 1: 55–80.

Hilton, Anne. 1985. *The Kingdom of Kongo.* Oxford: Clarendon Press.

Hodgson, Dorothy L. 1986. "'My Daughter . . . Belongs to the Government Now': Marriage, Maasai and the Tanzanian State." *Canadian Journal of African Studies* 30, no. 1: 106–22.

Hodgson, Dorothy L., and Sheryl McCurdy. 1996. "Wayward Wives, Misfit Mothers, and Disobedient Daughters: 'Wicked' Women and the Reconfiguration of Gender in Africa." *Canadian Journal of African Studies* 30, no. 1: 1–9.

Hoehler-Fatton, Cynthia. 1996. *Women of Fire and Spirit: History, Faith and Gender in Roho Religion in Western Kenya.* New York: Oxford University Press.

Hoffer, Carol P. 1972. "Mende and Sherbo Women in High Office." *Canadian Journal of African Studies* 4, no. 2: 151–64.

Hogendorn, J. S., and Paul E. Lovejoy. 1988. "The Reform of Slavery in Early Colonial Northern Nigeria." In Miers and Roberts, *The End of Slavery in Africa.*

Hoppe, Kirk. 1993. "Whose Life Is It Anyway? Issues of Representation in Life Narrative Texts of African Women." *International Journal of African Historical Studies* 26 no. 3: 623–36.

House-Midamba, Bessie, and Felix K. Ekechi, eds. 1995. *African Market Women and Economic Power: The Role of Women in African Economic Development.* Westport, Conn.: Greenwood Press.

Hubbard, Dianne, and Colette Solomon. 1995. "The Many Faces of Feminism in Namibia." In Basu, *The Challenge of Local Feminisms.*

Hunt, Nancy Rose. 1988. "Le Bébé en Brousse: European Women, African Birth Spacing and Colonial Intervention in Breast Feeding in the Belgian Congo." *International Journal of African Historical Studies* 21, no. 3: 401–32.

————. 1989. "Placing African Women's History and Locating Gender." *Social History* 14, no. 3: 359–79.

————. 1990. "Domesticity and Colonialism in Belgian Africa: Usumbura's Foyer Social." *Signs* 15, no. 3: 447–74.

————. 1991. "Noise over Camouflaged Polygyny, Colonial Morality, Taxation and a Woman-Naming Crisis in the Belgian Congo." *Journal of African History* 32, no. 3: 471–94.

————. 1992a. "Colonial Fairy Tales and Knife and Fork Doctrine in the Heart of Africa." In Hansen, *African Encounters with Domesticity.*

————. 1992b. "Single Ladies on the Congo: Protestant Missionary Tensions and Voices." *Women's International Studies Forum* 13: 395–403.

Hunt, Nancy Rose; Tessie P. Liu; and Jean Quataert, eds. 1997. *Gendered Colonialisms in African History.* Oxford: Blackwell.

Hunwick, J. O., and Nancy Lawler Wilks, eds. 1997. *The Cloth of Many Colored Silks: Papers on History and Society.* Evanston, Ill.: Northwestern University Press.

Ifeka-Moller, Caroline. 1975. "Female Militancy and Colonial Revolt: The Women's War of 1929, Eastern Nigeria." In Ardener, *Perceiving Women.*

Ina, Koko Ete. 1992. "The Tax Crisis of 1929 in Ibiboland." *Transafrican Journal of History* 21: 171–81.

Inikori, Joseph. 1992. "Export versus Domestic Demand: The Determinants of Sex Ratios in the Transatlantic Slave Trade." *Research in Economic History* 14: 117–66.

Isaacman, Allen. 1972. *Mozambique: The Africanization of a European Institution, the Zambesi Prazos, 1750–1902.* Madison: University of Wisconsin Press.

————. 1996. *Cotton Is the Mother of Poverty: Peasants, Work, and Rural Struggle in Colonial Mozambique.* Portsmouth, N.H.: Heinemann.

Isaacman, Allen, and Barbara Isaacman. 1984. "The Role of Women in the Liberation of Mozambique." *Ufahamu* 13, no. 2–3: 128–85.

Isaacman, Barbara, and June Stephen. 1980. *Mozambique: Women, the Law and Agrarian Reform.* Addis Ababa, Ethiopia: United Nations Economic Commission for Africa.

Jacobs, Susan. 1989. "Zimbabwe: State, Class, and Gendered Models of Land Resettlement." In Parpart and Staudt, *Women and the State in Africa.*

Jacobs, Susan, and Tracey Howard. 1987. "Women in Zimbabwe: State Policy and State Action." In Haleh Afshar, *Women, State and Ideology.*

Janzen, John. 1992. *Ngoma Discourses of Healing in Central and Southern Africa.* Berkeley and Los Angeles: University of California Press.

Jeater, Diana. 1993. *Marriage, Perversion and Power: The Construction of Moral Discourse in Southern Rhodesia, 1894–1930.* Oxford: Clarendon Press.

Johnson, Cheryl [Johnson-Odim]. 1981. "Female Leadership during the Colonial Period: Madam Pelewura and the Lagos Market Women." *Tarikh* 7, no. 1: 1–10.

————. 1986. "Class and Gender: A Consideration of Yoruba Women during the Colonial Period." In Robertson and Berger, *Women and Class in Africa.*

*Johnson-Odim, Cheryl. 1991. "Third World Women and Feminism." In Mohanty, Russo, and Torres, *Third World Women and the Politics of Feminism.*

*————. 1992a. "Lady Oyinkan Abayomi." In Awe, *Nigerian Women in Historical Perspective.*

————. 1992b. "On Behalf of Women and the Nation: Funmilayo Ransome-Kuti and the Struggle for Women's Equality and Nigerian Independence." In Johnson-Odim and Strobel, *Expanding the Boundaries of Women's History.*

*Johnson-Odim, Cheryl, and Nina Mba. 1997. *For Women and the Nation: Funmilayo Ransome-Kuti of Nigeria.* Urbana and Chicago: University of Illinois Press.

Johnson-Odim, Cheryl, and Margaret Strobel, eds. 1992. *Expanding the Boundaries of Women's History: Essays on Women in the Third World.* Bloomington: Indiana University Press.

*Joseph, Helen. 1986. *Side by Side.* London: Zed Books.

Jules-Rosette, Bennetta. 1979. "Women as Ceremonial Leaders in an African Church." In Jules-Rosette, *The New Religions of Africa.*

―――. 1980. "Changing Aspects of Women's Initiation in Southern Africa." *Canadian Journal of African Studies* 13, no. 3: 389–405.

Jules-Rosette, Bennetta, ed. 1979. *The New Religions of Africa.* Norwood, N.J.: Ablex Publishing Co.

Kaplan, Flora Edowaye S. 1993. "Ioyoba, the Queen Mother of Benin: Images and Ambiguity in Gender and Sex Roles in Court Art." *Art History* 16, no. 3: 386–407.

Kaplan, Temma. 1996. *Crazy for Democracy: Women's Grassroots Movements in the United States and South Africa.* New York: Routledge.

Kapteijns, Lidwien. 1985. "Islamic Rationales for the Changing Social Roles of Women in the Western Sudan." In Daly, *Modernization in the Sudan.*

Kea, Ray A. 1982. *Settlements, Trade, and Polities in the Seventeenth-Century Gold Coast.* Baltimore and London: John Hopkins University Press.

Kemp, Amanda; Nozizwe Madlala; Asha Moodley; and Elaine Salo. 1995. "The Dawn of a New Day: Redefining South African Feminism." In Basu, *The Challenge of Local Feminisms.*

Kenyatta, Jomo. 1979. *Facing Mount Kenya: The Traditional Life of the Gikuyu.* London: Heinemann. First published 1938.

Kettel, Bonnie. 1986. "The Commoditization of Women in Tugen (Kenya) Social Organization." In Robertson and Berger, *Women and Class in Africa.*

Khasiani, S. A., and E. I. Njiro, eds. 1993. *The Women's Movement in Kenya.* Nairobi: AAWORD.

Kileff, Clive, and Margaret Kileff. 1979. "The Masowe Vapostori of Seki." In Jules-Rosette, *The New Religions of Africa.*

*Kimble, Judy, and Elaine Unterhalter. 1982. "'We Opened the Road for You, You Must Go Forward': ANC Women's Struggles, 1912–1982." *Feminist Review* 12: 11–35.

Kinsman, Margaret. 1983. "'Beasts of Burden': The Subordination of Southern Tswana Women, ca. 1800–1840." *Journal of Southern African Studies* 10, no. 1: 39–54.

Kirk-Greene, A. H. M., and S. J. Hogben. 1966. *The Emirates of Northern Nigeria: A Preliminary Study of Their Historical Traditions.* London: Oxford University Press.

Ki-Zerbo, J. 1981. "African Prehistoric Art." In Ki-Zerbo, *Methodology and African Prehistory.*

Ki-Zerbo, J., ed. 1981. *Methodology and African Prehistory.* Vol. 1 of General History of Africa. London: Heinemann.

Klein, Martin A. 1977. "Servitude among the Wolof and Sereer of Senegambia." In Miers and Kopytoff, *Slavery in Africa.*

*―――. 1997. "Women in Slavery in the Western Sudan." In Robertson and Klein, *Women and Slavery in Africa.*

Kobishchanov, Yuri. 1979. *Axum.* University Park: Pennsylvania State University Press.

Konnoh, Augustine. 1993. "Women and Politics in Africa: The Case of Liberia." *Proceedings and Papers of the Georgia Association of Historians* 15: 107–15.

Koopman, Jeanne. 1995. "Women in the Rural Economy: Past, Present and Future." In Hay and Stichter, *African Women.*

Koso-Thomas, Olayinka. 1987. *The Circumcision of Women: A Strategy for Eradication.* London: Zed Books.

Krige, J. D., and E. J. Krige. 1943. *The Realm of a Rain Queen.* London: Oxford University Press.

Kriger, Colleen. 1993. "Textile Production and Gender in the Sokoto Caliphate." *Journal of African History* 34: 361–401.

Kropacek, L. 1984. "Nubia from the Late Twelfth Century to the Funj Conquest in the Early Fifteenth Century." In Niane, *Africa from the Twelfth to the Sixteenth Century.*

Kruks, Sonia, and Ben Wisner. 1984. "The State, the Party and the Female Peasantry in Mozambique." *Journal of Southern African Studies* 11, no. 1: 106–27.

Kuzwayo, Ellen. 1985. *Call Me Woman.* San Francisco: Spinsters Ink.

*La Pin, Deirdre. 1995. "Women in African Literature." In Hay and Stichter, *African Women.*

Lan, David. 1985. *Guns and Rain: Guerrillas and Spirit Mediums in Zimbabwe.* Berkeley and Los Angeles: University of California Press.

Landau, Paul Stuart. 1995. *The Realm of the Word: Language, Gender, and Christianity in a Southern African Kingdom.* Portsmouth, N.H.: Heinemann.

Lapchick, Richard E., and Stephanie Urdang. 1982. *Oppression and Resistance: The Struggle of Women in Southern Africa.* Westport, Conn.: Greenwood Press.

Leacock, Eleanor Burke. 1981. *Myths of Male Dominance: Collected Articles on Women Cross-Culturally.* New York and London: Monthly Review.

Leclant, J. 1981. "The Empire of Kush: Napata and Meroë." In Mokhtar, *Ancient Civilizations of Africa.*

Lee, Richard. 1979. *The !Kung San.* Cambridge: Cambridge University Press.

Lerner, Gerda. 1986. *The Creation of Patriarchy.* New York: Oxford University Press.

Lesko, Barbara S. 1998. "Women of Ancient Egypt and Western Asia." In Bridenthal, Stuard, and Wiesner, *Becoming Visible.*

Le Vine, Sarah, in collaboration with Robert A. Le Vine. 1979. *Mothers and Wives: Gusii Women of East Africa.* Chicago: University of Chicago Press.

Levtzion, N., and J. F. P. Hopkins, eds. 1981. *Corpus of Early Arabic Sources for West African History.* Cambridge: Cambridge University Press.

Lewis, Barbara. 1984. "The Impact of Development Policies on Women." In Hay and Stichter, *African Women.*

Lightfoot-Klein, Hanny. 1989. *Prisoners of Ritual: An Odyssey into Female Genital Circumcision in Africa.* Binghamton, N.Y., and London: Harrington Park Press.

*Likimani, Muthoni. 1985. *Passbook Number F.47927: Women and Mau Mau in Kenya.* London: Macmillan.

Lindsay, Beverley. 1980. "Issues Confronting Professional African Women: Illustrations from Kenya." In Lindsay, *Comparative Perspectives of Third World Women.*

Lindsay, Beverley, ed. 1980. *Comparative Perspectives of Third World Women.* New York: Praeger.

Llewelyn-Davies, Melissa. 1982. "Two Contexts of Solidarity among Pastoral Masai Women." In Caplan and Bujra, *Women United, Women Divided.*

Lodge, Tom. 1983. *Black Politics in South Africa since 1945.* London and New York: Longman.

Lovejoy, Paul. 1977. "Fugitive Slaves: Resistance in the Western Sudan." In Okihiro, *In Resistance.*

———. 1981. "Slavery in the Sokoto Caliphate." In Lovejoy, *The Ideology of Slavery.*

———. 1986. *Salt of the Desert Sun: A History of Salt Production and Trade in the Central Sudan.* Cambridge: Cambridge University Press.

———. 1988. "Concubinage and the Status of Women Slaves in Early Colonial Nigeria." *Journal of African History* 29, no. 2: 245–66.

Lovejoy, Paul, ed. 1981. *The Ideology of Slavery in Africa.* Beverly Hills, Calif.: Sage Publications.

Lovett, Margot. 1994. "On Power and Powerlessness: Marriage and Political Metaphor in Colonial Western Tanzania." *International Journal of African Historical Studies* 27, no. 2: 241–72.

———. 1996. "'She Thinks She's Like a Man': Marriage and (De)Constructing Gender Identity in Colonial Buha, Western Tanzania, 1943–1960." *Canadian Journal of African Studies* 30, no. 1: 52–67.

Ly-Tall, M. 1984. "The Decline of the Mali Empire." In Niane, *Africa from the Twelfth to the Sixteenth Century.*

Maathai, Wangari. 1988. *The Greenbelt Movement in Kenya.* Nairobi, Kenya: Environment Liaison Centre International.

MacCormack, Carol P. 1975. "Sande Women and Political Power in Sierra Leone." *West African Journal of Sociology and Political Science* 1: 42–50.

Mack, Beverly. 1992. "Harem Domesticity in Kano, Nigeria." In Hansen, *African Encounters with Domesticity.*

*Magona, Sindiwe. 1990. *To My Children's Children.* Cape Town, South Africa: David Philip.

Maloka, Tshidiso. 1997. "*Khomo Lia Oela:* Canteens, Brothels and Labour Migrancy in Colonial Lesotho, 1900–40." *Journal of African History* 38, no. 1: 101–22.

Mandala, Elias. 1984. "Capitalism, Kinship and Gender in the Lower Tchiri (Shire) Valley of Malawi, 1860–1960: An Alternative Theoretical Framework." *African Economic History* 13: 137–69.

———. 1990. *Work and Control in a Peasant Economy.* Madison: University of Wisconsin Press.

Manicom, Linzi. 1992. "Ruling Relations: Rethinking State and Gender in South African History." *Journal of African History* 33, no. 3: 441–65.

Mann, Kristin. 1985. *Marrying Well: Marriage, Status and Social Change among the Educated Elite in Colonial Lagos.* Cambridge: Cambridge University Press.

———. 1991. "Women, Landed Property, and the Accumulation of Wealth in Early Colonial Lagos." *Signs* 16, no. 4: 682–706.

Mann, Kristin, and Richard Roberts, eds. 1991. *Law in Colonial Africa.* Portsmouth, N.H.: Heinemann.

Marks, Shula. 1994. *Divided Sisterhood: Race, Class and Gender in the South African Nursing Profession.* Johannesburg, South Africa: Witwatersrand University Press.

*Marks, Shula, ed. 1987. *Not Either an Experimental Doll: The Separate Worlds of Three South African Women*. Bloomington: Indiana University Press.

Marks, Shula, and Anthony Atmore, eds. 1980. *Economy and Society in Pre-Industrial South Africa*. London: Longman.

Marks, Shula, and Richard Rathbone, eds. 1982. *Industrialisation and Social Change in South Africa*. London: Longman.

Marks, Shula, and Stanley Trapido, eds. 1987. *Race, Class and Nationalism in Twentieth Century South Africa*. London: Longman.

Martin, Phyllis. 1994. "Contesting Clothes in Colonial Brazzaville." *Journal of African History* 35: 401–26.

Masemann, Vandra Lea. 1974. "The 'Hidden Curriculum' of a West African Girls' Boarding School." *Canadian Journal of African Studies* 8, no. 3: 479–93.

*Mashinini, Emma. 1991. *Strikes Have Followed Me All My Life: A South African Autobiography*. New York: Routledge.

Matory, J. Lorand. 1994. "Rival Empires: Islam and the Religion of Spirit Possession among the Oyo-Yoruba." *American Ethnologist* 21, no. 3: 495–515.

Matveiev, V. V. 1984. "The Development of Swahili Civilization." In Niane, *Africa from the Twelfth to the Sixteenth Century*.

Mba, Nina Emma. 1982. *Nigerian Women Mobilized: Women's Political Activity in Southern Nigeria, 1900–1965*. Berkeley: Institute of International Studies, University of California.

———. 1989. "Kaba and Khaki: Women and the Militarized State in Nigeria." In Parpart and Staudt, *Women and the State in Africa*.

Mbilinyi, Marjorie. 1972. "The 'New Woman' and Traditional Norms in Tanzania." *Journal of Modern African Studies* 10, no. 1: 57–72.

———. 1982. "Wife, Slave and Subject of the King: The Oppression of Women in the Shambala Kingdom." *Tanzania Notes and Records* 88/89: 1–13.

———. 1984. "'Women in Development' Ideology: The Promotion of Competition and Exploitation." *African Review* 2, no. 1: 14–33.

———. 1989. "'This Is an Unforgettable Business': Colonial State Intervention in Urban Tanzania." In Parpart and Staudt, *Women and the State in Africa*.

McCall, Daniel. 1961. "Trade and the Role of Wife in a Modern West African Town." In Southall, *Social Change in Modern Africa*.

*McCord, Margaret. 1995. *The Calling of Katie Makanya*. Cape Town, South Africa: David Philip.

McCurdy, Sheryl. 1996. "The 1932 'War' between Rival Ujiji (Tanganyika) Associations: Understanding Women's Motivations for Inciting Political Unrest." *Canadian Journal of African Studies* 30, no. 1: 10–31.

McLean, Scilla, and Stella Efua Graham. 1985. *Female Circumcision, Excision and Infibulation: The Facts and Proposals for Change*. London: Minority Rights Group.

Meade, Teresa, and Mark Walker, eds. 1991. *Science, Medicine and Cultural Imperialism*. New York: St. Martin's.

Meena, Ruth. 1989. "Crisis and Structural Adjustment: Tanzanian Women's Politics." *Issue: A Journal of Opinion* 17, no. 2: 29–30.

Meena, Ruth, ed. 1992. *Gender in Southern Africa: Conceptual and Theoretical Issues*. Harare, Zimbabwe: SAPES Books.

Meillasoux, Claude. 1997. "Female Slavery." In Robertson and Klein, *Women and Slavery in Africa*.

Memon, Pyar Ali, and Diana Lee Smith. 1993. "Urban Agriculture in Kenya." *Canadian Journal of African Studies* 27, no. 1: 25–42.

Mianda, Gertrude D. M. 1995. "Dans l'ombre de la 'démocratie' au Zaire: la remise en question de l'émancipation Mobutiste de la femme." *Canadian Journal of African Studies* 29, no. 1: 51–78.

Miers, Suzanne, and Igor Kopytoff, eds. 1977. *Slavery in Africa: Historical and Anthropological Perspectives*. Madison: University of Wisconsin Press.

Miers, Suzanne, and Richard Roberts. 1988. "Introduction: The End of Slavery in Africa." In Miers and Roberts, *The End of Slavery in Africa*.

Miers, Suzanne, and Richard Roberts, eds. 1988. *The End of Slavery in Africa*. Madison: University of Wisconsin Press.

*Mikell, Gwendolyn. 1995. "African Feminisms: Toward a New Politics of Representation." *Feminist Studies* 21, no. 2: 405–27.

Miller, Joseph C. 1983. "The Paradoxes of Impoverishment in the Atlantic Zone." In Birmingham and Martin, *History of Central Africa*.

*Mirza, Sarah, and Margaret Strobel, eds. 1989. *Three Swahili Women: Life Histories from Mombasa, Kenya*. Bloomington: Indiana University Press.

Mohanty, Chandra; Ann Russo; and Lourdes Torres, eds. *Third World Women and the Politics of Feminism*. Bloomington: Indiana University Press.

Mokhtar, G., ed. 1981. *Ancient Civilizations of Africa*. Vol. 2 of General History of Africa. Berkeley and Los Angeles: University of California Press.

Moran, Mary H. 1990. *Civilized Women: Gender and Prestige in Southeastern Liberia*. Ithaca and London: Cornell University Press.

Morgan, Robin, ed. 1984. *Sisterhood Is Global: The International Women's Movement Anthology*. Garden City, N.Y.: Anchor Press.

*Morrow, Lance F. 1986. "Women in Sub-Saharan Africa." In Duley and Edwards, *The Cross-Cultural Study of Women*.

Morrow, Sean. 1986. "'No Girl Leaves the School Unmarried': Mabel Shaw and the Education of Girls at Mbereshi, Northern Rhodesia, 1915–1940." *International Journal of African Historical Studies* 19, no. 4: 601–35.

*M'Poyo Kasa-Vuba, Z. J. 1987. "L'Evolution de la femme congolaise sous la régime colonial Belge." *Civilisations* 37, no. 1: 159–90.

Mueller, Martha. 1977. "Women and Men, Power and Powerlessness in Lesotho." *Signs* 3, no. 1: 154–66.

Mukurasi, Laeticia. 1991. *Post Abolished: One Woman's Struggle for Employment Rights in Tanzania*. Ithaca, N.Y.: ILR Press.

Munachonga, Monica. 1989. "Women and the State: Zambia's Development Policies and Their Impact on Women." In Parpart and Staudt, *Women and the State in Africa*.

Munalula, Margaret Mulela, and Winnie Sithole Mwenda. 1995. "Case Study: Women and Inheritance Law." In Hay and Stichter, *African Women*.

Muntemba, Maud Shimwaayi. 1982. "Women and Agricultural Change in the Railway Region of Zambia: Dispossession and Counterstrategies, 1930–1970." In Bay, *Women and Work in Africa*.

Murray, Colin. 1981. *Families Divided: The Impact of Migrant Labour in Lesotho*. Cambridge: Cambridge University Press.

Murray, Jocelyn. 1974. "The Kikuyu Female Circumcision Controversy, with Special Reference to the Church Missionary Society's 'Sphere of Influence.'" Ph.D. thesis, University of California, Los Angeles.

———. 1976. "The Church Missionary Society and the 'Female Circumcision' Issue in Kenya, 1929–1932." *Journal of Religion in Africa* [Netherlands] 8, no. 2: 92–104.

Murray, Stephen O., and William Roscoe, eds. 1998. *Boy-Wives and Female Husbands: Studies of African Homosexualities.* New York: St. Martin's Press.

Murray-Hudson, Anne. 1983. "SWAPO: Solidarity with Our Sisters." *Review of African Political Economy* 27/28: 120–25.

Musisi, Nakanyike B. 1991. "Women, 'Elite Polygyny,' and Buganda State Formation." *Signs* 16, no. 4: 757–86.

———. 1992. "Colonial and Missionary Education: Women and Domesticity in Uganda." In Hansen, *African Encounters with Domesticity.*

Naanen, Benedict. 1991. "'Itinerate Gold Mines': Prostitution in the Cross River Basin of Nigeria, 1930–1950." *African Studies Review* 34, no. 2: 57–80.

Nelson, Barbara J., and Najma Chowdhury, eds. 1994. *Women and Politics Worldwide.* New Haven: Yale University Press.

Nelson, Nici. 1982. "'Women Must Help Each Other.'" In Caplan and Bujra, *Women United, Women Divided.*

Nelson, Nici, ed. 1981. *African Women in the Development Process.* London: Frank Cass.

*Ngcobo, Lauretta. 1991. *And They Didn't Die.* New York: Braziller.

Ngocongco, L. D., with the collaboration of J. Vansina. 1984. "Southern Africa: Its Peoples and Social Structures." In Niane, *Africa from the Twelfth to the Sixteenth Century.*

Niane, D. T., ed. 1984. *Africa from the Twelfth to the Sixteenth Century.* Vol. 4 of General History of Africa. London: Heinemann; Berkeley and Los Angeles: University of California Press.

Niane, D. T. "Mali and the Second Mandingo Expansion." In Niane, *Africa from the Twelfth to the Sixteenth Century.*

*Nnaemeka, Obioma, ed. 1998. *Sisterhood, Feminisms, and Power: From Africa to the Diaspora.* Trenton, N.J.: Africa World Press.

Northrup, David. 1988. "The Ending of Slavery in the Eastern Belgian Congo." In Miers and Roberts, *The End of Slavery in Africa.*

*Ntantala, Phyllis. 1993. *A Life's Mosaic: The Autobiography of Phyllis Ntantala.* Berkeley and Los Angeles: University of California Press.

Nurse, Derek, and Thomas Spear. 1985. *The Swahili: Reconstructing the History and Language of an African Society, 800–1500.* Philadelphia: University of Pennsylvania Press.

*Nwapa, Flora. 1966a. *Efuru.* Portsmouth, N.H.: Heinemann.

*———. *Idu.* 1966b. London: Heinemann.

*———. *Once Is Enough.* 1981. Enugu, Nigeria: Tana Press.

———. 1998. "Women and Creative Writing in Africa." In Nnaemeka, *Sisterhood, Feminisms, and Power.*

Nzomo, Maria. 1989. "The Impact of the Women's Decade on Policies, Programs, and Empowerment of Women in Kenya." *Issue: A Journal of Opinion* 17, no. 2: 9–17.

O'Barr, Jean. 1975/76. "Pare Women: A Case of Political Involvement." *Rural Africana* 29: 121–34.

O'Barr, Jean, ed. 1982. *Perspectives on Power: Women in Africa, Asia and Latin America.* Durham, N.C.: Duke University, Center for International Studies.

150    Sources

*O'Barr, Jean, and Kathryn Firmin-Sellers. 1995. "African Women in Politics." In Hay and Stichter, *African Women.*
*Obbo, Christine. 1980. *African Women: Their Struggle for Economic Independence.* London: Zed Books.
———. 1986. "Stratification and the Lives of Women in Uganda." In Robertson and Berger, *Women and Class in Africa.*
Oboler, Regina Smith. 1985. *Women, Power, and Economic Change: The Nandi of Kenya.* Stanford: Stanford University Press.
Oduol, Wilhelmina. 1993. "Kenyan Women in Politics: An Analysis of Past and Present Trends." *Transafrican Journal of History* 22: 166–80.
Oduol, Wilhelmina, and Wanjiku Mukabi Kabira. 1995. "The Mother of Warriors and Her Daughters: The Women's Movement in Kenya." In Basu, *The Challenge of Local Feminisms.*
Ofei-Aboagye, Rosemary Ofeibea. 1994, "Altering the Strands of the Fabric: A Preliminary Look at Domestic Violence in Ghana." *Signs* 19, no. 4: 924–38.
Offen, K.; R. R. Pierson; and Jane Rendell, eds. 1991. *Writing Women's History.* Bloomington: Indiana University Press.
Ogbomo, Onaiwu W. 1995. "Essan Women Traders and Precolonial Economic Power." In House-Midamba and Ekechi, *African Market Women and Economic Power.*
*Ogot, Grace. 1966. *The Promised Land.* Nairobi, Kenya: East African Publishing House.
*———. 1968. *Land without Thunder.* Nairobi, Kenya: East African Publishing House.
Ogunbiyi, I. A. 1969. "The Position of Muslim Women as Stated by 'Uthmān b. Fūdī." *Odu: A Journal of West African Studies* n.s., no. 2: 43–60.
*Ogundipe-Leslie, Molara. 1994. *Re-creating Ourselves: African Women and Critical Transformations.* Trenton, N.J.: Africa World Press.
*Okali, Christine. 1983. "Kinship and Cocoa Farming in Ghana." In Oppong, *Female and Male in West Africa.*
Okeyo, Achola Pala. 1980. "Daughters of the Lakes and Rivers: Colonization and the Land Rights of Luo Women." In Etienne and Leacock, *Women and Colonization.*
Okhamafe, E. Imafedia. 1990. "African-Style Feminisms in Contemporary African Literature." *Africa Today* 37, no. 1: 73–75.
Okihiro, Gary Y., ed. 1986. *In Resistance: Studies in African, Caribbean and Afro-American History.* Amherst: University of Massachusetts Press.
Okonjo, Kamene. 1983. "Sex Roles in Nigerian Politics." In Oppong, *Female and Male in West Africa.*
Olivier de Sardan, Jean-Pierre. 1997. "The Songhay-Zarma Female Slave: Relations of Production and Ideological Status." In Robertson and Klein, *Women in Slavery in Africa.*
Olmstead, Judith. 1997. *Woman in Two Worlds: Portrait of an Ethiopian Rural Leader.* Urbana and Chicago: University of Illinois Press.
*Oosthuizen, Ann, ed. 1987. *Sometimes When It Rains: Writings by South African Women.* London and New York: Pandora Press.
Oppong, Christine. 1974. *Marriage among a Matrilineal Elite: A Family Study of Ghanaian Civil Servants.* London and New York: Cambridge University Press.
Oppong, Christine, ed. 1983. *Female and Male in West Africa.* London: George Allen and Unwin.

Otieno, Wambui Waiyaki, ed. With an introduction by Cora Ann Presley. 1998. *Mau Mau's Daughter: A Life History.* Boulder, Colo.: Lynne Rienner.

Palmer, Robin, and Neil Parsons, eds. 1977. *The Roots of Rural Poverty in Central and Southern Africa.* Berkeley and Los Angeles: University of California Press.

Pankhurst, Richard. 1961. *An Introduction to the Economic History of Ethiopia.* Addis Ababa, Ethopia: Lalibela House.

Parpart, Jane L. 1986. "Class and Gender on the Copperbelt: Women in Northern Rhodesian Copper Mining Communities, 1926–1964." In Robertson and Berger, *Women and Class in Africa.*

———. 1994. "'Where Is Your Mother?' Gender, Urban Marriage, and Colonial Discourse on the Zambian Copperbelt, 1924–1945." *International Journal of African Historical Studies* 27, no. 2: 241–72.

Parpart, Jane L., and Gloria A. Nikoi, eds. 1989, *Women and Development in Africa: Comparative Perspectives.* Lanham, Md.: University Press of America.

Parpart, Jane L., and Kathleen A. Staudt, eds. 1989. *Women and the State in Africa.* Boulder, Colo.: Lynne Rienner Publishers.

Parpart, Jane L., and Sharon Stichter, eds. 1988. *Patriarchy and Class: African Women in the Home and the Workforce.* Boulder, Colo.: Westview Press.

Parreira, Adriano. 1990. *Economia e sociedade em Angola na epoca da rainha Jinga seculo XVII.* Lisbon: Editorial Estampa.

Paulme, Denise, ed. 1971. *Women of Tropical Africa.* Berkeley and Los Angeles: University of California Press.

Peires, J. B. 1982. *The House of Phalo: History of the Xhosa People in the Days of Their Independence.* Berkeley and Los Angeles: University of California Press.

———. 1989. *The Dead Will Arise: Nongqawuse and the Great Xhosa Cattle-Killing Movement of 1856–7.* Bloomington: Indiana University Press.

Peires, J. B., ed. 1981. *Before and After Shaka.* Grahamstown, South Africa: Institute of Social and Economic Research.

Pellow, Deborah. 1990. "Sexuality in Africa." *Trends in History* 4, no. 4: 71–96.

Penvenne, Jeanne. 1983. "Here Everyone Walked with Fear: The Mozambican Labor System and the Workers of Lourenço Marques, 1945–1962." In F. Cooper, *The Struggle for the City.*

———. 1986. "Making Our Own Way: Women Working in Lourenço Marques." Boston: Boston University, African Studies Center Working Papers, No. 114.

Peters, Pauline. 1983. "Gender, Development Cycles and Historical Process: A Critique of Recent Research on Women in Botswana." *Journal of Southern African Studies* 10, no. 1: 100–22.

Phillipson, David W. 1974. "Iron Age History and Archaeology in Zambia." *Journal of African History* 15, no. 1: 1–25.

———. 1993. *African Archaeology.* Cambridge: Cambridge University Press.

Porteres, R. and J. Barrau. 1981. "Origins, Developments and Expansion of Agricultural Techniques." In Ki-Zerbo, *Methodology and African Prehistory.*

Posnansky, Merrick. "The Societies of Africa South of the Sahara in the Early Iron Age." In Mokhtar, *Ancient Civilizations of Africa.*

Potash, Betty. 1995. "Women in the Changing African Family." In Hay and Stichter, *African Women.*

Potash, Betty, ed. 1986. *Widows in African Societies: Choices and Constraints.* Stanford: Stanford University Press.

Power, Joey. 1996. "'Eating the Property': Gender Roles and Economic Change in Urban Malawi, Blantyre-Limbe, 1907–1953." *Canadian Journal of African Studies* 29, no. 1: 78–106.

Presley, Cora Ann. 1986. "Labor Unrest among Kikuyu Women in Colonial Kenya." In Robertson and Berger, *Women and Class in Africa.*

———. 1992. *Kikuyu Women, the Mau Mau Rebellion, and Social Change in Kenya.* Boulder, Colo.: Westview Press.

Ramphele, Mamphela. 1989. "The Dynamics of Gender Politics in the Hostels of Cape Town: Another Legacy of the South African Migrant Labour System." *Journal of Southern African Studies* 15, no. 3: 393–414.

*———. 1996. *Across Boundaries: The Journey of a South African Woman Leader.* New York: Feminist Press.

Ranchod-Nilsson, Sita. 1994. "'This, Too, Is a Way of Fighting': Rural Women's Participation in Zimbabwe's Liberation War." In Tétreault, *Women and Revolution in Africa, Asia and the New World.*

Reiter, Rayna, ed. 1975. *Toward an Anthropology of Women.* New York and London: Monthly Review.

Ribeiro, Maria Aparecida. 1992. "A Mulher e a cidade: Uma Letura da narrativa Angolana." *Revista Critica das Ciencas Sociais* 34: 85–97.

Richards, Audrey I. 1956. *Chisungu: A Girls' Initiation Ceremony among the Bemba of Northern Rhodesia.* London: Faber and Faber.

Robbins, Catherine. 1979. "Conversion, Life Crises and Stability among Women in the East African Revival." In Jules-Rosette, *The New Religions of Africa.*

Roberts, Penelope A. 1987. "The State and the Regulation of Marriage: Sefwi Wiawso (Ghana), 1900–1940." In Afshar, *Women, State and Ideology.*

Roberts, Richard. 1984. "Women's Work and Women's Property: Household Social Relations in the Maraka Textile Industry of the Nineteenth Century." *Comparative Studies in Society and History* 26, no. 2: 48–69.

———. 1988, "The End of Slavery in the French Soudan, 1885–1914." In Miers and Roberts, *The End Of Slavery in Africa.*

Robertson, Claire. 1987. "Changing Perspectives in Studies of African Women, 1976–1985." *Feminist Studies* 13, no. 1: 87–136.

*———. 1990. *Sharing the Same Bowl: A Socioeconomic History of Women and Class in Accra, Ghana.* Ann Arbor: University of Michigan Press.

———. 1993. "Ideology and the Creation of a Militant Female Underclass in Nairobi, 1960–1990." *Journal of Women's History* 4, no. 3: 9–42.

*———. 1995. "Women in the Urban Economy." In Hay and Stichter, *African Women.*

———. 1996. "Women, Genital Mutilation, and Collective Action, 1920–1990." *Signs* 21, no. 3: 615–28.

———. 1997a. "Post-Proclamation Slavery in Accra: A Female Affair?" In Robertson and Klein, *Women in Slavery in Africa.*

———. 1997b. *Trouble Showed the Way: Women, Men and Trade in the Nairobi Area, 1890–1990.* Bloomington: Indiana University Press.

*Robertson, Claire, and Iris Berger, eds. 1986. *Women and Class in Africa.* New York: Africana Publishing Co.

*Robertson, Claire, and Martin A. Klein, eds. 1997. *Women and Slavery in Africa*. Portsmouth, N.H.: Heinemann. First published 1983.

Robins, Gay. 1993. *Women in Ancient Egypt*. Cambridge: Harvard University Press.

Rodney, Walter. 1970. *A History of the Upper Guinea Coast, 1545 to 1800*. London: Oxford University Press.

Rogers, Barbara. 1980. *The Domestication of Women*. London: Tavistock.

Rogers, Susan G. [Geiger]. 1980. "Anti-Colonial Protest in Africa: A Female Strategy Reconsidered." *Heresies* 3, no. 9: 22–25.

———. 1982. "Efforts toward Women's Development in Tanzania: Gender Rhetoric vs. Gender Realities." *Women and Politics* 2, no. 4: 23–41.

*Romero, Patricia W., ed. 1988, *Life Histories of African Women*. London: Ashfield Press.

Rosenfeld, Chris Prouty. 1986. *Empress Taytu and Menilek II: Ethiopia, 1883–1910*. Trenton, N.J.: Red Sea Press.

*Russell, Diana E. H. 1989. *Lives of Courage: Women for a New South Africa*. New York: Basic Books.

Rybalkina, I. G. 1990. "Women in African History." *Africa* 29, no. 3–4: 83–91.

Sacks, Karen. 1982. *Sisters and Wives: The Past and Future of Sexual Equality*. Urbana and Chicago: University of Illinois Press.

Salama, P. 1981. "The Sahara in Classical Antiquity." In Mokhtar, *Ancient Civilizations of Africa*.

Sargent, R. A. 1991. "Found in the Fog of the Male Myths: Analyzing Female Political Roles in Pre-colonial Africa." *Canadian Oral History Association Journal* 11: 39–44.

Scarnecchia, Timothy. 1996. "Poor Women and Nationalist Politics: Alliance and Fissures in the Formation of a Nationalist Political Movement in Salisbury, Rhodesia, 1950–6." *Journal of African History* 37, no. 2: 283–310.

Schapera, Isaac. 1966. *Married Life in an African Tribe*. Evanston, Ill.: Northwestern University Press.

*Schildkrout, Enid. 1983. "Dependence and Autonomy: The Economic Activities of Secluded Hausa Women in Kano." In Oppong, *Female and Male in West Africa*.

Schiller, Laurence. 1990. "The Royal Women of Buganda." *International Journal of African Historical Studies* 23, no. 3: 455–73.

Schlegel, Alice, ed. 1977. *Sexual Stratification: A Cross-Cultural View*. New York: Columbia University Press.

Schmidt, Elizabeth. 1988. "Farmers, Hunters, and Gold-Washers: A Reevaluation of Women's Roles in Precolonial and Colonial Zimbabwe." *African Economic History* 17: 45–80.

———. 1992. *Peasants, Traders, and Wives*. Portsmouth, N.H.: Heinemann.

Schoenbrun, David L. 1993. "We Are What We Eat: Ancient Agriculture between the Great Lakes." *Journal of African History* 34, no. 1: 1–31.

———. 1997. "Gendered Histories between the Great Lakes: Varieties and Limits." *International Journal of African Historical Studies* 29, no. 3: 461–92.

Schoepf, Brooke Grundfest. 1987. "Social Structure, Women's Status and Sex Differential Nutrition in the Zairan Copperbelt." *Urban Anthropology* 16, no. 1: 73–102.

Schroeder, Richard. 1996. "'Gone to Their Second Husbands': Marital Metaphors and Conjugal Contacts in the Gambia's Female Garden Sector." *Canadian Journal of African Studies* 30, no. 1: 69–87.

Schuster, Ilsa. 1979. *New Women of Lusaka.* Palo Alto, Calif.: Mayfield.

———. 1982. "Marginal Lives: Conflict and Contradiction in the Position of Female Traders in Lusaka, Zambia." In Bay, *Women and Work in Africa.*

Scully, Pamela. 1995. "Rape, Race, and Colonial Culture: The Sexual Politics of Identity in the Nineteenth-Century Cape Colony, South Africa." *American Historical Review* 100, no. 2: 335–59.

———. 1996. "Narratives of Infanticide in the Aftermath of Slave Emancipation in the Nineteenth-Century Cape Colony, South Africa." *Canadian Journal of African Studies* 30, no. 1: 88–105.

Seager, Joni. 1997, *The State of Women in the World Atlas.* Revised ed. New York: Penguin.

Seidman, Gay W. 1984. "Women in Zimbabwe: Post-Independence Struggles." *Feminist Studies* 10, no. 3: 419–40.

*———. 1993. "'No Freedom without the Women': Mobilization and Gender in South Africa, 1970–1992." *Signs* 18, no. 2: 291–320.

*Sembene, Ousmane. 1982. *God's Bits of Wood.* London: Heinemann.

Shaw, C. T. 1981. "The Prehistory of West Africa." In Ki–Zerbo, *Methodology and African Prehistory.*

Sheldon, Kathleen. 1991. "A Report on a 'Delicate Problem' Concerning Female Garment Workers in Beira, Mozambique." *Signs* 16, no. 3: 575–86.

———. 1992. "*Creches, Titias,* and Mothers: Working Women and Child Care in Mozambique." In Hansen, *African Encounters with Domesticity.*

———. 1994. "Women and Revolution in Mozambique: *A Luta Continua.*" In Tétreault, *Women and Revolution in Africa, Asia, and the New World.*

———. 1996. "Urban African Women: Courtyards, Markets, and City Streets." In Sheldon, *Courtyards, Markets, City Streets.*

*Sheldon, Kathleen, ed. 1996. *Courtyards, Markets, City Streets: Urban Women in Africa.* Boulder, Colo.: Westview Press.

Shepard, Gill. 1987. "Rank, Gender, and Homosexuality: Mombasa as a Key to Understanding Sexual Options." In Caplan, *The Cultural Construction of Sexuality.*

Sherif, N. M. 1981. "Nubia before Napata (-3100 to -750)." In Mokhtar, *Ancient Civilizations of Africa.*

Shettima, Kole Ahmed. 1995. "Engendering Nigeria's Third Republic." *African Studies Review* 38, no. 3: 61–98.

*Shostak, Marjorie. 1983. *Nisa: The Life and Words of a !Kung Woman.* New York: Vintage Books.

Sibisi, Harriet. 1977. "How Women Cope with Migrant Labor in South Africa." *Signs* 3, no. 1: 167–77.

Sikainga, Ahmad A. 1995. "Shari'a Courts and the Manumission of Female Slaves in the Sudan." *International Journal of African Historical Studies* 28, no. 1: 1–24.

Simons, H. J. 1968, *African Women: Their Legal Status in South Africa.* Evanston, Ill.: Northwestern University Press.

Skidmore-Hess, Cathy. 1995. "Queen Njinga, 1582–1663: Ritual, Power and Gender in the Life of a Precolonial African Ruler." Ph.D. dissertation, University of Wisconsin–Madison.

Skinner, David E. 1980. *Thomas George Lawson: African Historian and Administrator.* Stanford: Hoover Institution Press.

Slocum, Sally. 1975. "Woman the Gatherer: Male Bias in Anthropology." In Reiter, *Toward an Anthropology of Women.*

Smith, M. G. *The Affairs of Daura.* 1978. Berkeley and Los Angeles: University of California Press.

Smith, Mary F. 1981. *Baba of Karo: A Woman of the Muslim Hausa.* New Haven: Yale University Press. First published 1954.

Songue, Paulette Beat. 1996. "Prostitution, a *Petit-Métier* during Economic Crisis: A Road to Women's Liberation? The Case of Cameroon." In Sheldon, *Courtyards, Markets, City Streets.*

Southall, Aidan, ed. 1961. *Social Change in Modern Africa.* London: Oxford University Press.

Spaulding, Jay. 1982. "The Misfortunes of Some, the Advantages of Others: Land Sales by Women in Sinnar." In Hay and Wright, *African Women and the Law.*

Stamp, Patricia. 1986. "Kikuyu Women's Self-Help Groups." In Robertson and Berger, *Women and Class in Africa.*

———. 1991. "Burying Otieno: The Politics of Gender and Ethnicity in Kenya." *Signs* 16, no. 4: 808–45.

———. 1995. "Mothers of Invention: Women's Agency in the Kenyan State." In Gardiner, *Provoking Agents.*

Standing, Hilary, and Mere N. Kisekka, eds. 1989. *Sexual Behaviour in Sub-Saharan Africa.* London: Overseas Development Administration.

Staudt, Kathleen. 1982. "Women Farmers and Inequities in Agricultural Services." In Bay, *Women and Work in Africa.*

———. 1986. "Stratification: Implications for Women's Politics." In Robertson and Berger, *Women and Class in Africa.*

———. 1995. "The Impact of Development Policies on Women." In Hay and Stichter, *African Women.*

Staunton, Irene. 1990. *Mothers of the Revolution: The War Experiences of Thirty Zimbabwean Women.* Bloomington: Indiana University Press.

Steady, Filomina Chioma. 1985. "The Black Woman Cross-Culturally: An Overview." In Steady, *The Black Woman Cross-Culturally.*

———. 1987. "African Feminism: A Worldwide Perspective." In Terborg-Penn, Rushing, and Harley, *Women in Africa and the African Diaspora.*

Steady, Filomina Chioma, ed. 1985. *The Black Woman Cross-Culturally.* Rochester, Vt.: Schenkman.

Stichter, Sharon. 1975–76. "Women and the Labor Force in Kenya 1895–1964." *Rural Africana* 29: 45–67.

Stichter, Sharon, and Jane Parpart, eds. 1988. *Patriarchy and Class: African Women in the Home and the Workforce.* Boulder, Colo.: Westview Press.

*Strobel, Margaret. 1979. *Muslim Women in Mombasa, 1890–1975.* New Haven: Yale University Press.

———. 1982. "African Women: Review Essay." *Signs* 8, no. 1: 109–31.

*———. 1995. "Women in Religion and Secular Ideology." In Hay and Stichter, *African Women.*

———. 1997. "Slavery and Reproductive Labor in Mombasa." In Robertson and Klein, *Women and Slavery in Africa.*

———. 1998. "Gender, Race, and Empire in Nineteenth- and Twentieth-

Century Africa and Asia." In Bridenthal, Stuard, and Wiesner, *Becoming Visible.*

Sudarkasa, Niara. 1973. *Where Women Work: A Study of Yoruba Women in the Marketplace and in the Home.* Ann Arbor: University of Michigan Press.

——. 1977. "Women and Migration in Contemporary West Africa." In Wellesley Editorial Committee, *Women and National Development.*

Summers, Carol. 1991. "Intimate Colonialism: The Imperial Production of Reproduction in Uganda, 1907–1925." *Signs* 16, no. 4: 787–807.

Sutton, J. E. G. 1981. "East Africa before the Seventh Century." In Mokhtar, *Ancient Civilizations of Africa.*

Swantz, Marja-Liisa. 1985. *Women in Development: A Creative Role Denied?* New York: St. Martin's Press.

Sweetman, David. 1984. *Women Leaders in African History.* London: Heinemann.

Sylvester, Christine. 1995. "African and Western Feminisms: World-Traveling the Tendencies and Possibilities." *Signs* 20, no. 4: 941–69.

Tadesse, Zenebeworke. 1980. "The Impact of Land Reform on Women: The Case of Ethiopia." In Beneria, *Women and Development.*

Terborg-Penn, Rosalyn; Fanny Rushing; and Sharon Harley, eds. 1987. *Women in Africa and the African Diaspora.* Washington, D.C.: Howard University Press.

Tétreault, Mary Ann, ed. 1994. *Women and Revolution in Africa, Asia, and the New World.* Columbia: University of South Carolina Press.

*Thiam, Awa. 1996. *Black Sisters, Speak Out: Feminism and Oppression in Black Africa.* London: Pluto Press.

Thomas, Lynn M. 1996. "'*Ngaitana* (I will circumcise myself)': The Gender and Generational Politics of the 1956 Ban on Clitoridectomy in Meru, Kenya." *Gender and History* 8, no. 3: 338–63. Also in Hunt, Liu, and Quataert, *Gendered Colonialisms in African History.*

Thompson, J. Malcolm. 1990. "Colonial Policy and the Family Life of Black Troops in French West Africa, 1817–1904." *International Journal of African Historical Studies,* 23, no. 3: 423–53.

Thornton, John. 1983. *The Kingdom of Kongo: Civil War and Transition, 1641–1718.* Madison: University of Wisconsin Press.

——. 1991. "Legitimacy and Political Power: Queen Njinga, 1624–1663." *Journal of African History* 32: 25–40.

——. 1992. *Africa and Africans in the Making of the Atlantic World, 1400–1680.* Cambridge: Cambridge University Press.

Tripp, Aili Mari. 1997. *Changing the Rules: The Politics of Liberalization and the Urban Informal Economy in Tanzania.* Berkeley and Los Angeles: University of California Press.

*Turnbull, Colin. 1962. *The Forest People.* New York: Natural History Library.

——. 1981. "Mbuti Womanhood." In Dahlberg, *Woman the Gatherer.*

Turrittin, Jane. 1988. "Men, Women, and Market Trade in Mali, West Africa." *Canadian Journal of African Studies* 22, no. 3: 583–604.

——. 1993. "Aoua Keita and the Nascent Women's Movement in the French Soudan." *African Studies Review* 36, no. 1: 59–90.

Turshen, Meredith. 1995. "Women and Health Issues." In Hay and Stichter, *African Women.*

Turshen, Meredith, and Clotilde Twagiramariya, eds. 1998. *What Women Do in Wartime: Gender and Conflict in Africa.* London: Zed Books.

United Nations Economic Commission for Africa. 1975. "Women and National Development in African Countries: Some Profound Contradictions." *African Studies Review* 18, no. 3: 47–70.

Urdang, Stephanie. 1979. *Fighting Two Colonialisms: Women in Guinea-Bissau.* New York: Monthly Review Press.

———. 1983. "The Last Transition? Women and Development in Mozambique." *Review of African Political Economy* 27/28: 8–32.

———. 1985. "The Role of Women in the Revolution in Guinea-Bissau." In Steady, *The Black Woman Cross-Culturally.*

*———. 1989. *And Still They Dance: Women, War, and the Struggle for Change in Mozambique.* New York: Monthly Review Press.

*———. 1995. "Women in National Liberation Movements." In Hay and Stichter, *African Women.*

Vail, Leroy, and Landeg White. 1991. *Power and the Praise Poem: Southern African Voices in History.* Charlottesville: University Press of Virginia.

*Van Allen, Judith. 1976. "'Aba Riots' or Igbo 'Women's War'? Ideology, Stratification, and the Invisibility of Women." In Hafkin and Bay, *Women in Africa.*

van der Vliet, V. 1984. "Staying Single: A Strategy against Poverty?" Carnegie Conference Paper no. 116.

Vanderspuy, Patricia. 1991. "Gender and Slavery: Towards a Feminist Revision." *South African Historical Journal* 25: 184–95.

van Onselen, Charles. 1982. *Studies in the Social and Economic History of the Witwatersrand, 1886–1914.* 2 vols. New York: Longman.

van Sertima, Ivan, ed. 1985. *Black Women in Antiquity.* New Brunswick, N.J.: Transaction Books.

Vansina, Jan. 1983. "The Peoples of the Forest." In Birmingham and Martin, *History of Central Africa.*

Vaughan, Megan. 1985. "Household Units and Historical Process in Southern Malawi." *Review of African Political Economy* 34: 35–45.

———. 1987. *The Story of an African Famine: Gender and Famine in Twentieth-Century Malawi.* Cambridge: Cambridge University Press.

Venema, L. B. 1986. "The Changing Role of Women in Sahelian Agriculture." In Creevey, *Women Farmers in Africa.*

Verdon, Michel. 1982. "Divorce in Abutia." *Africa* 52, no. 4: 48–66.

VerEecke, Catherine. 1988. "From Pasture to Purdah: The Transformation of Women's Roles and Identity among the Adamawa Fulbe." *Ethnology* 28: 53–73.

———. 1995. "Muslim Women Traders of Northern Nigeria: Perspectives from the City of Yola." In House-Midamba and Ekechi, *African Market Women and Economic Power.*

Vidal, Claudine. 1977. "Guerre des sexes à Abijan: Masculin, feminin, CFA." *Cahiers d'Etudes Africaines* 8, no. 1: 121–53.

Wachtel, Eleanor. 1975/76. "A Farm of One's Own: The Rural Orientation of Women's Group Enterprises in Nakuru, Kenya." *Rural Africana* 29: 69–80.

Walker, Cherryl. 1992. *Women and Resistance in South Africa.* 2nd ed., revised. New York: Monthly Review.

———. 1995. "Conceptualising Motherhood in Twentieth Century South Africa." *Journal of Southern African Studies* 21, no. 3: 417–38.

*Walker, Cherryl, ed. 1990. *Women and Gender in Southern Africa.* London: James Currey.

Wallman, Sandra. 1996. *Kampala Women Getting By: Wellbeing in the Time of AIDS*. Athens: Ohio University Press.

*Ware, Helen. 1983. "Female and Male Life-Cycles." In Oppong, *Female and Male in West Africa*.

Watterson, Barbara. 1991. *Women in Ancient Egypt*. New York: St. Martin's Press.

Weiss, Ruth. 1986. *The Women of Zimbabwe*. London: Kesho Publications.

Wellesley Editorial Committee, eds. 1977. *Women and National Development: The Complexities of Change*. Chicago: University of Chicago Press.

Wells, Evelyn. 1969. *Hatshepsut*. Garden City, N.Y.: Doubleday and Co.

Wells, Julia. 1982. "Passes and Bypasses: Freedom of Movement for African Women under the Urban Areas Act of South Africa." In Hay and Wright, *African Women and the Law*.

———. 1983. "Why Women Rebel: A Comparative Study of South African Women's Resistance in Bloemfontein (1913) and Johannesburg (1958)." *Journal of Southern African Studies* 10, no. 1: 55–70.

———. 1986. "The War of Degradation: Black Women's Struggle against Orange Free State Pass Laws, 1913." In Crummey, *Banditry*.

*———. 1993. *We Now Demand! The History of Women's Resistance to Pass Laws in South Africa*. Johannesburg, South Africa: Witwatersrand University Press.

———. 1998. "Eva's Men: Gender and Power in the Establishment of the Cape of Good Hope, 1652–74." *Journal of African History* 39, no. 2: 417–37.

White, E. Frances. 1987. *Sierra Leone's Settler Women Traders: Women on the Afro-European Frontier*. Ann Arbor: University of Michigan Press.

White, Landeg. 1987. *Magomero: Portrait of an African Village*. Cambridge: Cambridge University Press.

White, Luise. 1984. "Women in the Changing African Family." In Hay and Stichter, *African Women* (1st ed., 1984).

*———. 1990a. *The Comforts of Home: Prostitution in Colonial Nairobi*. Chicago: University of Chicago Press.

———. 1990b. "Separating the Men from the Boys: Constructions of Gender, Sexuality, and Terrorism in Central Kenya, 1939–1959." *International Journal of African Historical Studies* 23, no. 1: 1–25.

*Wilks, Ivor. 1988. "She Who Blazed a Trail: Akayaawa Yikwan of Asante." In Romero, *Life Histories of African Women*.

Wilmsen, Edwin N. 1989. *Land Filled with Flies: A Political Economy of the Kalahari*. Chicago: University of Chicago Press.

Wilson, Amrit. 1991. *The Challenge Road: Women and the Eritrean Revolution*. London: Earthscan.

Wilson, Francile Rusan. 1982. "Reinventing the Past and Circumscribing the Future: *Authenticité* and the Negative Image of Women's Work in Zaire." In Bay, *Women and Work in Africa*.

Wilson, John A. 1951. *The Culture of Ancient Egypt*. Chicago: University of Chicago Press.

Wipper, Audrey. 1971. "Equal Rights for Women in Kenya?" *Journal of Modern African Studies* 9, no. 3: 429–42.

———. 1972. "African Women, Fashion and Scapegoating." *Canadian Journal of African Studies* 6, no. 2: 329–49.

———. 1975. "The Maendeleo ya Wanawake Organization: The Co-optation of Leadership." *African Studies Review* 18, no. 3: 99–120.

————. 1975/76. "The Maendeleo ya Wanawake Movement in the Colonial Period." *Rural Africana* 29: 195–214.

————. 1982. "Riot and Rebellion among African Women." In O'Barr, *Perspectives on Power.*

*————. 1995. "Women's Voluntary Associations." In Hay and Stichter, *African Women.*

Wright, John. 1981, "Control of Women's Labour in the Zulu Kingdom." In Peires, *Before and After Shaka.*

Wright, Marcia. 1983. "Technology, Marriage and Women's Work in the History of Maize Growers in Mazabuka, Zambia: A Reconnaissance." *Journal of Southern African Studies* 10, no. 1: 71–85.

————. 1993. *Strategies of Slaves and Women: Life-Stories from East/Central Africa.* New York: Lilllian Barber.

————. 1997. "Bwanikwa: Consciousness and Protest among Slave Women in Central Africa, 1886–1911." In Robertson and Klein, *Women in Slavery in Africa.*

Yates, Barbara. 1982. "Colonialism, Education, and Work: Sex Differentiation in Colonial Zaire." In Bay, *Women and Work in Africa.*

Young, Sherilynn. 1977. "Fertility and Famine: Women's Agricultural History in Southern Mozambique." In Palmer and Parsons, *The Roots of Rural Poverty in Central and Southern Africa.*

Yoyotte, J. 1981. "Pharaonic Egypt: Society, Economy and Culture." In Mokhtar, *Ancient Civilizations of Africa.*

Zulu, Lindiwe. 1998. "Role of Women in the Reconstruction and Development of the New Democratic South Africa." *Feminist Studies* 24, no. 1: 147–57.

# CONTRIBUTORS

**Iris Berger** is professor of history, Africana studies, and women's studies at the University at Albany, State University of New York. She is also past director of the Institute for Research on Women and recently completed a term as president of the African Studies Association. Her research centers on African history, with an emphasis on women and gender, labor, religion, and popular culture. She is author of *Threads of Solidarity: Women in South African Industry, 1900–1980* and the award-winning book *Religion and Resistance: East African Kingdoms in the Precolonial Period,* and co-editor of *Women and Class in Africa.*

**Cheryl Johnson-Odim** is professor of history and chairs the Department of History at Loyola University Chicago. She co-authored *For Women and the Nation: Funmilayo Ransome-Kuti of Nigeria* and co-edited *Expanding the Boundaries of Women's History.* She has published many articles and chapters on African women's history and on feminist theory. She is a past member of the board of directors of the African Studies Association and the American Council of Learned Societies and serves on the editorial boards of the *Journal of Women's History* and *Chicago Women, 1770–1990: A Biographical Dictionary.*

**Margaret Strobel** is professor of women's studies and history at the University of Illinois at Chicago. Her book *Muslim Women in Mombasa, 1890–1975* won the African Studies Association's Herskovits Award in 1980. She is author of *European Women and the Second British Empire* and co-editor of *Three Swahili Women: Life Histories from Mombasa, Kenya; Western Women and Imperialism: Complicity and Resistance;* and *Expanding the Boundaries of Women's History.* She serves on the editorial board of *Chicago Women, 1770–1990: A Biographical Dictionary,* and is working on a book about the Chicago Women's Liberation Union.

**E. Frances White** is professor and dean of the Gallatin School of Individualized Study at New York University. She writes on African women's history and feminist theory. Her publications include *Sierra Leone's Settler Women Traders: Women on the Afro-European Frontier* and "Africa on My Mind: Gender, Counter Discourse and African American Nationalism." For many years she taught at Hampshire College, where she was dean of faculty from 1994 to 1998.

# INDEX